INSIDE CONGRESSIONAL COMMITTEES

INSIDE
CONGRESSIONAL
COMMITTEES

FUNCTION AND DYSFUNCTION
in the
LEGISLATIVE PROCESS

MAYA L. KORNBERG

Columbia University Press
New York

Columbia University Press
Publishers Since 1893
New York   Chichester, West Sussex
cup.columbia.edu

Library of Congress Cataloging-in-Publication Data
Names: Kornberg, Maya, 1991- author.
Title: Inside congressional committees : function and dysfunction
in the legislative process / Maya L. Kornberg.
Description: New York : Columbia University Press, [2023] |
Includes bibliographical references and index.
Identifiers: LCCN 2022025712 (print) | LCCN 2022025713 (ebook) |
ISBN 9780231201827 (hardback) | ISBN 9780231201834 (trade paperback) |
ISBN 9780231554282 (ebook)
Subjects: LCSH: United States. Congress—Committees. |
Legislative hearings—United States.
Classification: LCC JK1029 .K67 2023 (print) | LCC JK1029 (ebook) |
DDC 328.73/0765—dc23/eng/20220815
LC record available at https://lccn.loc.gov/2022025712
LC ebook record available at https://lccn.loc.gov/2022025713

Columbia University Press books are printed on permanent and
durable acid-free paper.
Printed in the United States of America

Cover image: Sipa / AP Images

TO MY PARENTS, FOR THEIR CONTINUAL
FAITH AND CEASELESS SUPPORT

CONTENTS

ACKNOWLEDGMENTS

I would like to acknowledge the support of those who made this book possible. *Inside Congressional Committees: Function and Dysfunction in the Legislative Process* is based on previous research completed in 2019 at Oxford University's Department of Politics and International Relations, under the supervision of Professor Desmond King. The institutional, financial, and academic support therefore also formed a base for this book.

This book would not be possible without the many interviewees who graciously volunteered their time and insights. I am indebted to them for taking part in the research. I would also like to thank my friend Amir Malka, whose generous help with coding proved invaluable to the data collection process.

I owe a debt of gratitude to Desmond King, Nigel Bowles, and Sven Siefken for their valuable comments and suggestions on the manuscript. Their early feedback greatly strengthened the book.

I am also grateful to Stephen Wesley and Columbia University Press for the continuous support throughout the process.

To my dear friends—Sarah, Lili, Elle, Marta, Keren, Corinne, my brothers, and the many other voices of encouragement along the way—thank you for your friendship.

I am thankful for my family, near and far, for their presence and inspiration.

And to Noam, thank you for brightening my days and my writing process.

INSIDE CONGRESSIONAL COMMITTEES

INTRODUCTION

Society is a living organism and must obey the laws of life, not of mechanics; it must develop . . . a nation is a living thing and not a machine.

—WOODROW WILSON, 1912[1]

Wilson saw a country in a state of evolution. *Inside Congressional Committees: Function and Dysfunction in the Legislative Process* rests on the assumption that Congress, the legislative core of American society, acts as a living thing rather than a rulemaking machine. As the American nation changes and develops, so too does its legislative center. Scholars of historical institutionalism Stephen Skowronek and Karen Orren write that "to create something new in politics is, in the nature of things, to displace institutions." And these displacements accumulate over time, "magnifying distances and departures from points of origin."[2] This book explores congressional committees today after centuries of displacement and evolution.

Signs point to a contemporary Congress in which displacements have stirred increased partisanship and reduced legislative productivity. In an analysis of roll call voting that extends back to 1789, political scientists Keith T. Poole and Howard Rosenthal showed extremely high levels of polarization in Congress, almost as high as it was during and immediately after the Civil War.[3] Congress is also passing fewer pieces of legislation. In the late 1960s, members of the House of Representatives introduced an average of almost fifty bills per Congress. Today, that number is fewer than twenty.[4] Moreover, members of Congress are not spending their time legislating. A recent study found that members of Congress today spend only a third of their time in Washington, DC, legislating. Political scientists George Connor and Bruce Oppenheimer compared three Congresses, the 68th (1923–1925), 84th (1955–1957), and 96th (1979–1981) and showed that the number of hours spent debating each bill on the floor dropped.[5] They also looked at attendance for division votes (in which members receive no prior notice) as an indication of attendance at debates and found declining turnout as well as fewer speakers in attendance. Their study points to a marked decline in deliberation. In their 2006 book, *The Broken Branch*, scholars of Congress Thomas Mann and Norman Ornstein portray a Congress crippled by the filibuster and partisan gridlock. Congress is passing fewer laws, spending less time legislating and deliberating, and increasingly constrained by party lines.

What has made Congress impotent? *Inside Congressional Committees* focuses on committees as an important part of the story. Once a center of congressional power and bipartisanship, congressional committees slowly lost their power as Congress declined. Nonetheless, they still form a legislative concourse leading up to bill passage and account for a significant portion of legislators' schedules. This book peeks under the legislative hood. It examines the purpose and procedure of contemporary congressional committees, and follows dramatic changes to committee procedure over the twentieth century that undermine their roles as centers of congressional deliberation, learning, and bipartisanship.

THE DECLINE OF COMMITTEES: A CENTURY OF REFORM

In one of the major books on parliamentary committees, legislative studies scholars John Lees and Malcolm Shaw open with the following definition: "A committee is a body to which some task has been referred or committed by some other person or body. . . . There is inherent in the notion of a committee some idea of a derived . . . nature . . . it acts on behalf of or with responsibility to another body."[6] Committees have been essential institutions in Congress since its inception, acting as suborganizations to perform specific duties. As congressional scholar Nelson Polsby underlined in "The Institutionalization of the US House of Representatives," they formed organically as Congress itself institutionalized.[7] Polsby stresses that institutionalization led to decentralization of power and encouraged more legislators from both parties to be active participants in the crafting of policies. By 1825, Congress contained twenty-eight standing committees, with many of their modern responsibilities (overseeing the executive, amending legislation, etc.). In 1833, Scottish author Thomas Hamilton visited the United States and wrote a book about "men and manners" in the new country. He wrote that the "real business of the country" now took place in committees. "No bill connected with any branch of public affairs could be brought into Congress with the smallest prospect of success, which had not previously received the initiative approbations of these committees,"[8] Hamilton observed.

In the contemporary Congress, the Senate and House of Representatives have twenty-one and twenty standing committees, respectively. Most committee jurisdictions are divided based on policy issues, although a minority of committees focus on procedural issues (e.g., House Rules Committee).[9] Over the course of the last two centuries, as the Congress changed and developed, so did its committees. As Bryan D. Jones, Frank R. Baumgartner, and Jeffrey C. Talbert explain in their study of Congress, "committees, like other institutions of government, are dynamic structures. Fixed at any single time, they nonetheless change over the years."[10]

The survey of committee history in *Inside Congressional Committees* originates at the beginning of the twentieth century, when a dramatic shift in the power and function of committees began. The first half of the twentieth century was marked by the strengthening of committees and the deepening of their expertise. As a result of the 1910 Cannon revolt, in which Republican representatives joined the Democratic minority (hard to fathom today) to overthrow Speaker Joseph Cannon (R-IL), known as the czar, committees gained legislative power and autonomy. Early that year, the formidable progressive Democrat, Representative Oscar Underwood, framed the struggle as follows: "We are fighting a system, and that system is the system that enables the Speaker, by the power vested in him, to thwart and overthrow the will of the majority membership of this House."[11] As a result of both this upheaval and the Democrats taking back the House in 1911, the Speaker lost his power over committee assignments. This gave rise to a system in which member seniority (rather than the personal preferences of the Speaker) prescribed committee chairmanship. These two years were a turning point. This change gave committees greater autonomy because power filtered down from the party leadership directly into the hands of committees.

The second important "displacement," as Skowronek and Orren would say, was the 1946 Legislative Reorganization Act (1946 LRA). Spearheaded by New York Democrat James Wadsworth in a Republican majority House, the LRA was a bipartisan effort to improve Congress. American politics scholars Eric Schickler and Ruth Bloch Rubin contend that it may have resulted from the push to combat the growth in presidential power during World War II and the New Deal.[12] Among its many provisions, the LRA introduced several important changes to congressional committees. It reduced the number of committees and clarified committee jurisdictions. It also supplied each committee with its own professional staff. These changes to the organization, number, and staff support of committees strengthened them, and soon they became more specialized and more expert within those specialties. It enhanced congressional resources in the face of greatly augmented presidential authority and power.

While the 1910 and 1946 reforms bolstered committee power and specialization, the next set of displacements achieved the opposite goal. During the forty-year period of Democratic party control of the House of Representatives (1955–1995) and under the leadership of Carl Albert and Tip O'Neill, several rules changed. Committee leaders became less autonomous as the subcommittee and minority committee members were emboldened.

The 1970 Legislative Reorganization Act (1970 LRA) empowered the minority, allowing them to hire staff and call witnesses. It also required committees to set regular meeting days, allowing for more members to add items to the agenda. This reduced the power of the majority chair. Subcommittee chairs were also no longer appointed by chairs and therefore gained a degree of independence. The Subcommittee Bill of Rights, passed in 1973, also gave subcommittee chairs the right to hire staff and organize hearings. The devolution of power within committees directly disempowered committee chairs.

Second, the seniority system, which had once dictated committee assignments, was undermined as party leadership gained influence over assignment. This change resulted partly from pressure to reform imposed by the so-called Class of '74, the large group of freshmen members of Congress elected in the aftermath of the Watergate scandal. Changes to committees went hand-in-hand with strengthening of party leadership and increased party cohesion. The Speaker's authority was augmented in two respects: first, appointment of the chair of the Rules Committee was henceforth his or hers; second, the Speaker was permitted to refer a bill to more than one committee. In addition, steering committees were established as instruments of the party leadership with the authority to decide on the chair and membership of each committee. These steering committees, which include the party leader and other prominent party members, remain powerful institutions in the third decade of the twenty-first century. As a result of these changes, chairs became more dependent on the party for political survival and advancement; accordingly, they became more prone to partisanship. As the post–Cannon revolt seniority system waned, party leaders won back some of their prerevolt powers.

As party leadership consolidated power, committees continued to lose their autonomy, their power, and their place as a platform for members of Congress to gain specialization and expertise. Political scientist and pioneer of the study of Congress, Richard Fenno argued in *Congressmen in Committees* that the greater a committee's autonomy, defined as relative influence of the committee members, the more it will emphasize expertise.[13] It would follow that the loss of committee autonomy would result in the loss of expertise. The 1970 LRA simply abolished many committees, directly impairing representatives' ability to specialize in those topics. Committee staff was reduced by a third, and subcommittees were forbidden from hiring staff. Instead, staff people were hired only by the chair, who was appointed by the Speaker. These changes meant that representatives no longer had a strong network of staff to help them gather information and specialize. The centralization of staff hiring led to higher turnover and a potentially less diverse group, both of which make for less specialization.

After decades of Democratic control, the Republican party retook control of the House of Representatives in 1994, and the trends that started under Democratic reform intensified. In 1995, Newt Gingrich became the Republican Speaker of the House. Gingrich was, according to Polsby, "a self-identified bomb thrower" and the leader of a group who believed other Republicans had become "too acquiescent to their minority status and needed to pursue a strategy of overt obstreperousness."[14] He had long been identified with this type of tactic. In 1978, he addressed a group of Republican lawmakers in Atlanta, saying that "one of the great problems we have in the Republican party is that we don't encourage you to be nasty." He went on to explain that repairing the party could be achieved by "raising hell" instead of being nice.[15] When he became Speaker, he was intent on carrying out his plan by dismantling committees and norms of bipartisanship. He doubled the number of votes that the party speaker had on the steering committee, further solidifying the Speaker's grip on chair selection. Emphasizing the sweep of the changes, Fenno wrote: "The new Speaker abolished some committees and subcommittees, appointed the committee chairs, extracted loyalty pledges from committee leaders, controlled committee staff, selected committee members, created and staffed ad hoc task forces to circumvent committees, established committee priorities and timelines, and monitored committee compliance."[16]

The procedure for bill passage changed dramatically as a result of the aforementioned reforms during the second half of the twentieth century. Instead of bills passing gradually through subcommittees and committees and then being referred to the chamber for voting, bills began to be pushed down from the leadership into the committees and then forced quickly back to the chamber with few hearings—a pattern that continues today. The number of committee hearings has shrunk dramatically over the past several decades. According to a Brookings Institution report, during the 93rd Congress (1973–1974), committees and subcommittees held a total of just fewer than 6,000 meetings. By the 108th Congress (2003–2004), this number declined to a little over 2,000 meetings.[17] In an interview with me, a former Democratic congressman who served in Congress from 1989–2017, recalled:

Before the change in '94, for fifty years the chairs ran things. The Speaker gave them direction, but the chairs were really powerful. And when Gingrich came in, he took all the power to the Speaker's office. [Gingrich] told the chairs . . . what bills he wanted and in many instances gave the specifics of what he wanted in the bills. And so, it changed rather dramatically. Power was pulled up into the speakership. It had been that way under people in the far distant past, but it hadn't been that way for probably twenty-five years. And so the change in the power structure by taking it away from the chairs really made the committees almost irrelevant.

The former congressman went on to explain that Democrats kept these changes in place when they finally retook the House in 2006. He said, "When we retook the House in 2006, because at that point most people had only been under the Republicans and that's the way it was done, they said f**k 'em. We will do it that way too. And we did it exactly the same way." The congressman's reflection is a vivid indication of both the partisan strife in Congress and the continued decline in the power of committee chairs.

The changes instituted under Republican leadership had ramifications for committee learning. The graph in figure 0.1 emphasizes the marked decline in the size of congressional support staff over the past four decades.[18] According to the Brookings Institution's vital statistics on Congress, in 1979 there were between 8,500 and 9,000 total staff members working in the House. By 2015, the number had fallen to between 7,200 and 7,900. In 1979 there were approximately three and a half times as many personal staff members as committee staff members. By 2015, there were five times as many personal staff as committee staff. As congressional scholars Timothy LaPira and Lee Drutman explain, Gingrich "understood that long-standing expert committee staffers . . . gave individual members of Congress independent power bases." So, "he slashed

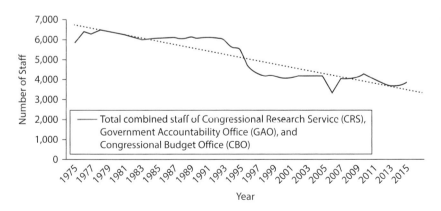

FIGURE 0.1 The size of the congressional support staff has declined over time.

Source: Brookings Institution, *Vital Statistics on Congress*.

committee staffing levels. . . . Congress has not yet recovered from the institutional brain drain."[19]

Gingrich also defunded the Office of Technology Assessment, which supplied Congress with expert analysis of science and technology, and he reduced funding to key institutions such as the Government Accountability Office (GAO) and Congressional Research Service (CRS). The GAO experienced an 18 percent reduction in budget after the Republicans regained control of the House of Representatives in 1994.[20] As one Democratic congresswoman who served in the House at the time of Gingrich's takeover recalled in an interview with me, "During the Gingrich era, he took the gavel as Speaker. He was I think really quite cunning in terms of eliminating long-time organizations inside Congress that did a great deal of the research." As a result of this loss of resources, the learning function of committees declined.

The changes in Congress also had a notable impact on bipartisanship. As Polsby explains, committees were once run by bipartisan coalitions. He describes the scene as "sharply restrained partisanship that had evolved into a subculture grounded in a bipartisan consensus. It is difficult to overestimate the power of this subculture to shape the attitudes of participants toward the political process."[21] He writes that some particularly bipartisan committees "took great pride in delivering to the floor proposals that had bipartisan cooperation in framing legislation."[22] This changed when the 1970s reforms shifted power into the hands of party leadership.

It is important to underline that some of the scholarly nostalgia for the bipartisanship of this period contains a racialized component. According to scholars of race and politics Desmond King and Rogers Smith, the bipartisanship described was a result of a consensus about segregation and race relations.[23] In the New Deal era preceding the 1970s reforms, President Roosevelt and congressional leadership agreed to sidestep addressing race issues in exchange for Southern support of the New Deal. With the start of the Civil Rights movement and the signing of the Civil Rights Act of 1964, there began a process of political realignment. The Democratic party lost a good deal of conservative Southern support. The composition of chairs also changed during this time period. In the mid-1960s, thirteen out of twenty committee chairs were Southern, but by 1980, only five chairs were from the South.[24] This compositional change was likely a result of continued Democratic control of the House, along with the Democratic loss of the South. Together, these political processes conspired to create a period of bipartisan committee relations followed immediately by one of partisan strife.

The combination of these racialized changes, together with the reforms of the 1970s and the Gingrich era, created a noxious environment for bipartisanship. John A. Lawrence identifies the 1970s as the beginning of the decline of bipartisanship in his book about congressional reform. He writes that "the large Democratic majority won in the aftermath of Vietnam and Watergate . . . created an unwarranted sense of confidence in . . . hegemony, which contributed to the failure to recognize the GOP threat."[25] Others place the bulk of the blame on Newt Gingrich's speakership in 1995. Gingrich harmed bipartisanship significantly by encouraging freshman Republican representatives not to bring their families with them to Washington. We can also see this change in the proportion of district staff versus Washington staff in the House, which rose from about one-third of total staff in 1979 to nearly half of the total staff in 2016. Before that time, most representatives brought their families and were likely to send their children to the same schools, have spouses who knew and were friendly with one another, and attend the same social gatherings. This personal interaction influenced political interaction. In Jonathan Haidt's investigation of the power of social contact across party lines in Washington, he explains that "intuitions come first, so anything we can do to cultivate more positive social connections will alter intuitions and thus, downstream, reasoning and behavior."[26] Once people's families and personal lives were no longer in Washington, there were fewer such opportunities to "cultivate more positive social connections" outside working hours, and therefore less bipartisan goodwill during working hours.

The Senate also underwent similar changes over the last century. Schickler and Rubin explain that, while many scholars treat the early twentieth-century Senate as "mirroring the House's development,"[27] there is evidence to suggest that party leadership in the early twentieth-century Senate was less consolidated than in the House. They cite the fact that the first mention of an official Senate majority leader was only in 1913. They go on to characterize the Senate of the first half of the twentieth century as an increasingly decentralized chamber in which parties struggled to maintain control of their members as internal divisions grew.

As a result of too many committee assignments and a rising workload, deliberation in the Senate declined during the second half of the twentieth century.[28] According to a Brookings Institution report, the number of hours the Senate spent in session rose from about 1,500 during the 80th Congress (1947–48) to about 2,400 during the 91st Congress (1969–70).[29] This trend was so apparent that the Senate decided to reform its committee system. In 1977, the Stevenson committee, named for its chair, Senator Adlai Stevenson (D-IL), was created to study and suggest how to reorganize Senate committees. The Stevenson committee attempted to reduce the number of committees and consolidate assignments, but Mann and Ornstein explain that "there was modest progress but no fundamental change: the underlying pressure to spread power and resources continues largely unabated."[30] The fact that senators are spread thinly across committees and burdened with a heavy legislative workload has a direct effect on their ability to learn in committees. Without the necessary time and resources, they cannot specialize in their committee's topic. Although the overall number of Senate staff remained relatively similar, the number of staff working under party leadership increased by 263 percent between 1977 and 2016.[31]

The explosive rise of filibustering in the Senate during the 1960s and 1970s had detrimental effects on the quality and quantity of legislation, and it bruised bipartisanship. The term "filibuster" refers to an obstructive attempt to delay or block bills, amendments, or other measures through prolonged speeches or debates. As congressional scholars Sarah Binder and Steven Smith explain, the filibuster was first introduced into the Senate in 1837, and "today . . . a minority of the Senate can still exploit the right of extended debate to prevent a majority from casting a vote," such that "even the threat of a filibuster by a single senator is often powerful enough to thwart a time-constrained majority from pursuing portions of its legislative agenda."[32] The only antidote to filibusters is Rule 22, which was adopted in 1917 and permits the supermajority to end a debate by invoking cloture. Binder and Smith track the number of filibusters per Congress from 1789 to 1989 and find a marked increase in filibustering starting in the late 1960s and 1970s. They write that filibustering rose to unparalleled levels at this time and identify a number of possible reasons for this trend. First, they explain that the increasing number of bills introduced created more targets for filibustering. Indeed, the number of recorded votes in the Senate rose from 248 in the 80th Congress (1947–1948) to 667 in the 91st Congress (1969–1970).[33] Second, the Senate was under increasing time constraints as its workload rose. In order to alleviate some pressure, Majority Leader Mike Mansfield introduced the two-track system, which made it easier for the minority to filibuster bills without bringing the Senate to a complete halt. Under this system, the Senate could have more than one bill pending on the floor and therefore move past filibustered measures. As a result, filibustering increased rapidly, and the quantity of legislation passed fell dramatically. Binder and Smith write, "by making filibusters more tolerable and less costly to the filibustering senators . . . tracking also seems to have sparked an increase in filibustering."[34] Scholars therefore classify filibustering as both a result of partisanship and as fuel that continues to drive it. It encourages members to adhere to party lines in votes and quash legislation put forward by the opposing party.

Today, the Senate committees are also characterized by much of the same dependency on the leadership and legislative impotence as House committees. In an interview with me, a senior Democratic senator explained:

> When it comes to the authority of committee chairs in the House . . . and in the Senate, it is all in the hands of the Speaker and the Republican leader as to whether a matter is going to move from the committee to the floor and the committee chairs in their day were powerful enough to really put pressure on a leader to bring a measure before them . . . not so much anymore. Unless that leader feels he is about to lose his own caucus, they can just stop things from happening.

The senator's assessment underscores the power shift away from committee chairs and committees and toward party leadership.

Bipartisanship also declined as regional divisions became barriers to collaboration. This was a result of a fall in Southern Democratic membership. Regional divides compounded party divisions in the Senate and further exacerbated partisan strife. By 1982, then Senator Joe Biden said of the Senate, "There's much less civility than when I came here ten years ago. There aren't as many nice people as there were before. Ten years ago, you didn't have people calling each other sons of bitches and voting to get at each other. As you break down social amenities one by one, it starts expanding geometrically."[35]

The introduction of television cameras into Congress represents another displacement to congressional institutions. Although the first live coverage of a congressional proceeding took place in 1947, there were hardly any television cameras in Congress for three decades after this debut. The aforementioned 1970 LRA also permitted House and Senate committees to start broadcasting committee hearings live. In 1979, CSPAN began streaming live coverage of the House floor. In 1986, the Senate followed suit. In part, this decision originated in a desire to restore public confidence after Watergate.[36] Since then, the number and incidence of television and other broadcast media in committee hearings has skyrocketed. Polsby writes of how, in the early days of CSPAN coverage of the House, Newt Gingrich and others would give speeches to an empty chamber, just to get on camera and gain publicity. He writes, "to an untutored television spectator, wild allegations delivered to an empty House were indistinguishable from the real business of Congress. From the point of view of Gingrich and his colleagues, this offered a free gift of publicity."[37] This story illustrates the manipulation of cameras for political gain.

Today, committee hearings can serve as a publicity stunt in a way that they could not before CSPAN. A former congressman, who served in the House of Representatives for thirty years, underscored this point, recalling that he would come in a few minutes before his scheduled five-minute questioning time and make a speech. He said he wanted to "get my television time." Yet another former congressman spoke of the weight he attached to televised hearings as a result of viewership. He said that when he chaired hearings on popular topics picked up by the media like sports, he would get much more visibility and that is why those hearings were important. In the Senate, television had a similar effect. In an interview with me, a senior Democratic senator admitted, "We play to the cameras. We are all sensitive to the fact that even though the chambers are empty and the galleries sparsely populated, it's going out over CSPAN. Someone someplace suffering from insomnia is watching the speech." The introduction and increasing embeddedness of television cameras represents another major displacement that may have created more theatrical hearings. Chapter 7 explores this in greater detail. A century of evolution and displacement in the Senate and House of Representatives produced a more partisan and public facing, and less deliberative and specialized Congress by undermining the committee system.

STUDYING COMMITTEES TODAY

Inside Congressional Committees: Function and Dysfunction in the Legislative Process focuses on contemporary committees for two major reasons. Even though committees have lost power, members of Congress still spend precious time in hearings. As a recent American Political Science Association Taskforce on Congressional Reform report explained, "Members frequently spend just three nights a week in Washington (when the House is in session) and four nights in their districts."[38] Nearly all hearings then take place in a short span between Tuesday morning and Thursday morning. A few hours of the barely two and a half days members of Congress have in Washington (much of which is spent on fundraising and other tasks) represent precious legislating time.

In addition, scholars still identify committees as part of the legislative concourse leading up to bill passage.[39] Just as members spend a lot of time in committees, so do bills. Committees are still where bills are referred for members of Congress to gather data; speak to external experts; and discuss, mark up, and sculpt bills prior to voting. Congressional scholar Jonathan Lewallen explains that "lawmaking studies tend to focus on the final row or three steps of the process (floor votes, bicameral negotiations, and veto bargaining). Yet by the time a bill either becomes law or fails to, two of the institution's most important decisions—whether to make policy and how   have already been made."[40] His explanation underscores the significance of studying the process leading up to voting rather than focusing solely on outcomes. Congressional scholar Richard Hall makes the same point, asserting that "majoritarian voting tells us only part of what we need to know. Again, the distinction that bears emphasizing is between revealed preferences and revealed intensities. Votes capture the former, not the latter. But members who wish to affect specific outcomes have much more to invest than their votes. Their legislative time and energy, staff effort, and political capital."[41] In an interview with me, a former congressman and committee chair explained, "You will never understand who a congressman is or why he did it if you look only at voting statistics." Only a deeper exploration of the stories behind voting trends will tell the whole story of Congress, he told me. Although committees are only part of the legislative story, and simultaneous changes in political parties as well as other branches of government also shape Congress, committees nevertheless form an important part of the lawmaking process leading up to voting. Therefore, they allow for a deeper exploration of the "stories behind voting."

However, even though committees are a significant part of the lawmaking process, they have been systematically understudied in the modern era. Polsby (1968),[42] Fenno (1973),[43] Kenneth Shepsle (1978),[44] Keith Krehbiel (1992),[45] Hall (1996),[46] and the other landmark literature on committee procedures are nearly half a century old. They were written before monumental changes like television cameras and streaming, and in an era in which Congress represented an altogether different institution with dated committee and bill passage procedures. Schickler and Rubin have noted the need for "careful studies of committee processes that could speak to contemporary debates about the purposes of the standing committee system."[47] This book offers a modern addendum to the classic literature, exploring committees today.

In the context of the devolution of committees as a space for specialization and deliberation and centers of legislative power, this book focuses on two core issues: (1) how do contemporary congressional committees work? and (2) how (if at all) do they still matter?

The first part of the book (chapters 1–3) examines how committees work. It examines the following questions: What are the procedures guiding the work of committees in today's evolved and displaced Congress? Which voices do committees hear in hearings and why? The book demonstrates the significant variation in the contemporary committee mechanics, based on partisanship, individual personalities, and different informal norms. Partisanship, with regard to the policy issue and in the nature of the relationship between chairs and ranking members and committee staff members, influences the way in which hearing topics and witness panels are chosen, and the degree to which witness panels exhibit a balance of perspectives. Partisan affiliations also "label" witnesses, branding them by association and affecting both who is invited and how their testimony is received. This part of the book also illustrates the significance of the personalities involved. The personal networks, knowledge, and preferences of committee leadership and staff members guide hearing creation and shape the degree to which lobbyists infiltrate the process. The professional background of individual witnesses is also of great significance, shaping how they communicate and how persuasive their testimony may be to members of the committee. This part culminates with the introduction of a novel witness typology, drawing on the data to present a theory of the kinds of witnesses that committees hear.

The second part of the book (chapters 4–7) focuses on the second part of the question—how committees matter—by exploring if and under what circumstances contemporary committees still fulfill each of the following core committee functions: deliberation, education, theater, and personal connection. Legislative scholars have identified these as central purposes of committees in legislatures, and these are the same functions that have shifted over the past century.

Scholars identify committees as a deliberative forum. Woodrow Wilson once wrote that "the House virtually both deliberates and legislates in small section. It delegates not only its legislative but also its deliberative functions to standing committees."[48] Much congressional scholarship speaks of deliberation as a core function of committees. Arthur Maass's "deliberation model" of Congress places committees at the center of congressional deliberation.[49] Joseph Bessette's in-depth study of deliberation in Congress again placed committees at the center of congressional deliberation. He writes, "By design it is in committees and subcommittees that the most detailed and extensive policy deliberation occurs within Congress. The committee and subcommittee structure of the House and Senate is an institutional device intended to solve the fundamental deliberative problem that faces a finite legislative body entrusted with hundreds of . . . issues. It is within the committees that . . . true subject matter expertise can be developed."[50] In addition, Polsby's emphasis on congressional institutions as a platform for empowering a greater number of voices, a key component of deliberation, suggests that committees are a logical focus for a study of deliberative democracy in Congress.[51] Previous scholarship therefore points to deliberation as a core function of committees.

Congressional scholarship also identifies committees as the center of congressional information gathering and specialization.[52] Laura Perna et al. explain that committee "hearings ostensibly enable legislators to gather information, explore ideas, and assess support for potential policy positions."[53] Emma Simson's research on citations of social science research in the 112th Congress found ninety-six references to research in written testimony before committees and fourteen references in hearing transcripts, while there were only two references made in floor debates and only twenty in House and Senate reports.[54] Committees are traditionally where research is brought in and where learning and specialization takes place.

Committees are also one of the major bipartisan institutions in a partisan Congress, forming a space for members of Congress to cultivate personal relationships with each other and with witnesses. Their significance as a bipartisan body has been noted in previous studies of Congress. In an analysis of congressional gridlock, Binder writes that "if members were given the chance to develop reasonable compromises at the committee level, there would be fewer challenges to the leadership, the Rules committee, and during floor consideration . . . because more partisan deliberations in committee reduce the likelihood of bill passage, encouraging policy compromise would probably bolster legislative performance."[55] Binder's comment emphasizes the importance of committees as bipartisan institutions and as spaces for potential collaboration and connection across party lines.

Committees can act as what Woodrow Wilson termed "the theatre of debate upon legislation." As a senior staffer on the Senate Judiciary Committee explained, sometimes "the purpose of the hearing is to give a public forum to discussions that largely happened behind closed doors." Bessette's work on the core functions of committees identified them as a stage for debate to be shaped publicly. He juxtaposes "political" and "deliberative" explanations for congressional processes, asserting that the "political explanation" for committee hearings is "to publicize issues in order to mobilize support outside of Congress."[56] Bessette's work points to the importance of committees' theatrical role in the academic study of committees.

The previous section charted the decline of committee capacity for deliberation, education, and personal connection over the past several decades and the parallel increase in their propensity for theatricality. Chapters 4–7 explore under what circumstances committees still fulfill each of these core goals. It argues that contemporary congressional committees still deliberate, learn, and provide a space for bipartisan connection under certain circumstances. They can also act as an arena for political theater. These chapters draw on the data to explain what kinds of witnesses, policy topics, hearings, and committees are most likely to result in deliberation, education, personal connection, or theater.

Taken together, chapters 1–7 form a comprehensive exploration of the procedure and purpose of committees in the contemporary Congress. This understanding of how, when, and for what purpose contemporary committees work paves the way to use committees more effectively.

THE DATA

The aforementioned congressman said that political scientists miss out by looking only at voting trends because "political scientists do not have access to the stories of who we are and what shapes us." This book relies on a large and diverse data set in order to tell a story of committees today and the trends that shape them. The analysis draws on an original data set of 1,364 pieces of witness testimony, representing 456 hearings in eight congressional committees during the 112th–116th Congresses, as well as over sixty-five interviews with senators, representatives, staff members, witnesses, and other relevant actors.

The large interview sample is unique in the landscape of modern political science. The sample of members of Congress comprised both women and men, several nonwhite members, and represented thirteen states and over eighteen congressional districts. The sample included the only PhD scientist in Congress, the first woman and first person of color to serve as chair of the House Science Committee, and the only nonvoting member of the House Agriculture Committee (representing the Virgin Islands), and committee members from both parties. The two senators interviewed each served in Congress for nearly four decades, and one of them is a senior member of the Democratic Senate leadership. The sample also included the former chair of the House Agriculture Committee, two former chairs of committees not included in the sample, former two-time chair of the Senate Foreign Relations Committee, and the current ranking member and vice ranking member of the House Science Committee. The sample contained a wide range of both Republican and Democratic staff members on every committee, and they ranged in seniority level and specialization. Last, I interviewed witnesses from different professional backgrounds and political affiliations (a scientist skeptical of climate change, a hunger relief advocate, a representative of the tech industry, and others).

Since Fenno's landmark work in the 1970s, and even Hall's more recent use of interview-based research on Congress, scholars of Congress have employed quantitative methods in their focus on quantifiable outcomes (voting, etc.). In fact, in Paul Pierson's critique of the "marginalization" of qualitative research in the study of American politics, he notes that less than 6 percent of articles in the three leading American politics journals employ qualitative methods (based on data from the period 2000–2005). Pierson writes, "Qualitative 'classics' of the Congress literature, such as Fenno (1978) and Mayhew (1974), are still venerated, but their research practices are not emulated. The deployment of sophisticated techniques for analyzing roll calls has dominated scholarly discussion."[57] The size, diversity, and stature of my interview sample and the resulting conclusions of my work are consequently unique in the current landscape of contemporary American political science. (See appendix A for more information on the interview sample.) It allows for a thorough exploration of the stories that shape Congress and the legislative concourse leading to policy creation.

Committee records are also underused as data, and they form another unique component of the data set.[58] This book analyzes committee transcripts using two unique kinds of language analysis (explained in greater detail in chapter 3). Using the "dictionary method" of sentiment analysis, I create an original data set of "balance" scores for 456 hearings to capture the extent to which the witness panel was positive versus negative about the issue at hand. In addition to sentiment analysis, I used Language Inquiry and Word Count (LIWC) software to assess the transcripts of witness testimonies. LIWC is computerized text analysis software developed by computer scientist Yla Tausczik and social psychologist James Pennebaker; it uses the dictionary method to assess the analytical language, clout, certainty, and other relevant aspects of the language of testimony. Neither of these methods have been previously employed in this way in the context of congressional committees. The data set of witness testimony spans five congresses (112th–116th Congresses). *Inside*

Congressional Committees also relies on an original data set of witness professions for a sample of five committees in the 114th Congress. This allows for further of exploration of who is heard by Congress.

The data are drawn from a representative sample of eight committees: Senate Judiciary, Finance, Foreign Relations, Commerce, House Science, Ways and Means, Veterans Affairs, and Agriculture. These committees cover different chambers, topic areas, desirability, and degrees of partisanship. A representative sample allows for an analysis of the committee system as a whole. I tease out how variation in committee characteristics shape the function of committees, and I draw conclusions that hold true across committees.

The committees in the sample represent different major policy areas to account for differences arising from subject matter focus. Political scientists John Aldrich and David Rohde call attention to the differences in committee procedures and processes between the House and Senate, and therefore the sample includes four committees from each chamber.[59]

Committee desirability might also influence committee behavior. As journalists Emma Roller and Stephanie Stamm explain, "Congressional committees are a bit like the four houses of Hogwarts School of Witchcraft and Wizardry—some are more desirable to get into than others."[60] Indeed, committee assignment is a complex process and integral in the study of committees.[61] Of course, many criteria guide committee assignment, including expertise, constituent interests, loyalty to the party, seniority, electoral concerns, and more. The Ways and Means Committee, included in the sample, is one of the most desirable committees in the House. Part of the reason is that, as the tax-writing committee, its jurisdiction is exceptionally broad. The aforementioned article states that "more bills are referred to Ways and Means than any other committee. In the 112th Congress, nearly a third of bills were referred to Ways and Means. That could explain why members find it such a desirable club to join—between 1995 and 2011, roughly thirteen members joined the committee for every one member who left it."[62] Many scholars have put forward theories about what guides assignment.[63] What is clear is that members who secure assignments to desirable committees may engage differently from those in other committees.[64] Therefore, the sample in the book reflects a range of committee "desirability" based on Charles Stewart and Tim Groseclose's categorization.[65]

In addition, I chose committees of varying degrees of partisanship. As noted in the opening of this introduction, one of the major changes in Congress in general and in the context of committees is rising partisan polarization. Scholarship also shows that committees vary in their degree of partisanship.[66] In order to account for this core element in selecting committees, I assessed partisanship based on Christopher Deering and Steven Smith's categorization of levels of "perceived conflict" of committees.[67]

The breakdown of sample committee policy focus, desirability, partisanship, and chamber is shown in table 0.1. The sample of committees and the range of data employed therefore allow for a comprehensive exploration of committee process, procedure, and function in the contemporary Congress.

TABLE 0.1 Sample Senate and House Committees

Committee	Jurisdiction	Desirability	Partisanship
Senate Judiciary Committee	*Topics:* Federal courts, immigration, constitutional amendments, and other related topics. *Oversight:* Department of Justice, nominations to judicial positions and positions within the Department of Justice and its related agencies.	High/medium	High
Senate Finance Committee	*Topics:* Social Security, revenue sharing, deposit of public funds, tariffs, debt, and more. *Oversight:* Internal Revenue Service.	High	Medium
Senate Foreign Relations Committee	*Topics:* Foreign affairs and treaties. *Oversight:* Department of State and all diplomatic nominations.	High	Medium[1]
Senate Commerce, Science, and Transportation Committee[2]	*Topics:* Transport industries and activities (land, ocean, and aerial), sports, consumer affairs, and communications. *Oversight:* Department of Commerce and the Federal Communication Commission.	Medium	Medium
House Ways and Means Committee	*Topics:* Tax writing committee of the House of Representatives. It has a wide jurisdiction that includes Social Security, Medicare, child support programs, foster care, adoption, as well as unemployment benefits and other assistance programs.	High	Medium

TABLE 0.1 (*continued*)

Committee	Jurisdiction	Desirability	Partisanship
House Science, Space, and Technology Committee[3]	*Topics:* Scientific research and development, exploration of outer space, science scholarship, and general support of American science. *Oversight:* National Science Foundation, the National Institute of Standards and Technology, and NASA.	Medium/low	Medium
House Agriculture Committee	*Topics:* Farming, nutrition and hunger relief, rural development, agricultural development and research, animal and dairy industry, and forestry. *Oversight:* Department of Agriculture.	Medium/low	Medium
House Veterans Affairs Committee	*Topics:* Issues pertaining to veterans— rehabilitation and readjustment to civilian life, veterans hospitals and medical care, education, and so on. *Oversight:* Department of Veterans Affairs.	Medium	Low

Source: Author created.
[1] Deering and Smith classified it as high in 1997, but my interviews suggest it is less partisan in the contemporary Congress.
[2] Referred to in this book as the Senate Commerce Committee.
[3] Referred to in this book as the House Science Committee.

PLAN OF THE BOOK

Chapters 2–4 concentrate on how committees work. Chapter 2 describes all the elements involved in setting up a hearing, deciding on a topic, and inviting witnesses to testify (including the ways in which interest groups and lobbyists are enmeshed in the process), and explains what resulting hearings look like. Chapter 3 explores who Congress hears from in hearings and relies on a wide variety of data about witnesses. Chapter 4 draws on the preceding chapters to present a theory of the different types of witnesses testifying in hearings.

Chapters 4–7 examine the kinds of hearings that result from these processes. They present a series of parameters—partisanship (of committee and topic), structure (chamber and committee desirability), formality, the nature of the topic, types of witnesses—and explain how each of these parameters affects the likelihood of different kinds of hearings. Each chapter centers on a different function (hearings as a deliberative forum, an educational platform, a theatrical stage, and a space for personal connection) and utilizes illustrative examples and data to indicate when hearings are most likely to serve each of these functions and how each kind of hearing stands to affect members. Chapters 4–7 show how and when committees still matter.

Inside Congressional Committees: Function and Dysfunction in the Legislative Process demonstrates the relevance of the findings to the contemporary and future Congresses. It draws on the conclusions about how and when committees work to suggest reforms for more effective utilization of committees in the future. Chapters 2–7 connect results to contemporary congressional procedure and put forward recommendations for committee reforms that emerge from the findings. Chapter 8 discusses the implications and significance of the book's conclusions.

Inside Congressional Committees is a book about American congressional committees. In some instances, however, certain international examples are introduced to highlight the scope and relevance of my findings to legislative studies as a whole, or to substantiate claims by drawing on similar examples from other legislative committees. According to the Inter-Parliamentary Union *2022 Global Parliamentary Report*, over 72 percent of parliaments hold committee hearings.[68] Lawrence Longley and Roger Davidson write, "Committees figure significantly on all continents and in most countries of the world, increasingly serving as the main organising centre of both legislation and parliamentary oversight of government".[69] Therefore, it is logical to draw on legislative literature in analysis of American congressional committees. Some of the book's conclusions may also shed light on committees as a universal legislative institution.

1

SETTING UP A HEARING

No man can be a competent legislator who does not add to an upright intention and a sound judgement a certain degree of knowledge of the subjects on which he is to legislate.

—JAMES MADISON, *FEDERALIST*, NO. 53

At the heart of committee work are committee hearings. Committees hold hearings to hear from external witnesses and gather information on legislation, oversight, investigations, and nominations. Hearings are held every week in both the Senate and the House of Representatives on a range of topics.

The first step of the committee hearing process is deciding on hearing topics and selecting witnesses to testify. This chapter explores the mechanics driving the hearing process, a process essential to grasping fully how Congress operates in hearings and how committee members are affected by the testimony.

I collected data on witness selection through extensive conversations with committee staff and witnesses. I spoke to both majority and minority staff members on the committees, affording two different viewpoints on the process. In addition, I interviewed staff on different subcommittees in several of the committees. This allowed me to gauge the variation between full committee and subcommittee procedures as well as between different subcommittees. I also spoke to both former and current staffers (who have served on the committees for varying lengths of time) to get a sense of how the process has changed over time. Last, I interviewed witnesses who testified before the different committees about how they were approached and how they prepared for the testimony. This served as verification of the staff interviews and added an additional perspective.

As I embarked on my quest to uncover the process of witness selection, I was struck first and foremost by the unsystematic nature of the procedures. The conversations provided considerable evidence that, although there are formal rules, in reality the process is largely informal and varies by committee and time period.

SETTING THE AGENDA

At the start of the Congress, the first order of business is to set the agenda and decide what hearings will take place. The agenda is officially in the hands of the majority. They have full control over hearing topics and timings. When the majority and minority members and staff are on good terms, however, the minority can have some impact on the agenda. A minority staffer on the Commerce Committee described how, in recent years, minority and majority staff on the Commerce Committee work sufficiently well together that a hearing topic recommended by the minority was sometimes accepted by the majority. Staff on other committees shared similar accounts, recalling instances of the minority influencing the topic of hearings when the environment in the committee remained collaborative. In some cases, there were stories about recent collaboration, and in other cases, staff told stories from previous terms. Despite isolated incidents of minority influence, the agenda remains almost entirely in the hands of the majority.

The topics that the majority chooses vary by committee, chair, and time period. A majority staffer on the House Science Committee explained that they usually have hearings on agencies under their jurisdiction, the budget, bills requiring reauthorization, and what the staffer referred to as the "unknown." She explained, "There's sort of the kind of unknown. Either it's that we think this is going to be a hot topic in science for this year so something we need to look at. And then there are the things that just happen . . . for example, we have some cybersecurity jurisdiction. Suddenly, well we have to have a hearing on that." When I posed the same question to a majority staffer on the Senate Foreign Relations Committee, he characterized their planning as a "combination of strategic planning and reactive planning." Some of the hearings are put together quickly as a reaction to a pressing event, and others are planned months in advance in an attempt to shape a policy debate. A staffer on the Senate Judiciary Committee described the hearing process thus:

> Picking out the hearings is going to be . . . part of a deliberate agenda. . . . If you've got a bill, it's very common to have a hearing on the legislation and how it works . . . whoever is in the majority has a specific agenda that they're trying to advance and pursue and dig into. And so the hearings are really an opportunity, whether it's looking at something going on in the world or whether it's looking at their legislation to keep pushing that forward to laying the groundwork.

He went on to explain that this agenda can result from specific events or specific interests of the chair:

> Sometimes there are events that just naturally lend themselves. . . . Other times the chair of the committee will just have an agenda . . . someone could be particularly interested in one specific area of what they cover in their committee. . . . We just had a hearing on election interference by Facebook and Twitter. That's obviously driven by the policy interests and preferences of the chair and the stuff that they want to focus on.

The staffer's remarks support previous research on hearings in earlier eras. In 1995, Kevin M. Leyden wrote that "many times chairs will hold these events to promote their own agendas and invite witnesses who can help facilitate this effort. In other instances, a chair may be interested in using the forum to gain insight and information about the consequences of various policy proposals, or simply to learn why a problem exists in the first place."[1] Venturing even further back in committee scholarship, in 1967, Lewis Froman and Paul A. Freund wrote that the "functions" of hearings depend on the legislation under consideration and the incentives of members and chairs and can include "attempts by the chair to provide public support or opposition for the bill (depending upon his predilections), to stall the legislative process, to act as a check on the executive branch, to 'test' the proposed law in terms of popular and interest group support, to provide citizens with an opportunity to make their views known, and to give a chair an opportunity to become visible to the general public."[2] These conclusions demonstrate that hearings (past and present) can serve different purposes depending on the policy issue at hand, the chair and staff, and timing.

The majority staffer on the Senate Foreign Relations Committee also explained that only a small number of the hearings are about legislation, remarking, "You would think, okay, the standard process is we're going to move a bill and therefore, let's do a hearing on it, [but] almost never." This fits with an overall historical trend of a decline in hearings linked to specific pieces of legislation.

Figure 1.1 draws on a data set from a study by Lewallen et al. in 2016 that analyzed 22,000 hearings starting in the 1970s.[3] It showed a dramatic drop in the number of hearings dedicated to policy solutions. Lewallen et al.'s study demonstrated that two-thirds of hearings in the 1970s were dedicated to policy solutions, whereas only one-third of hearings in recent years focused on policy solutions. Lewallen's additional study of committee hearings in 2020 further demonstrated the decline of legislative

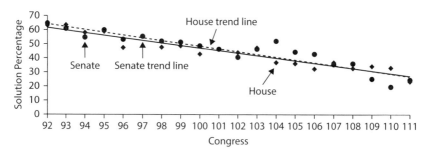

FIGURE 1.1 Hearings on policy solutions, 92nd to 111th Congress. Congress is holding fewer hearings devoted to exploring solutions to policy problems.

Note: This graph is taken from a June 2017 article by Jonathan Lewallen, Sean Theriault, and Bryan Jones in *Vox*. The graph in the article is based on the same data set employed in the 2016 Lewallen et al. study.

Source: Jonathan Lewallen, Sean M. Theriault, and Bryan D. Jones, "The Senate's Disastrous Process for Crafting the AHCA Fits a Historic Pattern," *Vox*, June 21, 2017, https://www.vox.com /the-big-idea/2017/6/21/15843352/senate-hearings-secrecy-ahca-debate-stealth.

hearings and a parallel rise in oversight hearings.[4] The decline in the number of hearings is in line with the general trends discussed in the introduction: a degeneration of congressional deliberation and a restructuring
of the legislative process over the past several decades. Scholars of American politics have noted that, instead of laws originating in committees
and passing to the chamber, bills are now pushed down from the party
leadership, hurried through committees, and taken straight to the floor
for voting.[5] The decline in hearings on legislative topics makes sense in
this context. Interviews with staff members confirm this shift in the way
committee hearings are used.

BETTER TOGETHER—PARTISANSHIP AND WITNESS PANELS

Once the hearing topic is decided, the staff decide on witnesses to invite.
Witness testimony forms the nucleus of any congressional hearing. In a
traditional hearing, several witnesses provide testimony and then committee members and witnesses engage in dialogue.

The official rules of the House and Senate entitle the minority to one
witness. House Rule 9 states that "whenever a hearing is conducted by a
committee on a measure or matter, the minority members of the committee shall be entitled, upon request to the chair by a majority of them
before the completion of the hearing, to call witnesses selected by the
minority to testify with respect to that measure or matter during at least
one day of hearing thereon."[6] The number of witnesses that the majority invites changes, but averages around three to four witnesses. These
remain the official rules, but the interviews showed that, in reality, the
numbers largely depend on the personal relationships of the majority and
minority staff.

When relationships stay collegial, majority and minority staff members
may put together a joint list. Interviewees for the Senate Commerce Committee and Senate Foreign Relations Committee said that this was standard. A senior staffer on the Senate Commerce Committee shared that
this happens regularly on their committee because of their long-standing relationships with each other and their shared understanding of
what "types" of witnesses certain topics call for. The staffer reflected that

approximately half of the time they create a joint list, usually for hearings on less contentious issues. He added that, even when they disagree, they try to "disagree without being disagreeable." On the Senate Foreign Relations Committee, a minority staffer explained:

> The minority can always invite their own witness and the majority can invite their own witness, and sometimes, we will agree to a third consensus candidate. . . . The majority could come back to us and say, we want two witnesses, you can have one, they could. But because for so long, this committee worked on parity, they're unlikely to do that, because when we're in the majority again, we could make life difficult for them by doing the same thing.

The staffer's comments depict a long-standing and pervasive culture of collaboration in the Senate Foreign Relations Committee, an environment in which the official rules are overshadowed by informal traditions of cooperation. In certain instances, certain subcommittees within partisan committees also exhibit similar tendencies. For example, a staffer on the Antitrust Subcommittee of the Senate Judiciary Committee explained:

> Senators Lee and Klobuchar have had a pretty good working relationship for a long time. And so there have been a lot of examples of our offices working very closely on hearings, even if we approach issues from a different angle. We keep in touch pretty well, and there hasn't been too much of like here's the witness list. This is the bill. Here's what it is. Take it or nothing you can do about it. Let us know who your one person is.

Interviews revealed that other committees also have joint lists for certain nonpartisan hearings. A veteran House Agriculture Committee staffer explained that joint lists can happen "if it's something where we can all agree, and the data is fairly uniform." A staffer on the Antitrust Subcommittee of the Senate Judiciary Committee explained, "If you agree on an issue, then, you know, maybe you, like it's much easier to agree on who the witnesses are. And you're always going to want to have at least somebody from the other side. . . . You don't want to have it completely stacked just for credibility's sake. But if you're so . . . if you're in total agreement, that can make it easier to pick the witnesses. If you're more divided than you might, then it gets harder." Another staffer on the Senate Judiciary Committee explained:

> Depending on the issue there might be more collaboration on who the witnesses were, so, for instance, one of the issues I focused on was property. There tends to be less of a partisan divide on IP [intellectual property] issues than there is on some other issues. Say there would be six witnesses. Grassley would pick three witnesses, Feinstein would pick three with the three witnesses. . . . I think that there was more collaboration between majority and minority staff in terms of scheduling. And just, you know, Grassley would say, okay, these are the three witnesses I want. Who are the three witnesses you want?

Witnesses on the House Science Committee echoed this idea. For example, in September 2017, the House Science Committee had a hearing on the solar eclipse over the United States. Several interviewees identified this as a bipartisan hearing. The congressional relations staffer of the National Science Foundation (who was previously a staffer on the House Science Committee) even comically referred to this hearing as a "love fest." The majority staffer explained the process of constructing a joint list for the eclipse hearing, saying, "I talked to my minority counterpart and I told her who I was thinking about for witnesses. And she said, 'What do you think will be good?' I said, 'Well, I'm kind of thinking education base.' So she went out and found an education person. So sometimes it's done that way." This example shows that joint lists have the potential to be both more diverse and more cohesive. I also heard several stories across different committees of the majority deciding on categories or types of witnesses, and sending the list to the minority for suggestions.

In the absence of personal staff relationships, the formal rules assume a greater weight. A minority staffer on the House Science Committee Subcommittee on Energy and Environment stressed that his subcommittee is less collegial in relation to the other House Science Committee subcommittees. He described how, in his subcommittee, the minority stick to their one allotted witness and they do not work together to form a joint list. He told me that in the previous Congress there was "absolutely no coordination . . . if we had a hearing on Thursday, they would let us know two weeks before at 4:59." This last point about timing highlights another way in which relationships affect rules. In this case, the minority and majority had no relationship, so the minority got the minimum official notice for the hearing. In cases where the minority is more involved in the planning, the minority staff may get more notice and therefore more time to plan. These examples underscore the power of personal relationships and the importance of informal norms.

THE CHAIR

One of the most significant factors in staff relationships is the chair because they control the hiring process.[7] This influences the types of witnesses invited. As the two-time chair of the Senate Foreign Relations Committee explained, "The power of chair comes from determining how the time of the committee will be spent, who will be heard, what subjects will be heard, what witnesses will be called." The chair accomplishes these goals through their staff, and the chair has full power to hire staff and to determine the number and professional background of their staff. A staffer on the House Agriculture Committee explained that the chair is given a budget and they can choose to hire either a few senior staffers or a larger number of junior staffers. Some chairs might prefer several junior staffers at the expense of one seasoned staffer. The staffer explained that, whereas Chair Lucas (2011–2015) kept many of the staff, Chair Conaway (2015 to the present) laid off two-thirds of the staff. This had grave consequences for relationships and witness lists. Another House Agriculture Committee staffer, who has worked in the majority and then the minority, explained that she used to have a personal relationship with members of the other staff, and she recalled how she lost those long-standing relationships when the staff were fired.

Staff members across different committees spoke about how staff retention guides cross-party staff relations. Staff told stories of working with the other side productively until a new chair came and hired completely new staff members, with the result that collaboration ground to a halt. One longtime staffer who has worked on both majority and minority staff of the House Science Committee for over a decade, told me in detail about her personal relationship with her counterpart. She said that when she was in the minority, her relationship with her majority counterpart enabled her to shape witness panels from the minority. She described how this process remained the same when she transitioned from the majority to the minority because of their collaborative relationship. This changed, however, when the new chair brought in different staff members she did not know, and the bipartisan process disintegrated.

Staff turnover also has other implications for the hearing process. On the Senate Finance Committee, a staffer reflected on the power of retaining staff from one chair to the next, saying, "Chair Grassley knew he only had two years left in his term limit as chair. And so, you know, I think he kind of looked at it as people that have already been there and working on the issues would be most helpful for him in a short period of time . . . so having people that already knew this committee's rules and time lines meant that they could get set up more quickly and through the right channels." The damage resulting from the loss of this staff knowledge was explained by the ranking member of the House Science Committee, who compared her relationship with Chair Ralph Hall to her relationship with Chair Lamar Smith, saying:

> We had a much [better] understanding because [Chair Hall] would take the time to discuss issues before . . . he would be responsive towards questions. It is very clear that a conservative and a so-called liberal are not going to be together on many things, but working together we can come to an agreement on what we can live with and with Ralph Hall we were able to do that, but with Lamar there are times he gives me the impression he doesn't know what is in some of the deals. I don't know whether this is driven by him or his staff. The staff has totally turned over since he has been there, so he does not have much institutional knowledge from the staff.

Indeed, a staffer on the House Science Committee confirmed that Smith fired an unusually large number of staff members when he became chair. The congresswoman's reflection, although only her own evaluation, calls attention to the detrimental effects of turnover. When staff members leave, the chair loses their institutional knowledge and expertise: among the costs of that loss can be the chair's relationship with the ranking member and the relationships between respective staffs. On the Republican side, chairs turn over more quickly because of the GOP's self-imposed term limits. The Republican conference permits Republican chairs to serve a maximum of three consecutive terms in leadership, thereby creating even greater potential for staff turnover.

In addition to differences in hiring strategies, different chairs also have unique styles and distinct relationships with their subcommittee chairs and ranking members. For example, the majority staff of the House Science Committee shared that Chair Lamar Smith was very involved and reviewed every hearing and witness list. Some chairs may take a more hands-off approach and assume a less direct role in witness selection. A majority staffer on the Senate Foreign Relations Committee said of Chair Corker, "He's like a CEO by nature, so he actually . . . gives the staff a lot of room to run, you know. Or a lot of rope . . . just don't hang yourself with it." This statement is illustrative of the consequences that chair style has for staff selection of witnesses and hearings. Another difference is the degree of autonomy that chairs afford to subcommittee chairs in suggesting hearings or selecting witnesses. In addition, the relationship between the chair and the ranking member affects the degree to which the minority is involved in the witness selection and hearing process. A staffer on the Senate Finance Committee explained, "The minority definitely had . . . more input than other committees, perhaps . . . because I think a lot of different committees didn't coordinate as well and didn't have the repertoire the way we did. And it also came down to the ranking member, you know. There was just a very good relationships between the two senators." These stories of the importance of individual chairs in deciding staff and witness dynamics again underline the power of individual idiosyncrasies in the committee process.

WITNESS SELECTION

The interviews with witnesses and staff members illustrated several criteria for selecting witnesses. First, long-standing personal relationships with witnesses factor significantly into selection. In several cases, witnesses said that they knew the staff members prior to the hearing and had even been invited on multiple occasions. Several of the staff members I spoke to have worked in their committee for decades and gotten to know the professional community in their field very well. A longtime staffer on the Nutrition Subcommittee of the House Agriculture Committee shared that the world of nutrition policy is "a small community" and she either knows most of the relevant actors or knows someone who can connect her. A minority staffer on the House Science Committee echoed this, explaining, "It's all about relationships and negotiating and trying to understand . . . there is a finite world of people on which [the staff] can draw from."

A witness who testified before the House Veterans Affairs Committee representing a veteran's service organization explained that she frequently knows the other witnesses on the panel and even discusses testimony with them before a hearing. She said that "a lot of times, the witnesses are people that I work and interact with on a weekly basis, you'll interact with them before the hearings . . . we'll talk about what positions we're going to take . . . we know what's going to be said. So we're ready for it." The fact that all the witnesses know each other well enough to interact before the hearing indicates insular networks.

This confirms David Whiteman's research on congressional communication in which he argues that congressional "information networks" are narrow in the sense that they are skewed and they are deep because staff are well connected and well informed about the policy community in their field.[8] Jack R. Van Der Slik and Thomas C. Stenger similarly found in their study of committee witnesses that "respondents identified a great many people, agencies, or groups who provided positive assistance to them in obtaining the opportunity to appear as a witness. . . . Most of the 'assists,' 35 percent, came from congressional contacts, especially staff and members."[9]

The importance of personal relationships between policy professionals and staff members creates a bias toward witnesses who are based in and around Washington. Committees do not cover the cost of travel to Washington, so it is easier to find someone willing to come from Georgetown than from Palo Alto. All the staffers I spoke to stressed that their committees do not pay for witnesses to come testify. Although lobbying groups sometimes step in to cover the cost of travel (one scientist I spoke to explained that a science lobbying group paid for his flight from California to Washington), these financial considerations may distort the pool of potential witnesses.

The parochial interests of the chair and ranking minority member also affect witness selection. There may be a number of reasons why these interests would shape witness selection, including reelection concerns, fundraising connections, or personal proclivities. Staffers explained that they might first look for someone who has the expertise or perspective they want and who also comes from their chair or ranking member's district or alma mater. A senior minority staffer on the House Science Committee explained that her ranking member, Daniel Lipinski, prefers witnesses from his home state of Illinois or his alma mater institutions (Duke and Stanford). Therefore, she will first try to find someone from this area or from these universities who also has the necessary expertise or perspective. On the Senate Commerce Committee, the minority staffers shared similar accounts. A staffer explained that if there is a hearing that relates in some way to Florida, for example, they will try to invite a witness from Florida (the state of the ranking minority member, Senator Bill Nelson).

Second, the witnesses are selected for their subject matter expertise. If the topic pertains to a government agency, the committee staff will typically invite representatives of that agency (usually as part of a separate government witness panel). In addition to government representatives, staffers also seek other types of professional expertise. A minority staffer on the House Science Committee spoke of wanting to fill in "gaps of expertise" in the witness list in order to provide the necessary information to the members. She explained the importance of inviting people who can accurately inform members of Congress about the different dimensions of the issue, based on their specialized knowledge of the field. For example, in October 2017, the House Science Committee had a hearing on quantum physics, to which they invited experts on quantum physics to inform the representatives about the state of the field. The Senate Foreign Relations Committee had a hearing on the Islamic State of Iraq and Syria (ISIS) in June 2017, during which they heard from Dr. Dan Byman, a Georgetown professor and senior fellow at the Brookings Institution who studies terror. A senior Senate Judiciary Committee staffer on the Antitrust Subcommittee explained, "I mean, you want experts. If the hearing has to do with a specific company, you're going to ask them to submit somebody . . . you want the most senior person that you can get . . . you want people that are knowledgeable on the subject."

In addition to expertise, sometimes staffers seek a particular perspective. A Senate Commerce Committee staffer explained, "When you select a witness you know what they are going to say, what side they are going to take." Staffers did admit that they occasionally have a conversation with the witnesses about the scope of the hearing and the members' interests; however, they never tell them what assessment to present or what side to take. Once witnesses are invited, they put together written and oral testimony on their own. As a result, staff preselect witnesses based on prior knowledge of their perspectives. Conversations with staff members shed light on several examples of this type of selection. A majority staffer on the House Science Committee said that she tries to "tell a story" and selects witnesses who together can paint a picture of that story. Her allusion to "telling a story" indicates that she wants the information conveyed in a certain way. A staffer on the House Agriculture Committee spoke of the construction of the twenty-three hearings with over eighty witnesses on the subject of the Supplemental Nutrition Assistance Program (SNAP) over the course of two Congresses. She explained that, because SNAP is controversial, "you want to make sure that you have got your voice." Similarly, a staffer on the Senate Judiciary Committee explained, "You want people that are going to help support your interpretation of the issues at hand." Each side wants to tell their story and voice their concerns, and so they invite people who can articulate those concerns.

This calculus fluctuates depending on whether the staffer is choosing the list together or separately. If the minority and majority are not working in collaboration, the minority may feel compelled to invite someone who can either rebut or balance the majority witnesses. In the case of the House Science Committee's Energy and Environment Subcommittee, the staffer explained that the majority will bring in several witnesses to make distinct points on an issue, and for his one witness he will look for a generalist who is able to rebut the different points made by the majority witnesses. Other minority staffers echoed the notion of bringing in witnesses to offset the majority witnesses. In the Senate Commerce Committee, the minority staffer described a conscious decision to "balance" the majority witness list, saying that if the majority invites certain professional types such as industry representatives, the minority might seek "balance" by inviting stakeholders who represent the public interest. A staffer on the Senate Judiciary Committee Antitrust Subcommittee similarly explained,

"You don't want to be a witness panel full of academics, or a witness panel full of lawyers, or a witness panel full of consumer advocacy groups."

Yet another calculation is the opinion of the witness and the zeal with which he or she conveys it. The minority staff on the House Science Committee's Subcommittee on Energy and Environment gave the example of a hearing on climate change in March 2017, in which the majority invited Dr. Judith Curry, Dr. John Christy, and Dr. Roger Pielke Jr., three climate change skeptics. The minority staffer explained, "We thought to ourselves, if you are going to bring in these three people, we are not going to have a serious discussion about climate change. So we're going to bring in the loudest and most prolific person we can think of and that was Michael Mann. That was a deliberate choice by us because you have to fight fire with fire." This is an example in which the minority's choice of witness was based not only on professional expertise of the witness but also on his public association with a partisan issue and reputation as an ardent advocate for the issue.

REPRESENTATION

Congressional committees are gendered and racialized. Studies around the word show that women legislators are underrepresented as committee chairs and relegated to certain roles and issues. The 2020 Interparliamentary Union report on women in parliament found that, as of January 2021, women occupy 259 of the 934 committee chairs in the survey (about 28 percent). The number drops dramatically to about 19 percent of total chairs when gender equality committees are excluded.[10] Sociologist Catherine Bolzendahl surveyed forty years of committee data from Sweden, Germany, and the United States and found that women were chronically underrepresented as chairs. She found that in Germany, for example, even woman-dominated committees (culture, tourism, human rights) have 75 percent to 83 percent male chairs. She also found that women occupied the fewest leadership roles in committees focused on "masculine" issues (budget, economy, legal affairs). Figure 1.2, which was taken from Bolzendahl's study, demonstrates that the United States has consistently lagged far behind in terms of female chairs, but even Sweden and

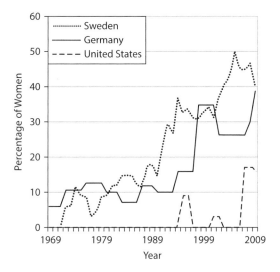

FIGURE 1.2 Percentage of women who chair or vice-chair legislative committees in Sweden, Germany, and the United States.

Source: Catherine Bolzendahl, "Opportunities and Expectations: The Gendered Organization of Legislative Committees in Germany, Sweden, and the United States," *Gender & Society* 28, no. 6 (2014): 847–876.

Germany do not achieve parity.[11] From a gender perspective, Bolzendahl explains:

> Organizations are not gender neutral, but systematically privilege men and (hegemonic) masculinity, marginalize women and the "feminine," and contribute to gender segregation. . . . Legislative committees may be structured in ways that create and maintain preferred gender constructions. . . . Specifically, women's overrepresentation on family committees may reinforce the notion that women deal with "soft" issues, simultaneously coding the issues "feminine" and thus of lesser power and prestige. Men's overrepresentation on defense or tax committees reaffirms their association with "hard" issues that convey power and mastery.[12]

In the United States, women are chronically and systematically underrepresented as committee chairs. From the 1st to the 115th Congress, only twenty women chaired a House committee and only thirteen women

chaired Senate committees.[13] Bolzendahl writes that gender discrimination in committees occurs "through unequal access to leadership positions, such as committee chair, where men's dominance as chairpersons
could block policy output by women members. . . . This process creates
women's internal exclusion despite a formal presence on the committee."[14]
Women are also usually newer members than their white male counterparts, which further undermines their power and specialization. It was
only in 1978 that the first woman was ever elected to the Senate without
her husband having served.[15] Bathroom facilities for women in the Senate were only provided in 1992. Prior to that time, female Senators such
as Margaret Chase Smith had to use public restrooms meant for tourists
visiting the Capitol.[16]

From a race perspective, Victor Ray explains that "race, as a multi-
dimensional concept, encodes schemas of sub- and super-ordination
that can be activated when connected to resources."[17] He gives historical
examples of "schemas of racial segregation" expressed as organizational
resources (buses, lunch counters, wages). Similarly, racial discrimination
guides the way in which resources are allocated in committees. Between
the 1st and 115th Congress, only 19 African Americans have chaired a
House committee and only one African American has chaired a Senate
committee.

There is also an overwhelming lack of diversity in staffing. Ninety-one
percent of congressional staff are white, and 64 percent are male.[18] A Joint
Roper report found that "people of color make up 38 percent of the U.S.
population, but only about 14 percent of staff. Both white Democrats
and white Republicans hire overwhelmingly white top staff, even though
their districts are surprisingly diverse." Senior staff positions are even
less diverse. No fewer than 88 percent of legislative directors are white.[19]
Women made up over half of all staff positions, but occupied only a third
of senior staff positions.

These extraordinary staff statistics are partially a result of the pipeline
to getting a congressional job. In their study of congressional staffers,
Alexander Furnas et al. found that nearly half of staffers had previously
worked as unpaid interns (either in the Washington, DC, office, on a
campaign, or in the district).[20] Who has the resources to start off with a
grueling unpaid internship? Young people who already come from priv-
ilege are those who can most afford an unpaid internship. If so many

staffers start as interns and work their way up, fewer unpaid interns of color eventually translate into fewer top staff of color. As former unpaid congressional intern Audrey Henson writes in her article, "Diversity on Capitol Hill Starts with Paying Interns," "I'd always thought the hardest part about one of these exclusive congressional internships would be getting it. What I learned is that the much more challenging piece is doing what it takes to keep it. Unless you have the financial means to make an unpaid internship work, Washington, DC, might not be for you."[21] She explains that she had to work two jobs just to afford to keep her job in Congress.

The lack of representation in chairs and staff has implications for committee hearing setup. This chapter has explained how the personal networks of staff and chairs shape witness selection. Chairs have great power in hiring staff, preferencing witnesses from their own towns, institutions, or personal circles, and choosing hearing topics. In an interview, the first woman and first African American ranking member of the House Science Committee explained that she makes a point of representing women and minorities as minority witnesses. A female witness who testified before the House Veterans Affairs Committee drew a direct connection between the female chair of the subcommittee on health and an emphasis on diversity in witness panels. She said, "It's very obvious by her legislation and just the things that she advocates for that equality and ensuring that all are seated at the table . . . [that she is] making an effort to make sure that there is more diversity in testimony."

That is not to say that women necessarily pick female witnesses or that minorities choose minority witnesses. In fact, even if one tried, in many fields, these same groups are underrepresented in expert roles. Nevertheless, when white male voices are not the only ones to design the stage, it is reasonable to imagine that members will hear a more representative set of voices and topics in hearing panels. This is backed up by research. Gender and politics scholar Susan Franceschet and Latin American expert Jennifer Piscopo showed that quota laws for female representation in the Argentine legislature led to an increase in the introduction of women's rights bills.[22]

Witness panels that reflect the makeup of the members may not only bring more voices to the table but also amplify them. One study showed that when women chair committees in conferences, more women spoke.[23]

On the other hand, a staffer from the parliament of Fiji explained the effect of chair gender on witnesses, saying, "When they go out for public hearings, I know sometimes the witnesses tend to . . . feel intimidated by a male-dominated committee. When there is a female MP [member of parliament] that is present with the committees, they tend to open up and give our submission to the committee members."[24]

Given the importance of individual identities in setting hearing agendas, hiring staff, and selecting witnesses, the lack of diversity in committee leadership and staffing has important consequences for the process.

THE POWER OF LOBBYISTS IN
THE HEARING PROCESS

Interest groups and lobbyists affect witness panels in myriad ways. It is difficult to identify and quantify the many subtle ways in which lobbyists are involved because these interactions largely take place behind closed doors. In fact, the difficulty of quantifying the effect of lobbying has been noted by other scholars of lobbying in Congress. In her survey piece on lobbying, lobbying expert Beth Leech examines the problem of accurately gauging lobby effects and explains that too often it is seen as a simple tit-for-tat interaction.[25] In his extensive study of lobbying, congressional scholar Lee Drutman asserts that "the lack of a direct, statistically significant correlation does not mean that there is no influence. It just means that the influence is unpredictable. The policy process is neither a vending machine nor an auction. Outcomes cannot be had for reliable prices."[26] Consequently, I do not attempt to quantify lobbying in this book but rather to use interviews as far as possible in order to shed light on some of the ways in which lobbyists shape witness selection and interactions between members of Congress and witnesses. In my own data collection, I reached out to many lobbying organizations in an effort to find out more about the way in which they influence witness selection. None of the organizations responded to my queries. I was able to interview a leading lobbyist for the auto industry, however, who previously worked on the Senate Commerce Committee. I also asked the staffers, witnesses, and politicians themselves about the involvement of lobbyists.

Several interesting effects emerged. First, although lobbyists may not select the witnesses, in many cases they have personal relationships with the staff members and that affects witness selection. In Leyden's research on committee hearings, one of the staffers he interviewed remarked:

> There are two ways people get to testify. They are either asked to testify or they ask to testify. The people who are asked [by us] to testify are the major players in a particular issue. The people who ask to testify are not always major players. This condition has to do with the way decisions are made . . . which depends on your relationship with [the committee]. If as a lobbyist you are doing your job right . . . for months or years before the issue comes up you have gone in to talk with the congressmen and the committee staff people before the hearing, so they know what your position is. You have to establish relations beforehand. . . . These are the types of interest groups that testify at hearings. If you don't have a good working relationship with the staff and the members, they're not going to know you exist and not going to know what your position is and therefore not going to seek you out.[27]

This reflection points to the deep ways in which long-standing relationships between lobbyists, staff members, and wider networks intimately shape hearing testimony.

Leyden's research also calls attention to the fact that, in some instances, lobbyists are the witnesses. A staffer on the Senate Judiciary Committee explained, "Oftentimes . . . the president or senior member of the trade association will be a witness." Lobbyists providing the testimony themselves is perhaps the most powerful indication of their involvement in hearings. In some cases, as with the interviewee who went from working on the Senate Commerce Committee to working for an auto lobby, the lobbyists are also the staff. Indeed, as Drutman points out, "Congressional staffers can usually at least double their salaries by 'going downtown.'"[28] For this reason, the trajectory of this staffer is reflective of the broader career trajectories of many committee staff members and is indicative of the power of money in shaping the entire committee ecosystem.

Leyden writes that "the types of organized interests most likely to testify are those that can afford to hire their own Washington-based lobbyists and supporting staff. These groups are more likely to have established contacts and to have the kind of policy or political information that makes a group a desirable participant. In addition, groups with PACs [political action committees] tend to participate in more hearings than groups without PACs. Committee members seeking to reward a group for its contribution [and perhaps hoping to maintain these contributions] may very well influence staffers' invitation decisions by suggesting that a contributor be permitted to testify."[29] His conclusions underline how deeply embedded lobbyists and financial interests are in witness selection.

Second, lobbyists may support witnesses in preparing for the hearings. The lobbyist for the auto industry explained that if there is a witness testifying on behalf of an auto company, he conducts what he termed "murder board type prep." He explained that he would grill them with possible questions to prepare them for the hearing because "you want to make sure the witness won't get any curve balls." He is uniquely positioned to do this because his experience on the committee allows him to say, "Of twenty, seven of these are going to be either vested in the issue or have a conflict with the issue or witnesses." This type of preparation is tremendously helpful in crafting effective testimony. A staffer on the Senate Finance Committee described how "some witnesses I think definitely have government relations teams and so [lobbyists are] probably very involved, especially if people on that team had been in the Senate or on whichever committee they're going to appear before. And so I assume that they would utilize those resources as much as I would hope, as much as possible." This corroborates Van der Slik and Stenger's findings regarding witness statements. They found that one-third of respondents received assistance from interest groups in crafting their statements.[30]

Third, the personal staffers shared that lobbyists may reach out with suggestions for questions to ask witnesses. The personal staffers would write suggested questions for their bosses, and so if they take the lobbyists' suggestions into account, this has the potential to elicit a different type of testimony. The frequency with which lobbyists send questions varies. On the Senate Judiciary Committee, a staffer put it at "30 percent of the time, probably a little less than half the time, folks would send us questions." On the Senate Finance Committee, on the other hand, a staffer said that "it was not common."

I asked several staffers and members of Congress about the degree to which they use the questions sent to them, and the responses varied. On the Senate Finance Committee, a staffer explained that "it wasn't really our style that we came up with questions." A Democratic congressman on the House Ways and Means Committee reflected that "I would say that less than 5 percent is external stuff that I use . . . like they want me to put a letter in the record of something that they said . . . or they want to highlight some point." On the Senate Judiciary Committee, a staffer explained, on the other hand, "I would usually read them at least just to see what sort of folks were interested in talking about my practice. And I think the practice of the other folks that were on Senator Hatch's staff on Judiciary, we always wrote our own questions." He went on to explain that "for any given hearing on the list of questions that we end up using, there is almost always at least one question that someone else has said to us. . . . I don't think I've ever been part of a hearing where, like most or even a significant number of the questions were from third parties. But it's not uncommon for there to be something that someone has submitted or suggested." One congressman on the House Science Committee even remarked that, in some climate change hearings, you see members reading "statements prepared by lobbyists."

As to why staff decided to use certain questions, the same Senate Judiciary Committee staffer explained, "If, like, some outside questions seemed really good, I might use them just because I thought they were good, not because they were like, oh, this is a question that, you know, the Chamber of Commerce wants to ask me to ask." Another staffer on the same committee explained, "We will see questions sent to us from lobbyists . . . most of the time they are already things that we're thinking about because you kind of know the lay of the land before going into these things." On the House Veterans Affairs Committee, a former personal staffer of a member said that whether he used suggested questions "just depended on, like, how good the questions were. Because a VSO [veterans service organization] sent a bunch of questions, we just didn't use them just because they sent them."

Fourth, lobbyists may share information with members throughout the hearing process that influences members' interaction with a given topic or witness panel. For example, the legislative director of a senator from Kansas explained that, in preparation for hearings, he will "reach out to lobbyists, stakeholder companies in Kansas, just about everybody I can think of who might have an interest in this. . . . Just to let them know there's a hearing coming up on this topic. Let us know if you have any, any questions about the hearing." A staffer who works on the Antitrust Subcommittee of the Senate Judiciary Committee said:

> Lobbyists would come by to sort of give us their pitch on the issue . . . my example I can think of are hearings of the Antitrust Subcommittee about mergers, proposed mergers. We would almost always be visited by representatives of the merging parties to talk about how great the merger was and how it was going to lower prices and all the stuff, trying to sort of make us feel favorably inclined toward the merger.

A member of the House Science Committee explained that lobbyists help him to "make the connection with the Midwest or a program that is important to me . . . [in] filling in more information." Although this reflection should be approached with the understanding that this congressman himself may be receiving financial support from such interest groups, his comment still shows that lobby information stands to influence his interaction with witnesses during the hearing. A Republican congressman on the House Science Committee remarked that "lobbyists get a bad name, but they are vital. Most of them have experience working on a committee or working on the Hill and so they get it in terms of making sure we get information."

The power of lobbyists' information has been well documented by scholars of American interest group politics. Political scientist Christine DeGregorio's research proved the value of information as a resource for members of Congress. One lobbyist she interviewed remarked, "Information has always been valuable to the members. It's amazing sometimes the things you can tell them that they are not familiar with. Outsiders provide a different perspective and a useful perspective."[31] Kevin Esterling's research also argued that lobbyists with more technical expertise are given greater access, suggesting that members of Congress value and learn from the information they provide.[32]

Although the full effect of lobbyists remains difficult to pinpoint, data from interviews showed four important ways in which lobbyists influence witness testimony. Lobbyists may suggest witnesses to committee staff, prepare witnesses to testify, send proposed questions to ask witnesses, and share information with committee members that may color their interactions with witnesses. These findings are increasingly important as the power of interest groups grows. As Drutman explains, "Lobbying grows because it has self-reinforcing stickiness . . . once companies invest in Washington, they rarely leave."[33] If interest groups and their lobbyists are not leaving the hearing process, it is important to understand how they shape it.

STAFF EXPERTISE

Staff expertise influences the susceptibility of Congress to external meddling. Drutman's study of lobbying links staff expertise to the power of lobbies. He concludes that staff "typically have neither the time to specialize nor the experience to draw on. As a result, staffers must rely more and more on lobbyists who specialize in particular policy areas . . . poorly informed staff are more likely to rely on shortcuts, or heuristics, when making decisions . . . for example, staff may make decisions by taking cues from party leaders, lobbyists, or the executive branch rather than relying on their own assessment of the situation."[34] Indeed, less than half (only 38 percent) of staffers hold advanced degrees, and only 2 percent hold PhDs. The average staffer has served in their current role for about three years.[35] The informational power of lobbyists is enhanced when lobbyists are met by an inexpert branch. On the Senate Judiciary Committee, a staffer seconded from the Justice Department described how his background knowledge of the issue made a difference to interactions with lobbyists:

> I do think that my expertise makes it easier to kind of sift through . . . the idea there is that various federal agencies have employees with expertise in the field that they deal with that your average staffer may not or likely doesn't have. So, I do antitrust. I'm an antitrust lawyer by trade. . . . I think one of the benefits of the arrangement is you don't have to outsource. . . . If you've got like a, you know, a twenty-three-year-old staffer fresh out of college, they don't know anything about banking law. And it's easy for a banking lobbyist to come in and say, hey, let me explain the world to you. Here you go. Here's a bill that does what you want. Just trust me.

His reflection draws a direct connection between inexpert staff members and the power of lobbyists.

On the other hand, staff expertise strengthens committees. The same staffer went on to recount a specific instance of a meeting with lobbyists who were not antitrust experts, saying, "It's like the companies walking into a chainsaw. . . . They're not ready to talk about the issues at the depth that we're trying to engage them, and they're not prepared for the kind of questions we have because they're used to having more inexperienced staffers." This further underscores how staff expertise can serve as ammunition against lobbyists. Jesse M. Crosson et al. reaffirm this in their study of the effect of staff experience on lawmaker effectiveness between 1973 and 2013 (operationalizing effectiveness using Alan E. Wiseman and Craig Volden's legislative effectiveness scores, which capture the ability to advance agenda items into law).[36] They conclude that, "on average, House members with more-experienced legislative staff appear to be somewhat more effective lawmakers. . . . Gaining about seven years of total legislative staff experience is equivalent to doing the work of an entire additional lawmaker or to shepherding another 'substantive and significant' bill into law." They go on to explain that "experienced staff may serve as a force multiplier. . . . Their knowledge of policy details and their connections with interest groups and with other lawmakers may allow chairs to take fuller advantage of their powerful positions."[37] This finding further suggests that staff experience and expertise lead to more effective lawmaking. In addition, they found that "committee chairs benefit from experienced legislative staff much more than do other legislators," further underscoring the relevance of these findings for congressional committees.[38]

Low and declining salaries represent one structural reason for the weakness of staff members' experience. For example, the average salary for a senior Senate staffer declined by $12,500 (in real 2016 dollars) between 2001 and 2015. Junior staff assistant salaries experienced a similar decline. A study of the salaries of 46,000 staffers between 2000 and 2014 found an 11 and 12 percent gender pay gap between male and female staffers in the House and Senate, respectively.[39] Pay gaps were even wider for senior positions ($11,000 in the House for top posts). Congressional staff salaries are now 35 percent lower than the median income in the Washington metropolitan area.[40] For this reason, in their analysis of staff career trajectories, Furnas et al. write, "Most staffers stay on Capitol Hill for a few years and move on, whereas a select few commit their professional lives to congressional service."[41] When asked where they would go after Congress,

22 percent of the respondents in Furnas et al.'s study said they hoped to move on to a lobbying firm as their "ideal next job."

THE HEARING

At the end of the planning process, once the hearing topic and witnesses are decided, the hearing takes place. Committee rooms are replete with grandeur and drama. A strict seating chart places the majority members on one side of the room and the minority on the other. Typically, members sit above the witnesses, casting questions down at them. Paintings of previous chairs or relevant figures (almost all white and almost all male) and engravings of sentences from biblical passages or well-known books line the walls.

Hearings follow a very precise agenda. They open with remarks from the chair and ranking member, followed by the oral testimony of witnesses. Each witness has five minutes to give oral testimony before he or she is questioned by committee members. Timing is closely monitored by a bright red timer, counting down in front of each witness. The witnesses are also required to submit written testimony several days before the hearing. Oral testimony normally resembles written testimony, but it does not have to be exactly the same. It often summarizes the main points that the written testimony may analyze in greater depth. Following the witness testimony, the chair and ranking member have five minutes to make a statement and/or ask questions (of a particular witness or the entire witness panel). Then all of the members in attendance are granted the same five minutes of questioning time.

Committees vary in the order of each member's questioning time. Sometimes seniority dictates order, while other times it depends on who arrived first, incentivizing members to arrive at the beginning of the hearing. Hearings vary substantially in length. They can last for many hours, but they average around two hours (depending on how many members show up to use their allotted five minutes of questioning time). After the hearing, the record remains open for two weeks for members to ask "questions for the record" (any additional or unanswered questions that witnesses can answer in writing). There is remarkably little variation in this recipe for congressional committee hearings.

CONCLUSION

This chapter set the scene and described how committee hearings are constructed. I add to the work by previous scholars, such as Van Der Slik and
Stenger (1977),[42] Leyden (1995),[43] Hall (1996),[44] and Lewallen (2016),[45] by
showing and explaining how the procedures work today in light of the
loss of committee power over legislation and the decline in bipartisanship.

Relying on extensive interviews with staff members, members of Congress, witnesses, and lobbyists, I identified the patterns characterizing
hearing construction and witness selection. Interview data illustrated
the importance of informal norms, personalities, and the personal bonds
of the committee staff and committee leadership. Both the partisan and
technical background of witnesses play a role in decisions to invite them.
I also uncovered several ways in which interest groups and lobbyists are
embedded in this process.

The data regarding the significance of informal norms in guiding committee procedures add to a growing body of recent work and draw attention to this often neglected aspect of legislative studies. It is a particularly
neglected area in modern scholarship. Because the hearing construction
process is largely informal and highly variable, the only way to parse out
this convoluted process is through qualitative research techniques. Sven
Siefken and Hilmar Rommetvedt write that "comparative overviews of
parliamentary committees have largely focused on formal institutions . . .
and the 'structural features.' . . . As parliaments are ever-evolving, such
studies need to be updated. . . . For a full understanding of the institutional
setting of committee work, it is necessary to look at more than only formal
rules in constitutions, laws, rules of procedure (RoP) or standing orders.
Such formalities serve as a necessary starting point, but established parliamentary customs have to be considered as well."[46] Recent legislative studies
have highlighted informal norms. For example, in Claire Bloquet's study
of committees in the French national assembly, interviewees told stories of
striking deals at the Assembly bar or through "informal talks in the corri-
dors."[47] In Ali Sawi's analysis of parliamentary committees in sixteen Arab
countries, he shows how personal relationships affect selection of committee chairs. Although committee chairs are formally elected by members,
85 percent of respondents in his study cited factors such as "tribal balances"

and "rapport" as deciding features in selection. He gives the example of a businessman in his seventies chairing the youth committee.[48]

Legislative studies also frequently focus on the power of committees to mold the relationship between the executive and the legislature. One of the major roles of committees is to conduct oversight. Legislative studies from around the world have shown that committees are weakened in relation to the executive when they do not have the information and expertise necessary to hold the executive to account. In many legislatures, committees must rely on the executive even for the staff itself. Israeli legislative scholar Reuven Hazan writes of the Israeli Knesset: "In order for committees to be able to assess a proposed bill, they must not be forced to rely on the government for information." Hazan recommends the Knesset "increase the budget, staff, and outside assistance available to committees."[49] Rachid Lemdower, an MP in the Moroccan House of Representatives similarly urges that "there is a pressing need to provide committees with competent advisors and skillful staff, as members of the committees would not have the capacity, energy or objectivity to put together reports assessing government performance."[50] My research showed that lack of independent expertise exposes committees in the U.S. Congress to external meddling. This chapter focused on meddling by lobbyists, but the same lack of expertise shapes other external relations, including with the executive branch. My findings therefore connect to a larger body of work in legislative studies and reaffirm the importance of staff capacity in strengthening the legislature vis-à-vis the executive.

RETHINKING CONGRESSIONAL STAFFING

This chapter demonstrated the centrality of staff to the hearing process. Furnas et al. write that "committees' ability to take up and accomplish legislative goals depends on whether they have the necessary staff resources to accomplish them."[51] In concluding this chapter, I will draw out several concrete recommendations for strengthening the hearing process by investing in staff. In order to mitigate the dangers of staff turnover and inexperience, each party could hire a number of expert staffers who can be retained past the tenure of the chair. The chair and ranking member would still be given part of the budget to hire some of their own staff, but the committee would allot a number of positions for expert, long-term staffers. Nelson Polsby's 1971 analysis of committees explains it best. He writes that "unswerving loyalty to the chair is seldom enough to produce technically advanced criticism of executive proposals, sophisticated insight into alternatives, or sensitive awareness of emerging problems in the world. Yet these are what Congress needs."[52] Polsby's argument makes the case for prioritizing professional expertise and experience over the chair's selection. In legislative scholar Malcolm Shaw's comparison of eight different committee systems, he points out that the Japanese Diet has the largest committee staff apart from the United States, and yet it is the weakest committee system in the study. He discerns that, although the staff is large in number, its members are divided in loyalty. The staff are loaned to the committee from other ministries and secretariats. The lack of an independent staff and corresponding body of expert information has implications for legislative power. Creating a number of permanent professional posts on each committee would go a long way toward creating the "sophisticated insight" that committees need. These permanent positions would hold salaries and job security that would enable staffers to "commit their professional lives to congressional service" in a way that the current system does note. As Crosson et al. write, "targeted effort to retain the most long-serving staff would likely be much more effective than would broad [and highly costly] attempts to increase staff size or staff compensation across the board."[53]

In January 2019, the House of Representatives introduced the Select Committee on the Modernization of Congress, a bipartisan committee tasked with suggesting recommendations to "make Congress more effective, efficient, and transparent on behalf of the American people."[54] The committee represents an exciting attempt to modernize Congress, the first concentrated congressional effort of this kind in over thirty years. My recommendations for bolstering staff support would also follow the Select Committee on Modernization's recommendations that:

1. Staff pay should no longer be linked to member pay and a new cap specific to staff should be established. (This recommendation was later adopted in August 2021.)
2. Congress should increase capacity for policy staff, especially for committees.

3. Committees should hire bipartisan staff approved by both the chair and ranking member to promote strong institutional knowledge, evidence-based policy making, and a less partisan oversight agenda.[55]

In addition to hiring permanent staff, committees could follow Polsby's recommendation to create outside advisory boards that would advise the chair on technical matters. The board would therefore serve not only the chair but the minority as well, and both sides would decide together which experts should sit on the panel. The advisory board for each committee would be composed of experts in that field, and it would outlive a single chair's term.

Such an advisory board would mitigate bias, educate staff, and strengthen professionalism. An outside panel would act as a check to mitigate this bias by introducing new ideas for witnesses and hearings. The advisory board could also help educate staff and professionalize the process. In interviews, expert witnesses accentuated their drive to effect policy change and the importance of their interactions with staff in accomplishing this goal. Advisory boards might consider similar bipartisan briefings to help educate staff members so that they have a comprehensive understanding of selecting hearing topics and witnesses. This would further professionalize the hearing process. It is one possible way of fulfilling the Select Committee on Modernization recommendation to "increase bipartisan learning opportunities for staff."[56] Of course, not all experts would take the time to join such an effort, but many of the expert witnesses I interviewed emphasized what an honor it is to testify. A senior fellow at Brookings with experience testifying on foreign affairs issues explained that testimony is a way for her to get her research and name publicized. Membership on the advisory board could be marketed similarly as an honor and a way to share one's work. The advisory boards, along with the permanent staff, would improve the quality of committee staff and allow for the "sophisticated insight" committees need.

Congress can also work to increase staff diversity. The 116th Congress saw the creation of the Office of Diversity and Inclusion. As the Select Committee on Modernization final report explains, "In addition to developing a comprehensive diversity plan, the Office of Diversity and Inclusion will collect staff demographic data . . . be responsible for assisting MCL offices to improve the recruitment and retention of a diverse workforce, develop best practices that can be utilized by offices, regularly survey staff, and provide recommendations for competitive compensation and benefits to House staff."[57] This office was made permanent in the 117th Congress and represents a major step forward.

The 117th Congress is also the most diverse in its membership, prompting hopes for more diverse staff. However, this is not a given. "I think that it requires members to be thoughtful in making sure that diversity and inclusion [are] at the center of their office hiring plan," says Don Bell, the director of the Black Talent Initiative at the Joint Center for Political and Economic Studies.[58] The Office of Diversity and Inclusion can incentivize offices to hire diverse staffs by requiring offices to report regularly on race, gender, and position of employees.

In addition to actively hiring a more diverse staff, salaries matter. Henson reflects on her internship experience: "When we don't invest in the congressional staffing pipeline, we end up with a congressional workforce that doesn't reflect the socioeconomic diversity of the country. We wind up staffing Congress only with people who come from money."[59] While certain individual offices have started to pay their interns (Alexandria Ocasio-Cortez made headlines with her promise to pay her interns $15 an hour), it is far from institutionalized practice.[60] The new Office of Diversity and Inclusion can address this by monitoring and holding individual offices accountable for reporting salaries that represent equal pay for equal work.

In the world of committee hearings, individuals are at the center. The personal relationships, partisan affiliations, preferences, lived experiences, and expertise of the chairs, ranking members, lobbyists, and staff members form the cornerstone of the hearing process. Reforms that create a system in which diverse and capable individuals join committees will strengthen the committee process.

2

WHO ARE THE WITNESSES?

Chapter 1 provided an understanding of how witness panels are created, and this chapter surveys some basic trends in the kinds of voices committees hear from. As with other components of contemporary hearings, this is an underexplored topic. Over three decades ago, Marc Landy, Marc Roberts, and Stephen Thomas evaluated the quality of debate on environmental policy in the 1970s and 1980s.[1] They used a normative unstructured framework to assess how media coverage, Environmental Protection Agency (EPA) statements, and congressional debates informed policy makers, and they concluded that environmental policies were directly damaged by distorted evidence.

I explore the evidence presented to members of Congress today. Who do they hear from in committee hearings, and what is the quality and diversity of information presented? To answer these questions, I gathered data on the witnesses, their professional backgrounds, the language they use when addressing committees, and how they compare to the other witnesses on their panel.

PROFESSIONAL BACKGROUNDS

The first important feature of the witnesses is their profession. While there has been research addressing witness testimony, there is a dearth of comparative work on witnesses' professional background.[2] Jonathan Lewallen tracked the number of witnesses testifying in each hearing and found that "committees heard from an average of fifteen witnesses across five panels in legislative hearings in the early 1980s, but between six and eight witnesses on average on two panels in the 2010s."[3] He argues that the declining number of witnesses shows that members of Congress are exposed to fewer sources of information.

My analysis of the professions of the witnesses explores precisely what sources of information members of Congress hear. I chose to focus this part of the analysis on five committees in the sample representing different kinds of policy areas and professional communities in order to assess how professional breakdown might vary by committee and committee policy jurisdiction. I also chose only hearings during the 114th Congress that pertained to substantive issues (excluding nominations hearings). This allowed for a more comparable data set across committees because some have more nominations hearings than others. The professional classification itself proved straightforward because all of the information about the witnesses' professions is accessible on the committees' websites. For the House Science, Senate Commerce, House Agriculture, and Senate Foreign Relations committees, the witness categories were as follows: nonprofit, government, academia, lobby/association, private sector, and other. Figure 2.1 shows, for the 114th Congress, the witness list for each of these four committees, broken down by profession.

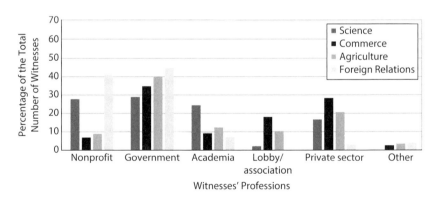

FIGURE 2.1 Professions of witnesses before four congressional committees during the 114th Congress, as a percentage of the total number of witnesses.

Source: Original data set created by the author.

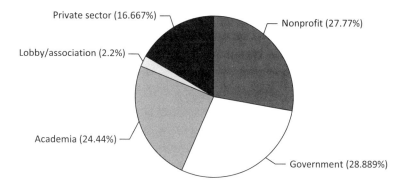

FIGURE 2.2 Professional breakdown of witnesses before the House Science Committee.
Source: Original data set created by the author.

For the House Veterans Affairs Committee, the professional categorization was adjusted because of the unique specialization of the committee and the resulting skew toward military and veteran witnesses. The professional categories were as follows: veterans affairs/military (representing witnesses who came from the Department of Veterans Affairs or the U.S. military), private sector, nonprofit, lobby/association, other, and government (nonmilitary) (representing all other government witnesses). Figures 2.2 to 2.6 present pie charts showing the professional breakdown of witnesses before each of the five committees.

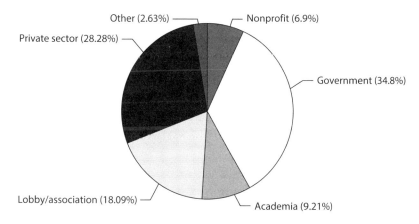

FIGURE 2.3 Professional breakdown of witnesses before the Senate Commerce Committee.
Source: Original data set created by the author.

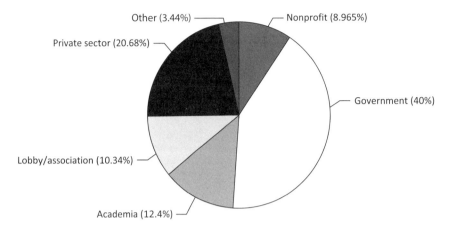

FIGURE 2.4 Professional breakdown of witnesses before the House Agriculture Committee.
Source: Original data set created by the author.

The pie charts emphasize the pronounced variance in the professions between the four committees. Some of the divergences are expected given the differences in the subject matter specialization of the committees. The House Science Committee hears from the most academics, with about 25 percent of its witnesses coming from academia (compared to 8 percent

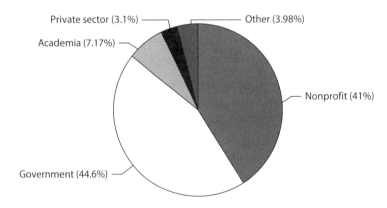

FIGURE 2.5 Professional breakdown of witnesses before the Senate Foreign Relations Committee.
Source: Original data set created by the author.

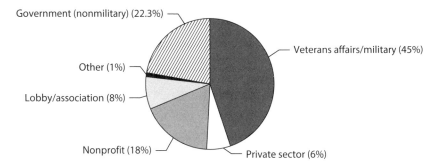

FIGURE 2.6 Professional breakdown of witnesses before the House Veterans Affairs Committee.

Source: Original data set created by the author.

to 12 percent in the other three committees). This is reasonable to expect given their jurisdiction over the National Science Foundation and their specialization in scientific topics. On the other hand, nearly 33.3 percent of the Senate Commerce Committee witnesses come from the private sector, compared to 3 percent to 20 percent in the other committees. This is also natural in view of their subject area.

Analysis of the professional breakdown of witnesses testifying before the Veterans Affairs Committee further underscores that witnesses' professional backgrounds vary greatly by committee jurisdiction. As illustrated by the pie chart in figure 2.6, almost 50 percent of the witnesses are either members of the Department of Veterans' Affairs or the U.S. military. It is also important to note that across all other categories, an overwhelming majority of the witnesses were still from organizations relating to veterans' affairs of the U.S. military. For example, nearly all the non-profit category represents organizations such as Wounded Warriors Project, American Legion, Disabled American Veterans, Veterans of Foreign Wars, Vietnam Veterans of America, and many similar organizations. The lobby/association category is also largely comprised of organizations like Blinded Veterans Association, the National Guard Association, and similar organizations. The House Veterans Affairs Committee has a uniquely narrow topical focus and thus a fittingly narrow band of professional sectors represented on its witness panels. Whereas committees like Science or Commerce hear from many different professional sectors, the House Veterans Affairs Committee hears mostly from veterans or those working with veterans.

All of the committees heard from a large number of government witnesses. The agencies these witnesses represented varied based on the agencies under each committee's jurisdiction. The Senate Foreign Relations Committee heard from the State Department, the Senate Commerce Committee heard from many port authorities, the House Science Committee heard from the National Science Foundation, the House Agriculture Committee heard from the Department of Agriculture, the House Veterans Affairs Committee heard from the Department of Veterans Affairs. All committees heard from government witnesses at least one-third of the time. This holds true even though this data set did not include hearings about nominations to government positions and focused only on hearings on substantive issues. The House Veterans Affairs Committee heard from government witnesses the most (67 percent of witnesses were government or military personnel). The predominance of government witnesses is not surprising given the responsibility of committees as oversight mechanisms as well as the large number of hearings involving legislation about government agencies.

The nonprofit category of witnesses included think tanks and charitable organizations. There was also variation in the types of nonprofits represented in the witness pool, which is not accounted for in the graphs. For example, the Senate Foreign Relations Committee heard from many think tank experts. It has a relatively low number of academic witnesses, perhaps because it draws on think tanks rather than academia for subject matter expertise.

The witnesses categorized as "other" were not listed in committee documents with a profession or organization. Some were listed with previous professions, for example, retired members of the military and others simply with the name of their town. These witnesses were likely not there to share professional expertise but rather to tell their personal stories. Examples of witnesses that were categorized as "other" in this analysis include writers, recipients of food assistance, a plaintiff in a lawsuit, former National Aeronautics and Space Administration (NASA) astronauts, and former airline captains. This category included only a handful of witnesses (2 percent to 4 percent) for each committee.

A striking finding is that the Senate Commerce and House Agriculture and Veterans Affairs committees heard from many witnesses who spoke on behalf of an association or lobby, whereas the Senate Foreign Relations and House Science committees had almost none of these witnesses. These types of witnesses can represent an entire sector. An auto industry lobbyist referred to association witnesses as "ambassadors for companies without having to put a company name on it." As explained in chapter 1, lobbyists provide information throughout the legislative process, including appearing as witnesses. This builds on the findings explained in chapter 1, suggesting that they may be more influential in certain policy areas or committees. This and the other differences in profession may have implications for the types of testimony given and therefore the type of hearing and its effects on members of Congress.

LINGUISTIC INQUIRY AND WORD COUNT ANALYSIS

A second component of the witness voice is the language that witnesses employ. I analyzed the witness testimony using Linguistic Inquiry and Word Count (LIWC) language analysis software. This computerized text analysis software assesses different psychological dimensions of text. It utilizes the dictionary method of text analysis, which rests on the assumption that the sentiment of a text can be determined from the sentiment of the words in a text. LIWC reads pieces of written or transcribed text and uses an existing dictionary to look for the incidence of certain words that convey different sentiments. It relies on a set of dictionaries that were created and honed over years by Yla R. Tausczik and James W. Pennebaker and their team to identify the various emotions and social styles contained in a given piece of written text. The dictionaries were developed using judges to categorize and cross-validate text.[4] Like other computerized text analysis software, LIWC is not perfect. It ignores irony, sarcasm, idioms, and context. Still, it is useful in making sense of a large volume of texts and has been used widely by academics in social psychology, health, and political science.[5]

Automated text analysis methods have also been used specifically by scholars of Congress to increase the scope of data on legislatures.[6] In their automated analysis of 118,000 congressional speeches, Kevin Quinn et al. explain that human-human or human-computer intercoder reliability is around 70 percent to 90 percent, whereas the automated approach they suggest is 100 percent reliable and replicable. Any extrapolations based on methods that are 100 percent reliable will doubtless be more forceful.[7] However, language analysis has yet to be applied widely in political science or in the study of Congress in particular. This application is therefore a new use of this software.

The sample of text that I tested comprised 1,364 pieces of written testimony drawn from 456 hearings held in the eight committees (the testimony was taken from each committee's website). I first tested the sample on the LIWC summary dimensions: analytical language and clout. The LIWC manual states that these summary variables are "derived from previously published findings from our lab and converted to percentiles based on standardized scores from large comparison samples."[8] It should be noted, however, that the explanation ends there, and the creators of LIWC acknowledge that the summary metrics are the only "non-transparent dimension" of the software.

The first summary dimension, analytical language, captures the degree to which speakers employ language that suggests formal, logical, and hierarchical thinking patterns. People who score low on this dimension are likely to use a more narrative style, focused on the present. This metric has been used in a wide range of subjects, for example, to assess the analytical level of Facebook posts by pro- and anti-vaccine activists.[9]

Clout aims to capture the speaker's confidence. The metric was developed based on studies of personal interaction.[10] One such study, conducted by Ewa Kacewicz et al. in 2014, examined language used in a variety of social interactions (emails, informal chats between participants, a decision-making task in which they were randomly assigned to leadership roles, and even letters written by Iraqi soldiers who served under Saddam Hussein). This diverse set of data sources allowed them to look at trends in confident language across different kinds of linguistic situations, communication styles, and cultural contexts.[11] This variation is accounted for in the LIWC metric. Clout also captures expertise. For example, Meina Zhu et al. found that students' clout scores improved during a course as they gained knowledge and understanding of the subject matter.[12] In addition, clout has been used as a barometer for social status and leadership.[13] Higher clout scores are linked to higher social status.

In order to further understand the results, I look at them in the context of the average scores of different types of written information presented in the LIWC manual. The manual explains that the sample comprises writings of over 80,000 writers from the United States, Australia, England, Canada, and New Zealand. Table 2.1 presents the average analytic and clout scores for the LIWC sample of blog writing, expressive writing, novels, natural speech, *New York Times* articles, and Twitter posts. These are distinct forms of written information and hence they present a useful comparison.

In addition to the summary variables for the psychological dimensions, I explored linguistic characteristics further by using LIWC word counts of specific psychological processes. LIWC has specialized dictionaries for words conveying certainty (i.e., *always*, *never*), tentativeness (i.e., *maybe, fairly, perhaps*), and insight (i.e., *think, how*). For these categories, LIWC gives a score representing the percentage of total words that fit into each dictionary category. I use these word counts as additional evidence about the complexity and certainty of witness testimony. These same indicators were used by Ryan Owens and Justin P. Wedeking in their analysis of the complexity of U.S. Supreme Court opinions between 1983 and 2007.[14]

Certainty and tentativeness are of particular interest in witness testimony because scholars have identified them as deciding factors in the use of evidence in policy making. In his study of the use of evidence in British policy making, Alex Stevens identifies "uncertainty" as a major

TABLE 2.1 LIWC analysis of different types of written language

Category	Blogs	Expressive writing	Novels	Natural speech	New York Times	Twitter
Analytic	49.89	44.88	70.33	18.43	92.57	61.94
Clout	47.87	37.02	75.37	56.27	68.17	63.02

Source: James W. Pennebaker, Ryan L. Boyd, Kayla Jordan, and Kate Blackburn, "The Development of Psychometric Properties of LIWC2015," University of Texas at Austin.

reason that policymakers eschew academic research. He explains that policy makers were averse to uncertainty and preferred information in which the bottom line was clear. He writes that civil servants are taught to communicate with their superiors through "killer charts," constructed "by choosing data carefully and by restricting the number of cases and categories that were shown. The policy implications of the data should be immediately apparent from the graph alone."[15] Adnan Hyder et al. conducted a cross-national study in Argentina, Egypt, Iran, Oman, and Malawi using data from eighty-three interviews with policy makers in these countries, and they too discovered that the poor packaging and communication of research were major impediments to its uptake.[16] Several of the interviewees explained that researchers should be taught to convey complex information clearly and concisely, even when such a distillation of laborious and lengthy studies may seem irreverent and painful. Given these findings with regard to the importance of the levels of certainty and complexity used to convey information, I take a closer look at these aspects of witness testimony.

The results of the LIWC analysis for eight congressional committees are summarized in figures 2.7 and 2.8. Figure 2.7 presents the summary score metrics on a scale of 1 to 100 (low to high). These are summary scores constructed by the LIWC rather than raw instances of word usage. Figure 2.8 presents certainty, tentativeness, and insight scores as incidence of raw usage.

A number of interesting trends emerge about the committees in general. First, all of the committees have similar summary metric scores, with little variation. All of the committees receive high analytic language scores, suggesting that the witnesses are in fact presenting analytical and logical testimony. The average analytical score is 93.7, and the levels for all of the committees are similar to the analytical language in *New York Times* articles. This is an important finding in the context of the wider debate about the information presented to congressional committees.[17] In the subsequent chapters, I will explore in greater detail the degree to which congresspeople listen to witnesses and how they are affected by this information. Nonetheless, the high analytical scores of the testimony are noteworthy in and of themselves. Contradicting the argument that Congress does not access quality analysis, they point instead to highly logical and analytical information presented to Congress.

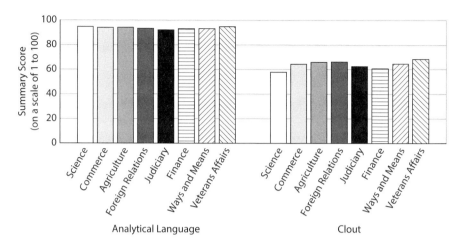

FIGURE 2.7 LIWC Analysis of summary metrics.

Source: Original data set of LIWC scores constructed by the author for the purpose of this study.

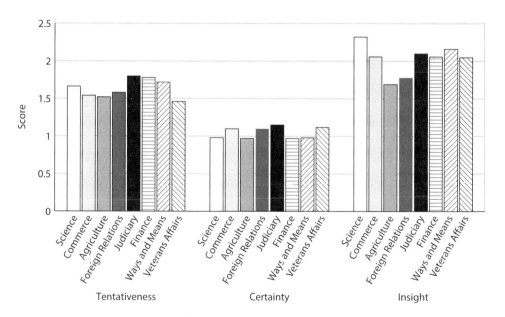

FIGURE 2.8 LIWC analysis of psychological processes.

Source: Original data set of LIWC scores constructed by the author for the purpose of this study.

All of the committees also receive similar clout scores (the average clout score is 63.7). The score lies between the confidence of pieces that people publish with a specific idea to espouse (a Twitter post, an article, or a full-length novel) and less pointed pieces (natural speech, expressive writing). This is logical in light of the space that witness testimony occupies: somewhere between a formal predetermined piece and a free-flowing statement. The clout scores indicate that witnesses exhibit a certain degree of confidence, status, and expertise in their speech.

CAUTIOUS SCIENTISTS

The House Science Committee has one of the highest levels of tentative language and the second lowest level of certainty. The tentativeness and certainty scores appear logical inverses of each other in all of the committees. The science committee scores may seem surprising because some would expect that scientific facts are conveyed with high levels of certainty. In addition, the House Science Committee has a high level of insightful language and a correspondingly high analytical score.

These findings may be explained by the profession of the witnesses. The House Science Committee heard from the largest number of academics. One academic witness I spoke to lamented the confusion regarding what type of language to use. He stressed that academics communicate with a different tone and demeanor than politicians and so what they say may be lost in translation. A congressman on the House Science Committee and former physicist explained that, as a scientist, he goes through the scientific references in the written testimony in great detail and is able to understand the professional academic jargon of the academic witnesses much better than his nonacademic colleagues. He regretted that, although he could understand the scientists' buzz words, scientists do not simplify in order to make their explanations more accessible. Another former House Science Committee staffer echoed this sentiment, recalling that the witnesses who stood out to her during her decade on the committee were those scientists who "answer questions directly and speak to you like a human." The aforementioned congressman and physicist explained that a "typical scientific presentation presents data and then a conclusion. As politicians, we have to lead with the conclusion . . . unlike in science where you say, 'How do I get to the truth?' It's much more like law, where you say, 'How do I convince the jury?'" His statement underscores the dissonance between lengthy academic explanations and pithy political presentations. Given that the scientific method is grounded in questioning and casting doubt, it makes sense that its advocates use tentative and uncertain language. Convincing the jury entails speaking with certainty. Witnesses from other professional backgrounds, such as the private sector, adept at selling their ideas, may indeed appear more self-assured than academics, who are trained as cautious truth seekers.

CONFIDENT SPEAKERS

The Senate Commerce Committee and House Veterans Affairs Committee have relatively high clout and certainty and low tentativeness scores. This may also be explained by the witnesses testifying. The Commerce Committee heard from many private sector witnesses and lobbyists. As explained in chapter 1, lobbyists may be more adept at testifying and therefore appear more confident.

Another interesting point in the context of the breakdown by profession are the unique characteristics of the House Veterans Affairs Committee. It has the highest clout score (68.32) and the correspondingly lowest tentativeness score (1.46). It also has the highest level of power language (references relevant to status, dominance, social hierarchy) and the use of first-person pronouns. This is consistent with work showing that people with higher social status are more self-oriented and use more first-person pronouns.[18] In the aforementioned five Kacewicz et al. studies, the team found that people with higher social status used more first-person plural and fewer first-person singular pronouns (in fact one of their studies even drew on letters written by soldiers). The Veterans Affairs had a very high proportion of witnesses from military backgrounds.

These findings suggest a connection between a professional background related to the military and speech exhibiting higher social status and confidence. Former U.S. Marine and text analytics expert William Marcellino's analysis of discourse of Marine officers identified their speech as "highly certain" and found they frequently use first-person pronouns.[19] This assessment is substantiated by the firsthand account of a veteran who has testified before the House Veterans Affairs Committee. She said, "I'm a veteran, and one of the things that I've had to learn coming back into the civilian workforce and engaging on the Hill is, you know, in the military, you're very blunt and curt. . . . And I've had to learn to kind of gentle and be more personable in my correspondence and relationships on the Hill." Marcellino explains that "marines learn a way of speaking that has life and death stakes for them, and repeat that performance over their careers, even when speaking outside of their community to civilian audiences. Their values are implicated in their way of speaking, and thus when they speak in public deliberative forums, the epideictic dimension of their speech can be problematic."[20] This further underscores the power of professional culture in shaping language. Marines, veterans, scientists, and CEOs come to testify before a committee after "learning a way of speaking . . . and repeat that performance over their careers, even when speaking outside their community."

Taken together, the LIWC results further illuminate the kinds of evidence that congressional committees hear and the variations across topic, professional background of the witness, and committee.

BALANCE

Witnesses testify on a panel with other witnesses, and to assess the voice Congress hears, it is also necessary to step back and look at the panel as a whole. The conversations with staff members illustrate the importance placed on the witnesses as a group and the "balance" of the panel. The inclusive "voice" that Congress hears is the amalgamation of the witnesses on the panel. To assess this feature of hearings, I again employed the dictionary method of sentiment analysis. This time, rather than relying on existing software, I created original "balance" scores, with the use of a "dictionary" of positive and negative words. I used Minqing Hu and Bing Liu's opinion lexicon of 6,800 positive and negative words to determine the proportion of positively and negatively charged words in each testimony.[21] I computed balance scores at the level of committee hearings. I first scored each individual hearing transcript based on the numbers of positive and negative words. Then I scored each hearing based on the number of predominantly positive transcripts (those with more positive than negative words) divided by the total number of testimonies in that hearing. The method of constructing balance scores is novel and has not been used before to characterize committee hearings. The final data set consists of 456 hearings conducted in the eight committees during the 112th to the 116th Congresses. Each hearing included between one and nine witnesses, averaging around three and a half witnesses per hearing. (See appendix C for a full breakdown of data set of hearings by term and committee.) The balance scores allowed me to see how the witnesses compare to one another. Chapter 1 explained how the witness panels vary in setup. Sometimes staffers seek to balance out the other side's arguments. Other times, majority and minority staffers construct a balanced panel together. The balance scores help to answer the question: Are members of Congress really hearing the balance of perspectives that the staffers seek in their selection?

Table 2.2 and figure 2.9 present summary statistics for balance scores by committee (highest to lowest). A number of interesting trends in balance scores emerge. The average balance score for all eight committees for the 114th Congress was quite high, at 0.80. This is a high score on the

TABLE 2.2 Average committee balance scores

House Agriculture Committee	.95
House Veterans Affairs Committee	.87
Senate Commerce Committee	.87
House Science Committee	.85
Senate Finance Committee	.85
House Ways and Means Committee	.81
Senate Foreign Relations Committee	.76
Senate Judiciary Committee	.54
Average balance (all committees)	0.8
Average number of witnesses	3.5

Source: Original balance score data set constructed by the author for this study.

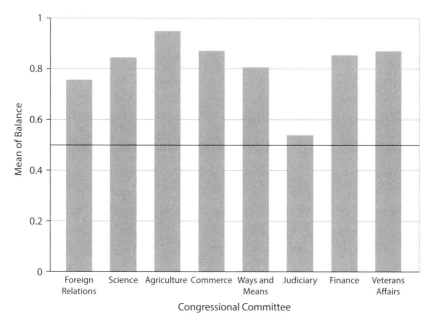

FIGURE 2.9 Average balance by committee.

Source: Original data set created by the author.

balance score spectrum because a score of 1 would signify that all the witnesses spoke in favor of the issue at hand. If the hearings were perfectly balanced, one would expect a 0.5 balance score. As referenced in chapter 1, the presence of positive sentiment is taken as an indication that the testimony is supportive of the legislation discussed. A testimony with primarily negative sentiment indicates that a speaker is opposed to the legislation. An average balance score of 0.80 indicates that Congress is hearing more from witnesses with a positive perspective on a given issue. This makes sense given the aforementioned trends in the witness selection. The official rules of both chambers specify that the majority controls the hearing agenda and invites all but one witness. As a result, it would follow that the majority chooses topics that they want to support. Even taking into account the practice of joint lists, the skew toward witnesses who support a given policy makes sense. In their analysis of witnesses testifying before committees, Jack Van Der Slik and Thomas Stenger asked 1,200 witnesses about the purpose of their testimony. They conclude that "of those who identified their purpose, only 5 percent came to oppose change in policy. Another 38 percent came as advocates of change."[22] The average balance scores in this study corroborate this finding in a contemporary context, underscoring the skew toward witnesses who speak in support of a policy. Nevertheless, the balance score is under 1, illustrating that, on average, there is at least part of the panel that has an opposing view. This suggests that there is at least some range of perspectives in the hearings.

As a robustness check, I also used the LIWC average positive and negative emotion scores. These two scores represent raw incidence of word usage based on the LIWC dictionary of positive and negative words. This is a different dictionary from the Liu and Hu dictionary used in my own sentiment analysis and so it is useful in cross-validating my results. I took the proportion of the average incidence of positive words divided by the average incidence of negative words for the entire set of witness statements for each committee. The average LIWC scores are given on a committee level rather than for each group of witness statements in a hearing, and therefore they may be slightly less accurate. Still, the results largely confirm the results of the balance score analysis. As with my own balance scores, the House Agriculture Committee had the highest proportion of positive relative to negative words (3.24), followed by the House Veterans Affairs Committee (3.05) and the Senate Commerce Committee (2.97). The lowest two scores were the Senate Foreign Relations Committee (1.79) and the Senate Judiciary Committee (1.65). These findings validate the ranking of the committees by my balance scores, as well as the skew toward positive emotion. Even the most proportional score (the Senate Foreign Relations Committee) had nearly twice as many positive words as negative words.

This initial analysis of balance scores points to two important conclusions. First, it shows that the balance of voices on a witness panel varies substantially by committee. Second, balance score results indicate that there is some, albeit a relatively small, degree of balance on witness panels. The balance scores tell the story of how the witnesses on a panel compare to one another, an important component of assessing the voice Congress hears. The following chapters will delve into balance scores in greater depth to explain the relationship between committee culture, chamber, policy topic, chairmanship, and balance, and will rely on balance scores to further explore committee deliberation.

CONCLUSION

This chapter answered the question: Who does Congress hear in committees? I used a variety of methods, including language analysis and examination of witness backgrounds, to address this question from various angles. The data presented are all original and were collected and analyzed entirely for the purpose of the study. Text analysis methods have not been previously applied either to congressional committees in general or to witness testimony in particular. This chapter also introduced a new method for analyzing whether committees are hearing a diverse set of opinions on the witness panel, a question left unanswered by previous work on the topic.

Several trends emerged. In light of work in evidence-based policy making on the lack of access to high-quality research by policy makers,[23] the high number of academic and think tank researchers who come to speak and the analytical language used would suggest that there is indeed access to high-quality research. The LIWC analysis shed light on how language varies based on the committee and professional training of the witnesses. Contrary to the narrative of entirely partisan information distorting Congress, my study finds that witness panels exhibit some degree of balance. Chapter 4 will show how the balance scores introduced in this chapter vary based on relationships between majority and minority factions and partisanship of topics. These findings are central to understanding the nature of information presented in committees in Congress today.

3

WITNESS TYPOLOGY

Drawing on the information from chapters 1 and 2 about the ways in which witnesses are chosen and the characteristic language, professions, and balance of witnesses, this chapter presents a theoretical framework of the witnesses that committees hear. This typology of witnesses will then be used to classify the different functions of hearings. It is important to note that these are Weberian ideal types, useful for theoretical purposes, and in reality, some witnesses can be a combination of more than one type. Such labeling based on ethnographic research harks back to Richard Fenno's *Congressmen in Committees*, in which he used extensive interviews to categorize committee member goals (classified as reelection, influence, and good public policy).[1] These broad categories form a map to understanding a convoluted system. They are based on the recurring themes in the respondents' answers when they are asked the same question. Similarly, the typology presented in this chapter is based on themes from interviews with participants in the hearings and data about witnesses. Just as Fenno's ethnographic research presented a series of categories for member motivation, the information from chapters 1 and 2 is used to categorize witnesses. Just as Fenno's labels provided a tool for future researchers to understand committee members, the typology in this chapter aims to make sense of committee witnesses. No similar typology exists to describe the witnesses who testify before committees.

NOTE ON DEFINING EXPERTISE

Before fleshing out the definitions of the first two types of witnesses, described as different types of experts, it is important to define the term *expert*. Several interviewees stressed that they see some witnesses as more "expert" than others and explained how they judge the "credibility" of witnesses. A Democratic congressman on the House Agriculture Committee remarked that "anybody can be deemed an expert. . . . So, just because someone's deemed an expert doesn't really necessarily mean that they're experts." His comments highlight the murkiness of expertise as a concept, and the potential dissonance between perception of expertise and genuine knowledge. He went on to explain the elements he looks at when determining the credibility of a witness:

> You're looking at what they're saying. You're looking at their expertise. You're looking at their intelligence. You're looking at how they kind of articulate themselves. You're looking at their demeanor basically when it comes to certain questions that are being asked towards them, be it by one side or the other and how far they push back, whether or not, they push back. Like I said, it's a number of elements that you look at in determining someone's credibility.

A senior Democratic congressman used words like *objective* and *dispassionate* to describe useful witnesses. Furthermore, expertise is frequently gendered and racialized. Research shows that female academic authors are less likely to be cited than their male colleagues.[2] Women are often passed over for "highly intellectual" roles. According to one study, the odds of a woman being chosen for a job dropped 38 percent when the word *intellect* was included in the job description.[3] This translates to the way women are perceived in legislative committees. In her research on legislative committees in the Colorado state legislature, Lyn Kathlene found that female witnesses opposing a bill are afforded fewer speaking opportunities than their male counterparts.[4]

By the same token, notions of competence are also racialized. African Americans face more scrutiny in work reviews than white employees and need to pass a higher bar in order to be judged as competent.[5] Résumés with stereotypically white names are twice as likely to receive a callback as an identical résumé with a stereotypically black name.[6] These studies reflect a societal bias in judging expertise and competence that permeates every interaction, including congressional committee assessments.

Because the term *expert* is loaded and structurally biased, and its definition remains imprecise, I define *expert* based on the staff's perception of expertise. As described in chapter 1, one of the motivations guiding staff invitations of witnesses is specialized knowledge of a given subject or field. Therefore, I define *expert* as anyone invited by the staff to share from their specialized knowledge of an issue.

TYPES OF WITNESSES

LABELED EXPERT

This type of expert is recruited by staff because he or she is known for publicly embodying a certain view on an issue or for the zeal with which he or she conveys it. As noted earlier, staff members sometimes choose witnesses to represent a particular perspective or to tell a story in the way they want it told. As a staffer on the Senate Judiciary Committee explained, "I think it's pretty rare to have, like, a neutral expert . . . every expert is always going to come down kind of on one side or the other."

Because the witnesses write their own testimony, the committee staff must rely largely on the brand the witness represents. Perhaps the witness has worked for a political administration or donated to a campaign. Maybe they are well known publicly for supporting a certain perspective on an issue (one that the staff is looking to represent). A staff member on the House Science Committee explained that in her preparatory conversation with witnesses, she wants to make sure they "serve our purpose." A Middle East expert at the Brookings Institution explained that when staff approach her to testify, "there is something they are looking for you to provide." She characterized their approach as "We need someone who can do X—can you?" I heard similar stories across professional disciplines.

Staffers achieve this goal by choosing people whose views are well known. One labeled witness, publicly known as a climate change skeptic, explained that the staffers she speaks to are definitely familiar with her blog, where she writes many pieces about the uncertainty of climate science. She said that when they approach her to testify, "they want to know what my ideas would be and if they like those ideas, they invite me to the hearing. I've never not been invited to a hearing after it being suggested there was one . . . they are pretty familiar with my point of view after reading my blog." She went on to explain that her testimony does in fact mirror other pieces she has written on her blog or elsewhere. Her comments illustrate that she is invited precisely because of her public association with a certain perspective that the staff members want to represent. The aforementioned choice of Michael Mann as the "loudest and most prolific person we can think of" is another illustration of this type of thinking. Staff then know beforehand what witnesses' perspective are. A staffer on the Senate Finance Committee explained that she knows witnesses' positions from "what they've said in the past, probably. I know that committee staff always look into witnesses' prior positions." She said that "all the staffers are very diligent on that."

The before-and-after story of former Israeli ambassador to the United States Michael Oren represents a telling example of the power of labeling. He testified in 2003 in a hearing on the Iraq War. At the time, he was an academic historian of the Middle East. Several years later, he also testified before Congress in his position as Israeli ambassador. He identified the marked difference between the two experiences, saying that in the hearing on the Iraq War "I was myself." He even recalled that the staff were surprised by the position he took in the hearing, an indication of the difficulty in assigning him a label before the hearing. He contrasted this with his experience testifying as an ambassador, when he represented the views of the Israeli government and was therefore clearly labeled.

The labeling is also picked up on by the committee members themselves and their staff. A former congressman who served in Congress for nearly thirty years recalled that "if [the witnesses] come from the Heritage Foundation, I know where they are coming from. They don't like social programs. They want to get rid of Medicare. Anything that came out of their mouth, I said 'I understand but you do not have an alternative.'" Another longtime senator who served in Congress for over thirty years, reiterated this, saying that "you already know what the Heritage Foundation will have to say." These statements reaffirm the significance of labeling experts. Another personal staffer to a senator on this committee spoke of his preparations to support his boss at these hearings, saying, "I would say frequently you kind of know going into these hearings where everybody is. . . . Most of the witnesses come from organizations that have longstanding positions on whatever issue that they're discussing. So, yeah, usually there are very few surprises that come up or witnesses who you're just totally blindsided by."

The tendency to invite labeled experts may indeed have implications for expertise in hearings. If the guiding question is "We need someone who can do X—can you?" rather than "Are you the foremost expert in X?," then it is plausible that sometimes staff members may compromise expertise in favor of perspective. However, interviews also made clear that being labeled does not necessarily mean one is not the foremost expert on a topic. The emphasis on labeling may but does not definitively dilute the quality of expertise.

UNLABELED EXPERT

As explained in the previous section, staff members may seek pure expertise in their selection. These experts are not associated with a specific ideology. They have not worked in previous political administrations or made significant donations to political campaigns. They are specialists sharing their expertise. The staff members explained that sometimes they specifically want an expert who is not publicly associated with a party or perspective. They told me that they explicitly sought this so that the members will listen to them more openly. A legislative director for a senator on the Senate Finance Committee explained that some experts present "the information from a scientific perspective that isn't necessarily a left or right position . . . presenting straight down the middle fair information and just their perspective that's not tied to an organization . . . there's a whole list of folks that do come in that we don't look at as left or right."

Witnesses who are invited because they are not labeled have caught on to this as well. A witness who testifies frequently before the bipartisan House Veterans Affairs Committee said that her organization actively avoids partisan issues because "if you start giving off partisan vibes, you're going to stop getting invited to the table. At least that's the impression I've got. No one has ever directly told me that, but it's been made very clear we are bipartisan and remain Switzerland."

Professional background assumes great weight in labeling. A label derives largely from the current and former professional affiliations of the witness, and certain organizations and sectors are more readily labeled. This is evident from information about professional backgrounds and the discussions with witnesses and staffers referred to in the previous sections. For example, the aforementioned congressman was quick to assert that the Heritage Foundation is associated with a certain ideology, and consequently its witnesses are branded. On the other hand, an academic witness from Johns Hopkins University explained that the university reminds faculty who are called to testify that they should not appear as though they are lobbying for a certain policy on behalf of the university. A staffer on the Senate Finance Committee further corroborated this, explaining:

> Witnesses that are professors or researchers would be of a different ilk than CEOs of drug companies and probably those in academia would be very prepared to answer any questions on their papers or their research. [You] have less of a need for an understanding of political overtones or whatever a government relations team would help other witnesses with. I keep going back to the drug pricing because that's what I know, but when the Senate Finance Committee had the academics in the first hearing, which I think was February 2019, they answered a lot of questions on the process of drug pricing in different countries for different drugs, and for different beneficiaries.

Her comments stress the difference between academic experts and witnesses from the private sector. The line of questioning she describes for academics suggests that these witnesses are less easily colored by political overtones. Her assessment is in line with previous research on academic witnesses. Laura Perna et al. explain that "unlike interest groups and overtly ideological think tanks, academic researchers are said to offer perspectives that are independent from a larger political agenda and based on fair and rigorous examinations of data."[7]

This is not to say that academic experts never have a label. In the previously mentioned case of the climate change hearing, all three of the majority witnesses were either current or former academics. The comments of the minority staff members indicated that they were publicly known as climate change skeptics and therefore labeled. In addition, academic experts can be labeled by virtue of their previous employment by a political administration or partisan cause. Nonetheless, universities and the academics representing those universities are less easily labeled than experts coming from partisan think tanks. This is noteworthy because of the difference in professional breakdown by committee discussed in chapter 2. Whereas the House Science Committee has more academic experts, the Senate Foreign Relations Committee hears from many more think tank experts.

In addition to professional field, certain topics may be more difficult to label. For example, an expert on terror, who works in both think tank and academic settings, stated that terror is a topic that is less prone to partisan divides. He explained that the professional community is united, and that the disagreement is more bureaucratic than political. Less politically contentious topics may be more likely to have experts who are unassociated with a partisan ideology.

PERSONAL STORYTELLER

Many hearings include a witness who comes to share a personal story of how a policy has affected her. As noted in the discussion on witness selection, staffers select for certain types of perspectives. They explained that they seek out this type of witness in order to humanize a given issue. A former Republican staffer on the House Agriculture Committee spoke of the witness selection for the Supplemental Nutrition Assistance Program (SNAP) hearings series, saying that "there is the human component. We can talk about at a higher-level perspective how things impact SNAP recipients, but maybe we should hear from an actual SNAP recipient. . . . You will see a number of people who testified as current recipients or as former recipients." The staffer stressed that this was a deliberate move in order to incorporate this type of perspective. She explained further that there may be a stereotype among some members that SNAP recipients are lazy but putting a face to the issue helps elucidate the nuances of the experience. Indeed, a congresswoman on the House Agriculture Committee who attended these hearings recalled an example of a witness who was a Women's National Basketball Association (WNBA) star raised on food stamps.

She remembered that a congressman pressed her about why her family was on food assistance, insinuating that her mother could have been working harder. According to coverage of the hearing, he said, "Why are parents having children, multiple children, if they can't have the responsibility to take care of them?" The witness responded that her family was abandoned by her father, explaining that "my mom obviously didn't intend to be a single parent. My father left." The congressman was taken aback.[8] The congresswoman recalled this example when asked if she could remember a specific example of a witness who affected her. This shows that the perspective of a personal storyteller is not only a purposeful staff decision but also holds the potential to shape a policy debate in a different way.

Frequently, personal storytellers tell stories of trauma meant to raise awareness about an issue. A Senate Commerce Committee staffer told the story of a gut-wrenching witness at a hearing about legislation meant to limit trafficking on the internet. The witness was the mother of a teenager who was trafficked on the internet and brutally murdered. The staffer explained, "That's an example of a hearing where you really want someone who can show the human [side] and the impact." Another witness on the same panel, who spoke on behalf of the tech industry lobby, recalled that she was so moved by this testimony that she felt a need to acknowledge it in her own testimony. This witness's reaction is strong confirmation of the influence of personal stories. In yet another example, I asked the longtime Republican member and former chair of the House Agriculture Committee to recall a witness who was exceptionally influential for him. He remembered, "In 2015, the House Judiciary Committee, which I chair, held a hearing on 'Planned Parenthood Exposed: Examining the Horrific Abortion Practices at the Nation's Largest Abortion Provider.' We heard from Gianna Jessen, whose mother was seven and a half months pregnant when she went to Planned Parenthood to have an abortion. Ms. Jessen survived that attempted late-term abortion and is now an outspoken advocate on prolife matters. Her testimony was extremely moving and impactful. While it was an emotional story to hear, her testimony underscored exactly why the hearing was being held that day." The congressman's comments emphasize the power of personal storytellers.

A senior Democratic senator and former member of the Senate Foreign Relations Committee, House Science Committee, and House Agriculture Committee explained that the six most important words in any speaking engagement are "Let me tell you a story." He went on to share several examples over his thirty years in politics of personal stories that shaped the legislative process. One particularly poignant example was from his battle to reform prison conditions. He explained that two witnesses testified about their traumatic experience in prison, saying that "they both talked about being back in that experience and what they saw. And really, I think [it] changed a lot of minds among the members of the committee when they heard about it."

My conclusions regarding the power of the personal narrative, typified by the preceding examples, reinforce findings of previous scholarly work. Allen Schick explains that policy narratives connect "ordinary knowledge" of daily experiences to policy relevant implications.[9] Carolyn Hughes Touhy writes, in her analysis of the narrative form in welfare policy, that "anecdotes are pervasive in political speech . . . an anecdote invites the audience to identify with the characters it portrays, and often with the narrator who positions himself or herself within the story, to experience the world in which the characters live."[10] Personal storytellers are invited in order to bridge this gap between daily experience and policy and make the subjects of the hearing more relatable. Previous scholarship has also situated such anecdotal speech in American political life. In her analysis of rhetoric in congressional welfare reform hearings from the 102nd, 103rd, and 104th Congresses (1992–1996), Lisa Gring-Pemble identifies anecdotal narratives as key to shaping the discussion of President Bill Clinton's Personal Responsibility and Work Opportunity Reconciliation Act.[11] Touhy similarly locates anecdotal stories in President Barack Obama's discourse about the Affordable Care Act. She writes that, "to enable the more privileged members of his audience to identify with characters whose situation was more precarious, Obama invited his audiences into the narratives."[12] She goes on to explain that he highlighted individual stories in order to achieve this goal, speaking about the experience of his own mother, of a small business owner who sought to provide coverage for his employees, or a boy whose mother died because she did not have insurance. The personal storyteller type that this typology introduces builds on earlier scholarship about the power and prevalence of personal stories in American politics.

However, the professional breakdown of the various committees suggests that, although personal storyteller witnesses may be powerful, they may be a rarity in recent congressional hearings. During the 114th Congress, only a handful of witnesses came before the committees who were listed on the witness list without a current professional affiliation; instead, they were listed with their former professions or their involvement with a certain issue. These are the witnesses who are likely there to tell personal stories. Of course, there may be witnesses who are invited for their professional expertise and who also weave personal experience into their testimony. For example, I heard one account of a journalist covering the Islamic State of Iraq and Syria (ISIS) who came to speak to the Senate Foreign Relations Committee based on personal stories of close interactions with the group. However, stories as personal as that of the journalist remain uncharacteristic of the professional testimony before Congress.

There are a number of potential reasons for the lack of personal storytellers. As referenced in chapter 1, staff selecting witnesses appear to place emphasis on expertise, power to convey a perspective, as well as their own networks and those of the chair. It stands to reason then that the mother of a sex-trafficking victim or a recipient of food stamps will not be high on their witness list both because they may not already know them and because staff may instead prefer either a subject matter expert or someone to promote a certain brand.

SPOKESPERSON

This type of witness comes to voice the perspective of a stakeholder group or cause. A spokesperson can speak on behalf of a lobby or association, such as one witness who spoke on behalf of the Internet Association at sex-trafficking hearings at the Senate Commerce Committee, or the spokespeople for the Fresh Produce Association at House Agriculture Committee hearings. As noted in chapter 1, one lobbyist explained that the benefit of lobby and association witnesses is that they "are ambassadors for companies without having to put a company name on it." A spokesperson can also speak on behalf of a cause. For example, witnesses from certain nonprofit or private sector organizations may come to impress upon the members of Congress the significance of acting on an issue. Conversations with committee staffers on all of the committees drew attention to the importance of representing the concerns of relevant stakeholder groups at congressional hearings.

CONCLUSION

This chapter has offered a typology of the major categories of witnesses who come to testify before Congress. Following in the tradition of Fenno's labeling of member motivations, the categories offered in this chapter are a general framework. There indeed may be witnesses who fall between the cracks, or witnesses who represent more than one category. It is not intended as gospel but rather as an analytical tool to assist in the study of the committee process.

Taken together, chapters 1–3 revealed several key themes. First, they showed that the process depends on the individuals involved. The idiosyncrasies, districts, professional and personal interests, and personalities of the chair and ranking member of each committee guide hearing agendas and witness lists. Likewise, the personal relationships between the chair and ranking member and their staffs decide whether the minority and majority collaborate on hearing agendas and witnesses or not. Second, because individuals are central to the process, there is also a great deal of informality and variability in the way hearings are designed and carried out. The partisanship of the topic taints the interactions between staff members on these topics, the choice of witnesses, and the way in which witnesses convey information. The data on witness testimony also demonstrated the diversity and analytical value of information that Congress hears and the range of styles in which it is conveyed. In a Congress in which the capacity to specialize has been undermined by years of structural reforms, this finding suggests that hearings can still present committee members with useful information. In a Congress in which legislators still spend precious time in committee hearings listening to witnesses, understanding how hearings are set up and who testifies is crucial to understanding what parts of this process work and how. Now that you have this understanding and have read about the typology of congressional witnesses presented in this chapter, chapters 4–7 will investigate when and how committees still fulfill core functions in the legislative process.

4

HOW CONGRESS LISTENS

The Different Hearing Types

Congress in session is Congress on public exhibition, whilst Congress in its committee rooms is Congress at work.

—WOODROW WILSON[1]

You can lead a man to Congress, but you can't make him think.

—MILTON BERLE[2]

This book explores the function of committees in today's Congress. Chapters 1–3 asked what and who Congress hears. Chapters 4–7 build on these findings to examine the functions of committee hearings and whether and how they might still matter. Each chapter will focus on the core functions of hearings, utilizing several key parameters to explain when each kind of hearing is most likely and showcasing several illustrative examples of hearings where each function is most likely. This book argues that these parameters are necessary, but they are not sufficient to create a perfectly deliberative or educational hearing. They can be used to explain partly when different hearing functions may be more likely rather than as clear-cut rules. It is also important to note that functions can coexist, and no hearing fits one function perfectly. However, certain parameters can

TABLE 4.1 Theoretical framework

Function of hearings	When are these types of hearings most likely	Possible effects
Deliberative forum	*Partisanship:* Bipartisan committees, bipartisan topic *Structure:* Senate	Legitimization, collaboration
Educational platform	*Partisanship:* Bipartisan topic *Structure:* Senate, desirability *Nature of topic:* Legislative status *Types of witnesses:* Unlabeled witnesses *Formality:* Informal	Learning, staff education
Theatrical stage	*Partisanship:* Partisan committees, partisan topic *Nature of topic:* Publicity *Types of witnesses:* Labelled witnesses, spokespeople	Voicing views
Space for personal connection	*Partisanship:* Bipartisan committees *Structure:* Senate *Formality:* Informal *Types of witnesses:* Personal storytellers	Empathy, committee collective

make certain kinds of hearings more likely. The presentation of ideal types allows us to better understand the purpose and effect of contemporary hearings. As with the typology of witnesses presented in chapter 3, these broad categories form a theoretical map to make sense of a complicated system.

Chapters 4–7 also rely on interview data to survey the possible effects of hearings on committee members. Table 4.1 summarizes the theory presented. The next section explains the core functions and the parameters used in chapters 4–7.

FUNCTIONS

DELIBERATIVE FORUM

As chapter 1 explained, displacements in committee structure and congressional structure have led to a decline in congressional deliberation. In a Congress that is less deliberative overall and whose committees still form the historical center for deliberation, when can committee hearings still serve as a deliberative forum? Chapter 4 answers this question.

EDUCATIONAL PLATFORM

There is an old saying that members of Congress are like the mouth of the Mississippi River, a mile wide and an inch deep. That is, they lack depth and expertise. Chapter 1 charted the systematic loss of committee capacity and the ramifications for learning. Chapter 5 asks whether and how members of Congress are still learning in contemporary committee hearings.

THEATRICAL STAGE

Committees are also a public forum and, as such, can function as a theatrical stage for politicians. Chapter 1 explained how the introduction of televised hearings changed political behavior in committees. Indeed, Woodrow Wilson once described the growing power of committees relative to the chamber as a shift of "the theatre of debate upon legislation from the floor of Congress to the privacy of the committee-rooms."[3] In the context of a televised contemporary Congress, chapter 6 explores when theatricality is most pronounced.

SPACE FOR PERSONAL CONNECTION

The opening chapter identified committees as a core bipartisan institution and explained the importance of personal relationships and positive social connections for cultivating bipartisanship. In the context of a hyperpolarized Congress, chapter 7 explores how committees can still serve as a space for bipartisan social connection and explores the power of personal connection in hearings more broadly.

PARAMETERS

When are hearings most likely to be theatrical? Deliberative? Educational? Or when do they act as a space for connection? This book focuses on the following core parameters in explaining when each hearing function is most likely—partisanship (of committee and topic), structure (of chamber and committee), nature of the hearing topic (legislative status and publicity of the issue), formality of the hearing, and the kinds of witnesses testifying. Chapters 4–7 rely on these parameters in explaining when hearings are most likely to serve different functions. The sections below briefly describe each parameter and how it is assessed in this book.

PARTISANSHIP (OF COMMITTEE AND TOPIC)

As noted in the opening chapter, partisanship is a core element of understanding the legislative process in the contemporary hyperpolarized Congress. The sample of committees analyzed in this book include committees and topics of varying partisanship in order to explore how partisanship affects the function of hearings in the contemporary Congress. Within committees, there is also variation in the partisanship of specific topics of the hearings. The partisanship of committee and topic of hearing are two of the parameters linked to which function is most pronounced. I rely on the balance score data introduced in chapter 2 as well as interviews to assess this parameter across and within committees.

STRUCTURE (OF CHAMBER AND COMMITTEE)

Desirability and Attendance

As explained in the introduction, not all committees are equally desirable to members of Congress. Members have very busy schedules and frequently spend only Tuesday to Thursday in Washington. Many hearings are scheduled at the same time (mostly Wednesday or Thursday mornings). Since the 110th Congress, members of Congress sit on an average of about five and a half committees and subcommittees.[4] As a result, members have to choose which hearings to attend and how long to stay. Members managing multiple committee assignments may prioritize an A-list for committee attendance. Kenneth Shepsle looked at how committees differ in regard to hearings and meetings and concluded that committees vary in the depth of their expertise and that many of the "minor" committees are comparatively inexpert bodies because turnover is high, and members are juggling other committee assignments simultaneously.[5]

The House Ways and Means Committee is both a highly desirable committee and is unique in that members of this committee only have one committee assignment and do not have to juggle conflicting hearing times. As a result, average member attendance is higher. A staffer on the House Ways and Means Committee confirmed that members of this committee attend most hearings and are engaged in the work. A Democratic congressman on the committee corroborated this:

> I now serve on the Ways and Means. I would say that I probably have 100 percent attendance for all full committee hearings. I don't stay for the entire hearing, but I often stay for much of it because I learn a lot at the hearings. Sometimes I leave to go for other appointments and come back. But I would say that I spend a lot more time with my committee hearings at Ways and Means. . . . So I'd say that because of the importance of the committee, because of my interest in the topics, and because I've decided to make it a focus of what I work on, that I have very high attendance at House Ways and Means Committee meetings.

He went on to compare this with previous committee assignments, saying, "I do the same with foreign affairs and armed services, but not quite as diligent. . . . I'd say I was more like at 75 percent for my other committees in the old days . . . some things that I just wouldn't have any interest in and it would be just out of my area of expertise or interest . . . in this committee [Ways and Means] I try to go to everything the full committee and subcommittee do." This illustrates the difference between A-list committees and other assignments, indicating a clear connection between desirability of committee and member attendance and engagement. If members attend more often, then the potential of discussions to engage them on an educational, deliberative, or personal level, or indeed any level, is greater. Therefore, desirability is a parameter that spans the hearing functions.

Chamber

The similarities between the Senate and House chambers were underscored in an interview with a senior Democratic senator who has served on three of the committees in my sample (the Senate Foreign Relations, House Science, and House Agriculture committees). He served in the House for fifteen years and in the Senate for over twenty years. When asked about the difference between chambers, he stressed that the "committee experiences extend across a wide spectrum" that spans both chambers. Other interviewees with experience working in or testifying before the two chambers reiterated the resemblance of committee experiences in both chambers. They also reaffirmed the resemblance between committees in the same chamber. I asked one Republican congressman who served on both the Science and House Agriculture committees if he could speak to the differences in his experiences on the two committees, and he responded, "I would think it would be similar . . . [it] just depends on subject." These comments highlight the similarity across chambers.

Nevertheless, research revealed several notable distinctions between Senate and House hearings. Due to the disparity in the sizes of the two chambers, members of the Senate are required to sit on more committees. Therefore, the nominal workload is much greater. Another structural difference between the chambers is the turnover in committee members and the voting rules. Senators serve six-year terms, and the average tenure of senators is longer than that of the average representative. According to a study conducted by the Congressional Research Service, from the first Congress all the way to the 115th Congress, the Senate maintained a longer average tenure per member than the House.[6] Congressional scholarship identifies a greater impetus for bipartisanship in the Senate, where politicians must work across the aisle in order to pass legislation.[7] These differences all have implications for the likelihood of education, deliberation, and personal connection between chambers. The subsequent chapters rely on interview data and balance score analysis to explain these structural differences.

NATURE OF THE HEARING TOPIC

Publicity

While all congressional hearings are recorded and (with the exception of the Intelligence Committee and other classified topics) all hearings are included in the public record, not all hearings attract the same amount of public attention. Some hearings have millions of Americans tuning in and make headlines in leading papers, whereas others are met with a scant audience and no media attention. Whether or not a hearing draws cameras and an audience (and protestors) may depend on different elements of the nature of the topic at hand (subject matter, timing, individuals involved). The level of publicity stands to affect the tendency toward theatricality, as chapter 6 will explain further.

Legislative Status

Some hearings pertain to specific pieces of pending legislation, whereas others aim to explore an issue area. Jonathan Lewallen defines "legislative" hearings as follows: "legislative hearings are those organized around recently introduced bills, sometimes called 'referral hearings.'"[8] On the other hand, many hearings do not pertain to a specific piece of legislation at all, or they connect to a topic for which legislation is not planned for the immediate future. Interview data showed that legislative status shapes behavior across party lines, resulting hearings, and effects on members. For example, one member of the House Science Committee said, "If you are talking about the far future, you can act in a much more bipartisan way. When you are talking about next year's budget or tribal issues like climate change, you immediately go into parties." This is further supported by research suggesting a greater potential for the minority to influence the majority opinion in cases in which the discussion is not aimed at reaching a specific decision.[9] This is just one example of how legislative status shapes behavior in committees. Chapters 5 and 7 will explain in greater detail how legislative status affects the tendency for educational hearings and personal connection.

FORMALITY OF THE HEARING

As explained in chapter 1, most hearings are highly formalized and have a very specific setup. They are public, proper, and to a certain degree predetermined. However, Richard Hall explains that "much of the committees' decision-making activity takes place in formal committee sessions . . . at the same time, much of a committee's decision-making activity occurs informally—outside the context of an official markup."[10] He describes how public forums may yield a different type of participation. There are indeed many informal and less public "hearing-like" settings in which members of Congress meet with witnesses.

Some examples of informal hearings include roundtables and listening tours. For example, the House Science Committee has off-the-record roundtable meetings. There are no television cameras or reporters. Unlike the formal hearings, members of Congress sit around one table with the witnesses and engage in a free-flowing discussion back and forth. They sit together with food, a demarcation of a social gathering. This scene differs from formal hearings in which the seating is assigned and members of Congress are divided, Democrats sitting on one side and Republicans on the other. The members of Congress are restricted to the apportioned discussion time. There is no food or casualness involved in such formal hearings.

Another example of informal hearings is the 2017 House Agriculture Committee listening tour. As the name suggests, the committee members traveled around the country listening to different perspectives on the farm bill. Unlike formal hearings, in which there is a handful of witnesses on a panel with regimented time, many of these meetings are set up as open-mic sessions where people can come in and voice their concerns on the farm bill. Other committees also hold the occasional field hearing outside Washington or even engage in similar tours to hear from constituents. I was able to interview several representatives who attended the farm bill listening tour and other such informal hearings about their experiences.

Chapters 5 and 7 will explain how formality influences the propensity for hearings to act as a space for learning or personal connection.

THE KINDS OF WITNESSES TESTIFYING

Chapter 3 presented a typology of the major types of witnesses who testify before committees. The kinds of witnesses who testify logically affect the resulting hearing and its effect on members. The subsequent chapters will draw on the typology in chapter 3 to explain in greater detail which kinds of witnesses lead to which kinds of hearings. The following chapters employ these five parameters (partisanship of committee and topic, structure of the chamber and committee, nature of the hearing topic, formality of the hearing, and the kinds of witnesses testifying) in an exploration of hearings and how they affect members. They draw on extensive interview data as well as balance score data sets.

COMMITTEE HEARINGS AS A DELIBERATIVE FORUM

"Congress is so strange," observed the Russian actor Boris Marshalov on one of his visits to the United States. "A man gets up to speak and says nothing. Nobody listens—and then everybody disagrees." Marshalov made this observation over a hundred years ago, but it appears all the more relevant today.[11]

This chapter explores the extent to which committees still act as a deliberative forum in an increasingly polarized Congress and investigates how contemporary committee deliberations might affect members. This section begins by explaining deliberation as a concept. It then shows why deliberative hearings might be most likely in bipartisan committees, for bipartisan hearing topics, and in the Senate rather than the House of Representatives. It also draws on interview data and two illustrative examples of deliberative hearings on different policy issues to show that, when deliberative hearings do take place, they may still encourage the legitimization of opposing views and cross-party collaboration.

WHAT IS MEANT BY *DELIBERATION*?

Deliberative democrats distinguish between deliberation and mere discussion and believe in the power of deliberation to transform opinions. Political philosopher Joshua Cohen explains that deliberation resorts to reason while discussion may be restricted to a mere pooling of information.[12] As John Dryzek and Valerie Braithwaite write, "deliberation induces individuals to think through their interests and reflect upon their preferences, becoming amenable to changing the latter in light of persuasion from other participants."[13] Philosopher Jürgen Habermas similarly contends that actors must be open to persuasion by better arguments and find reasoned consensus through reflective dialogue (for Habermas, the entire concept of rationality is based on how we acquire and use knowledge rather than simply the possession of knowledge).[14] In the congressional context, political scientists Lee Drutman and Timothy LaPira address congressional "deliberativeness" as "does Congress seek out and incorporate the best available information and reason through the causes and consequences of public problems?" They write that "high-quality deliberation is informed . . . and open to alternatives. Low-quality deliberation is purposely ignorant, with predetermined positions that are immune to the force of the better argument and new information."[15] This book draws on existing definitions and sees deliberation as an interactive process with the power to change opinions.

WHEN ARE HEARINGS MOST LIKELY TO BE DELIBERATIVE?

PARTISANSHIP

Using Balance Scores

Deliberative democrats agree that a core element of deliberation is that a variety of perspectives are included in the discussion. Habermas's ideal forum is one in which no one competent to make a contribution has been excluded, all participants are allowed to question assertions, and everyone is free to express themselves without any coercion.[16] Philosopher John Stuart Mill writes of the legislature as a "Congress of opinions" in which

> not only the general opinion of the nation, but that of every section of it, and, as far as possible, of every eminent individual whom it contains, can produce itself in full light and challenge discussion; where every person in the country may count upon finding somebody who speaks his mind as well or better than he could speak it himself—not to friends and partisans exclusively, but in the face of opponents, to be tested by adverse controversy; where those whose opinion is overruled, feel satisfied that it is heard.[17]

In his analysis of congressional deliberation, Edward Lascher explains that deliberative "hearings include participants with a variety of perspectives. Evidence of exclusion of certain views (e.g., those of people adversely affected by legislation) would lead to a lower assessment."[18] As described in chapter 2, balance scores provide an assessment of which hearings show both positive and negative perspectives and thus represent one way of determining whether there is a "variety of perspectives." The subsequent sections in this chapter rely on balance score analysis, in addition to interview data and other sources, to show how variation in partisanship of committee and topic may affect the potential for deliberative hearings.

BIPARTISAN COMMITTEES

Committee Culture and Balance

Chapter 1 described the ways in which the culture of the committee shapes the selection of witnesses and the resulting witness panel. As a senior Democratic congressman explained, "The nature and character of the expert witnesses [are] often reflective of the . . . nature and character of the committee. If it's not an ideological or a very partisan committee, you'll tend to have more nonpartisan witnesses." This characterization points to a connection between committee partisanship and resulting witness panels.

The effect of collegiality is reflected in a comparison of the balance scores of the committees. In interviews, the staff members on the Senate Foreign Relations Committee referred to the extensive collaboration between minority and majority staff members on the committee as well as the positive relationship between the chair and ranking member. This committee also boasts a relatively "balanced balance score." On the other hand, the Science and House Agriculture committees, in which staffers complained of poor relationships and high staff turnover, have less balanced scores. The two most contentious issues in the House Science Committee, climate change and oversight of the Environmental Protection Agency (EPA), both fall under the jurisdiction of the Energy and Environment Subcommittee. As mentioned in chapter 1, on this subcommittee, staff relations are especially weak, and there is hardly any collaboration.

The tone of staff relations is set in large part by the chair and ranking member. As chapter 1 explained, they hire and fire the staff. The importance of the chair and ranking member is demonstrated by an assessment of the DWNominate scores of the chair and ranking member of each of the sample committees. This metric, devised by Keith Poole and Howard Rosenthal, gives each member of Congress a composite score by averaging her roll call voting history, ranging from −1 (very liberal) to 1 (very conservative).[19] I chose to compare the chair and ranking member DWNominate scores as an indication of the overall committee and staff dynamics. Table 4.2 shows that the absolute value of the distance between DWNominate scores of the chair and ranking member largely follow the same rank order as the balance scores. This suggests that perhaps chairs and ranking members whose average score is closer to 0 (the center of the liberal to conservative scale) lead their committees in creating more balanced panels. One possible reason is that there may be more "joint lists" if the two sides can easily find common ground, and "joint lists" have the potential to be more varied.

A further illustration of the power of the chair can be found in a comparison of balance scores on the Senate Foreign Relations Committee between the 113th and 114th Congresses. Although the chairmanship in the Senate Foreign Relations Committee changed parties from Menendez to Corker, the average balance score remained relatively similar in both terms (0.78 in the 113th Congress and 0.74 in the 114th Congress). In addition, the histograms in figure 4.1 show that the distribution of balance

TABLE 4.2 DWNominate scores versus balance scores, 114th Congress

Committee	DWNominate (distance between chair and ranking member)	Balance score
House Agriculture Committee	.221	.95
House Veterans Affairs Committee	.17	.87
House Ways and Means Committee	.145	.81
Senate Commerce Committee	.108	.87
Senate Finance Committee	.052	.85
House Science Committee	.0335	.85
Senate Foreign Relations Committee	.03	.76
Senate Judiciary Committee	.013	.54

Source: DWNominate scores are taken from the voteview.com database and balance scores are taken from the original balance score data set constructed by the author for this study.

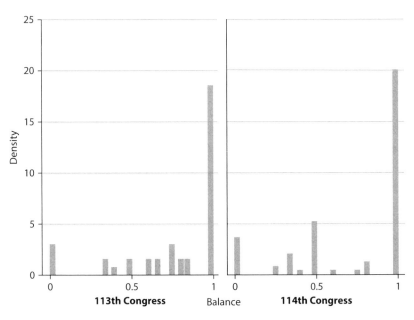

FIGURE 4.1 Balance in the Senate Foreign Relations Committee in the 113th and 114th Congresses.

Source: This figure draws on an original data set of balance scores constructed by the author.

scores for Senate Foreign Relations Committee hearings remained similar between the 113th and 114th Congresses. This is an indication that both sides are represented in hearings, regardless of party control of the chairmanship. The staff members of the Senate Foreign Relations Committee chalked this up to Menendez's and Corker's similar chairmanship styles, good relationship with each other, and their reliance on mostly the same staffers.

As noted in the opening chapters, polarization levels and personal collegiality may go hand in hand. Scholars of Congress point to a parallel decline in both spheres over the past several decades, writing of a deterioration in cross-party relationships between chairs and ranking members as well as rising polarization in Congress as a whole. The DWNominate scores illustrate how the partisanship of the chair, ranking member, and their respective staffers may affect the balance of witness panels. This finding connects the deterioration noted by previous scholars and highlighted by the interviews in my own research to the balance of committee hearings.

The combined effect of the chair and partisan dynamics is further evidenced by an intracommittee comparison across different terms. Examining variation in the balance score of the Senate Foreign Relations Committee across three terms (the 112th, 113th, and 114th Congresses) and the balance score of the House Ways and Means Committee across four terms (113th, 114th, 115th, and 116th Congresses) allows for a comparison of chairmanship change and shift in party control in two different chambers.

As noted earlier, the average balance score for the Senate Foreign Relations Committee during the 113th Congress was 0.78. During the 114th Congress, it fell to 0.74, and the committee leadership changed hands from Democratic Bob Menendez to Republican Bob Corker. The average balance score for the 112th Congress was identical to the balance score for the 113th Congress. The Democrats maintained control of the committee for both of these terms, but John Kerry was chair during the 112th Congress and Bob Menendez was chair during the 113th Congress. Figure 4.2 shows that there is a very small difference in balance between terms. This suggests that the partisan ideology and party of the chair may have a greater effect than the individual idiosyncrasies of any given chair.

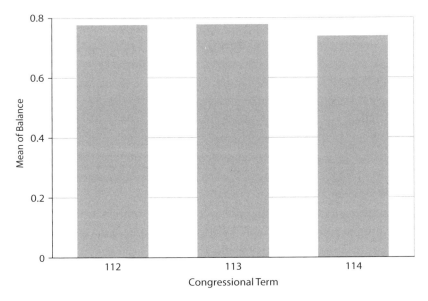

FIGURE 4.2 Senate Foreign Relations Committee balance, by term.

Source: This figure draws on an original data set of balance scores constructed by the author.

In the House Ways and Means Committee, chairmanship changed from Kevin Brady (Republican) to Richard Neal (Democrat) when Democrats regained control of the House of Representatives in 2018, and the balance score shifted from 0.85 to 0.80 with this change. Prior to Brady, Paul Ryan chaired the committee for half of the 114th Congress (January 2015 to October 2015), and Dave Camp chaired the committee during the 113th Congress. The balance scores for the 113th and 114th Congresses were 0.77 and 0.75, respectively (see figure 4.3). Even though Republicans maintained control of the committee for three congressional sessions, there were three different chairs, which may explain part of the continuous changes in balance scores.

Taken together, the analysis of the effect of chairs and ranking member dynamics suggests a connection between bipartisan committee culture and more closely aligned leadership and more balanced scores. Deliberation is premised on a discussion that includes a variety of perspectives. Therefore, the data imply that deliberative hearings may be more likely in bipartisan committees.

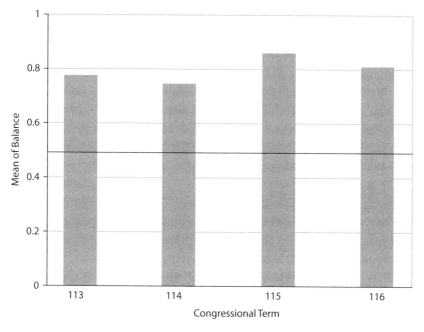

FIGURE 4.3 House Ways and Means Committee balance, by term.

Source: This figure draws on an original data set of balance scores constructed by the author.

Bipartisan Topics

Within committees, partisanship also varies by topic. The Senate Judiciary Committee provides an excellent example. Even though it is a partisan committee, there is variation in the partisanship of topics. Chapter 2
found that the Senate Judiciary Committee has the most balanced score of
all the committees in the sample, despite both scholars and pundits clas-
sifying it as a highly partisan committee. The previous section identified a
connection between partisanship of committee and balance score. So why
might the Senate Judiciary Committee be different? First, the data set of
hearings included only policy-related rather than nomination hearings.
As one staffer on the committee explained, "There's sort of two buckets
of hearings. There are hearings for judicial nominees and there's hearings
for like everything else. . . . I think there was going to be much more
collaboration on hearings for everything else versus hearings for nominations." This shows that, within the same committee, different topics elicit

different kinds of hearing dynamics and degrees of collegiality. Because nominations are so unique, they are explored separately and in greater detail in chapter 6.

The data set of balance scores for legislative hearings shows that even in a partisan committee, bipartisan topics may lead to more deliberative hearings. A staffer on the Antitrust Subcommittee of the Senate Judiciary Committee explained, "I think the Antitrust Subcommittee has been an exception to the rule for a while, just because antitrust is usually and ideally a bipartisan area of law where we try not to make it too partisan." His statement emphasizes the degree of variation in the partisanship of topic within the committee. Indeed, during the 114th Congress, many of the hearings were on less partisan topics such as drug abuse, adoption, and sexual assault. Figure 4.4 compares the balance scores for bipartisan and partisan topics (categorization is based on background research and conversations, along with close reading of the chair and ranking member opening statements). The figure shows that the more bipartisan topics within the committee receive more balanced scores, suggesting that even

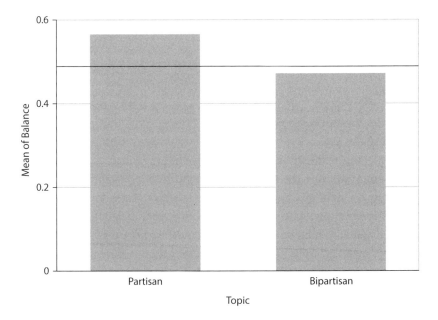

FIGURE 4.4 Senate Judiciary Committee balance, by topic.

Source: This figure draws on an original data set of balance scores constructed by the author.

in the Senate Judiciary Committee, the less contentious topics may lead to more balanced witness panels and, as a result, more deliberative hearings.

The significance of the bipartisanship of the hearing topics is further substantiated by an intracommittee comparison based on issues. To investigate the effect of topics further, I compared the balance of hearings on clearly bipartisan topics to hearings in general for the four "average committees" in the center of the Christopher Deering and Steven Smith partisanship ranking (House Science, House Agriculture, Senate Commerce, Senate Foreign Relations).[20] I relied on voting data as well as information gleaned from staff interviews to identify bipartisan topics in each committee. For the House Science Committee, the bipartisan topics were those in which there was a good deal of voting across party lines, such as fossil fuels, research, water pollution, and space exploration. For the Senate Foreign Relations Committee, bipartisan topics were those in which parties came together to pass bipartisan legislation (Iran, North Korea, human trafficking, and sexual abuse). In the House Agriculture Committee, interviews with staff and members from both parties confirmed that Supplemental Nutrition Assistance Program (SNAP) was the contentious issue of the 114th Congress. It was also the issue on which the committee held the largest number of hearings. Therefore, I chose topics that interviewees described as less partisan, such as an exploration of how to make better use of food waste, agriculture and national security, and agriculture and energy. For the Senate Commerce Committee, I similarly chose topics that interviewees described as bipartisan, such as the possibility of developing self-driving cars and improving cybersecurity.

Figure 4.5 shows that bipartisan topics have balance scores closer to 0.5 (perfectly balanced) than hearings in general during the 114th Congress. Within each committee, the bipartisan hearing panels are more balanced than the average hearing of the committee. This further suggests a connection between partisanship of topic and the likelihood of a deliberative hearing displaying a variety of perspectives.

This conclusion reaffirms previous research by Jürg Steiner et al. regarding polarizing issues and quality of deliberation. They write, "When legislators agree on policy fundamentals, it should be easier to engage in an open-minded deliberation than when there is sharp disagreement on an issue."[21] Steiner et al. also compared congressional debates on polarizing issues (partial birth abortion and minimum wage) to nonpolarizing issues

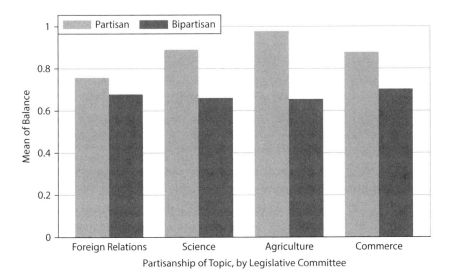

FIGURE 4.5 Balance by topic, 114th Congress.

Source: This figure draws on an original data set of balance scores constructed by the author.

(crime prevention and disability rights). They found that less polarizing issues lead to higher levels of respect and sophisticated justification in speech and concluded that there is a negative correlation between the degree to which an issue is polarizing and the quality of deliberation.

STRUCTURE: SENATE

There are also signs that the Senate has a greater propensity for deliberative hearings than the House of Representatives. Rules such as the Hastert
rule (which brings bills to a floor vote only if the majority will support
them) grant the majority enormous power to shape policy in the House of
Representatives. As a result, the majority party in the House may have less
incentive to work with the minority compared to their counterparts in the
Senate. As explained in chapter 1, when the staff members on both sides
work together on a joint list, there is a higher likelihood of a diverse and
balanced panel that features different witness types and points of view.
A stronger minority voice and more work across the aisle may translate

TABLE 4.3 Hearing balance by chamber, 114th Congress

Senate committees average balance	.77
House committees average balance	.85

to more deliberative hearings in the Senate. The comparison of the balance scores of each chamber for the same congressional session in table 4.3 shows that the four Senate committees have more balanced scores than the four House committees, substantiating the notion that the Senate displays more deliberation than the House of Representatives.

This conclusion regarding the greater capacity for deliberative hearings confirms Steiner et al.'s findings in their comparative analysis of parliamentary deliberation. They find that "second chambers" display higher levels of deliberative speech around the world. They attribute this to "institutional provisions as well as norms of civility."[22] The study quotes Senator Claiborne Pell from Rhode Island as saying, "The Senate has a long and established tradition of deliberation precisely because [of] its rules and procedures for legislating such difficult issues with thorough and adequate review."[23] The senator's reflection and Steiner et al.'s conclusion about deliberative speech further stress the Senate's propensity toward deliberation.

The contemporary Congress is perhaps less deliberative than its predecessor, but the evidence in this section suggests that, when deliberative hearings do occur, they are most likely to take place in bipartisan committees, on bipartisan topics, and in the Senate rather than the House of Representatives.

POSSIBLE EFFECTS

LEGITIMIZATION

How might these deliberative hearings affect committee members today? There is a rich body of work in social psychology on the power of exposure to a variety of perspectives. This work rests on the assumption that these instances may cause stimulation of "implicit attitudes" outside one's conscious awareness.[24]

Research suggests that showing people pro-attitudinal information strengthens their opinions. For example, political scientist Matthew Levendusky found that showing people like-minded media made them more extreme and more certain in their views and caused them to delegitimize and mistrust the other side.[25] Yet another study found that white people with racist beliefs showed even more racial prejudice after speaking to others with racial prejudice. On the other hand, white people with low levels of racial prejudice exhibited even less prejudice after speaking to other white people with low levels of prejudice.[26]

In addition to intensifying positions, interaction with only like-minded perspectives leads to the wrong conclusions. As political psychologist Philip Tetlock explains, "groupthink" occurs when "intense social pressures toward uniformity and in-group loyalty within decision-making groups can build to the point where they seriously interfere with both cognitive efficiency and moral judgment."[27] Irving Janis traced poor political decision-making cases (Bay of Pigs, escalation of the Vietnam War) and showed that the policy makers formed cohesive groups that inhibited independent judgment.[28] Tetlock later expanded on Janis's analysis and found that policy makers in groupthink situations evaluated the group they identified with more positively relative to policy makers in non-groupthink situations.[29] The work on groupthink illustrates that monolithic groups endanger both moderation and the quality of the decisions themselves.

On the other hand, there is work showing that exposure to conflicting people and perspectives holds the potential to sway positions. Psychologist Christopher Hsee et al. showed that joint evaluation of two different options causes people to reverse previous decisions.[30] Simply viewing two pieces of information side-by-side changes people's decisions. Legal scholar Cass Sunstein collected tens of thousands of judicial votes from federal judges who were on three-person panels that were either all Democrat, all Republican, or mixed. He found that sitting on a mixed panel makes a great difference in how people vote. While Democrats and Republicans have a 41 percent difference in voting on gay rights issues overall, Democrats on an all-Democrat panel and Republicans on an all-Republican panel show an 86 percent difference.[31] This suggests that seeing and understanding different positions may change one's opinion.

In sum, this work on exposure to like-minded versus different opinions demonstrates the power of variety to sway opinions. Deliberation may therefore prove impactful because it requires participants to grapple with different opinions. In her explanations of "pathways to deliberative transformation," political philosopher Iris Marion Young writes that "through listening across difference each position can come to understand something about the ways proposals and claims affect others differently situated . . . participants gain a wider picture of the social processes in which experience is embedded."[32] Young further explains that confrontation with different perspectives teaches the "partiality of my own." Deliberation therefore tends to reveal the full spectrum of opinions on a topic and cultivates a greater understanding of other views. Empirical studies of deliberation corroborate this. Political scientist Jason Barabas studied the effects of a deliberative forum on Social Security in Arizona in which more than 408 citizens gathered to deliberate about Social Security reform. He measured the political opinions before and after the forum and found that deliberation leads to moderation of opinions.[33] In his study of Canadian committees, Michael Rush also found that partisanship decreased when the committees heard outside evidence. He writes, "82 percent of respondents said there was some degree of internal specialization in committees that resulted in cooperation between members of opposing parties."[34] Rush's conclusion suggests that listening to different views stands to change the way members approach an issue.

Research points to a clear connection between communication across difference and transformation of opinions. But is any of this happening in Congress today?

Interviewees from both sides of the aisle referred to the capacity of hearings with diverse panels to help them understand the other side, appreciate the full spectrum of opinions on an issue, and even reassess their own view. As one congresswoman explained, "With good questioning you can get folks to flesh out their views." A senior Democratic congressman explained, "Expert testimony tends to give you . . . [opportunity] to consider, or at least understand, the opposing point of view or . . . consider the steps you need to take in mitigation. You might hear one of the majority experts make a point, [and] you think, wow, I hadn't thought about that, that makes a lot of sense. So, then you can go to the minority expert and say, 'Do you agree, do you not agree?'" This observation demonstrates that the testimony helps the congressman gain a wider picture of the opinions on a topic and how they relate to each other. On the other side of the aisle, a Republican congressman, a member of the House Science Committee and former member of the House Agriculture Committee, echoed this reaction. He said, "What I've learned in this job is that there are a lot of different perspectives and it's my responsibility to hear." He went on to say that in hearings, "it happens almost all the time where I'm listening to different perspectives and piecing them together." A senator said the same of Senate hearings. He explained that, in hearings, he thought of "new aspects of the problem or I realized who was for and who was against this. What sectors of our society that I might not have thought had an interest in this or had something to say about it." These remarks are all indicative of the ways in which hearings broaden and deepen members of Congress' understanding of different opinions on an issue.

Members of Congress even told me of instances where listening helped them to understand new elements of arguments they had wholeheartedly opposed. The Democratic vice-ranking member of the House Science Committee (a major proponent of fighting climate change) told me that even though he completely disagreed with climate change skeptics who came to speak at the hearings, he saw that "at least they had coherent arguments" and this added some legitimacy to some of their positions. This statement is particularly meaningful because in one of the climate change hearings, this congressman engaged with a climate change skeptic on the witness panel, asking her to clarify her points. He was one of the few Democrats in this hearing who questioned the Republican witness, and when I spoke to the witness herself, she shared that she felt he was genuinely trying to understand her rather than asking a "gotcha question." Their interaction signals that the congressman was trying to understand her argument, even if he did not necessarily agree. The congressman shared, "I really do try to listen carefully . . . they all opened my mind." There were also stories of confrontation with an opposing viewpoint leading to a reassessment of one's own view. A senior Democratic congressman ruminated, "I think genuine witnesses are useful no matter what point of view they share. And often, I'll listen to a majority expert and it will help me . . . to test my own opinion."

COLLABORATION

New opportunities for collaboration may also arise through learning where others stand. When one better understands where one's counterpart stands, one might discover shared goals or interests. Several members of Congress explained that the questioning and overall interaction between committee members and witnesses during hearings helps them to understand where their colleagues' views might overlap. This corresponds with Young's notion that "through listening across difference each position can come to understand something about the ways proposals and claims affect others differently situated . . . participants gain a wider picture of the social processes in which experience is embedded."[35] A freshman Democratic congressman on the House Agriculture Committee said that hearings "give me a good understanding based on the questions that they asked of any witness about what's important for them in their district." He then explained that this has positive legislative consequences because, as a freshman member, he can understand where his colleagues stand and that just as beneficial as what these experts say is to "hear the questions from the members." A senior Democratic congressman on the House Science Committee reflected that hearings are useful because they help him understand "the other side." He said that hearings allow him "to know what [the other side] are thinking and get their perspective on something, especially something that I'm very interested in. And if I know there's resistance to something that I would like to do and I'd like to see in a piece of legislation . . . listening to the questions to witnesses from Republicans gives me a better sense of what their objections are." His reflection demonstrates that listening to and understanding the other side through questioning can help to bridge areas of disagreement.

On the Senate side, the same trend emerges. The conversation and increased understanding pave the way for cooperation. Hearings act as a "way of illuminating where everyone stands," said a longtime Republican senator. A senior Democratic senator and former member of the Senate Foreign Relations Committee shared a similar account from the Senate. He explained that, for him, the most valuable aspect of committee hearings is hearing his colleagues ask questions. He went on to share a story of a major piece of legislation that he discussed with two Republican colleagues and was able to advance as a result of a hearing. He said, "That exchange was taking place at a committee hearing that was stacked against me. But at the end of it, there was a conversation." This comment exemplifies the collaborative potential of hearings. By the same token, a personal staffer for another senator on the Senate Foreign Relations Committee explained that, as a result of attending a hearing about the position for "women's issues" within the State Department, her boss was able to see which other members cared about this issue and then she could work with them to protect this position. Yet another personal staffer for a Democratic senator on the Senate Foreign Relations Committee told a story of a bipartisan bill to create a Senate Select Committee on Cybersecurity. He explained that, during the hearings, his boss noticed that "Senator Gardner was vocal about cyber. He would ask questions in fall 2016 and in January we introduced a bill for a select committee on cyber. That bill came out of seeing him question cyber issues and seeing he was interested in it." This example again shows the potential for collaboration as a result of questioning.

Critics may argue that in today's congressional battlefield, in which partisan votes demarcate fixed borders, these stories of legitimization and collaboration are exceptions rather than rules. Indeed, much of congressional scholarship rests on rational choice assumptions that render the effects of deliberation an "impossibility theorem."[36] Key thinkers such as David Mayhew saw members of Congress as solely interested in reelection. From this standpoint, there is little room to maneuver in today's gridlocked Congress. In light of the increasingly partisan nature of voting behavior in Congress, I do not argue that hearings always have the potential to change opinions or encourage legitimization. Yet these reflections from leading politicians about the "stories that shape them" leading up to the vote, as well as the illustrative examples of hearings presented in this chapter, show that there is still some space for deliberation and its effects in Congress, perhaps especially in certain committees, topics, and chambers—as referenced earlier.

EXAMPLES OF DELIBERATIVE HEARINGS

Below are two illustrative examples of recent deliberative hearings on different policy issues: a hearing in the House Science Committee on a piece of cybersecurity legislation and a hearing in the House Agriculture Committee on SNAP. The examples chosen in this chapter are hearings that received balance scores between 0.5 and 0.7, indicating that they included a near even split of positively and negatively charged text.

I also coded transcripts for the following deliberative characteristics: reference to earlier points made by witnesses, reference to earlier points made by other members of the committee, inquisitive questioning, and purposeful inclusion of more than one witness. This coding scheme is grounded in Lascher's explanation of deliberation in Congress.[37] I define inquisitive questions as questions that seek new information. Questioning is only categorized as inquisitive when the committee members do not ask yes or no questions or questions with clear agendas, such as questions that start with "wouldn't you agree that . . ." This assessment is based on a thorough reading of the transcript. Purposeful inclusion of more than one witness means that committee members explicitly pose questions to more than one witness. In order for a hearing to be categorized as deliberative, a critical mass of speakers displaying one or more of the aforementioned deliberative characteristics is required. This is not to say that there cannot be one or two speakers who do not follow the pattern. Rather, it should be clear that the majority of speakers exhibit deliberative discourse. Each transcript was coded several times to assess reliability. Lascher also suggests that an additional way to assess deliberation is to ask participants whether they felt they had the opportunity for genuine questioning. Therefore, I also asked respondents for such opportunities in the hearings.

After identifying examples, I use these examples to further test how deliberative hearings stand to affect members, relying on content analysis of the transcripts and interviews with the members of Congress in attendance.

THE CYBERSECURITY HEARING

Balance Score: 0.66

On June 15, 2017, the House Science Committee held the hearing, "Bolstering the Government's Cybersecurity: Lessons Learned from WannaCry."[38] After the WannaCry ransomware attack and in the lead-up to the NIST Cybersecurity Framework, Assessment and Auditing Act (H.R. 1224), the committee held a series of hearings. The bill directed the National Institute of Standards and Technology (NIST) to conduct audits and evaluate whether federal agencies are complying with the NIST cybersecurity framework. The bill was a partisan issue. It was authored by Republican Ralph Abraham and supported by all Republican members. Every Democratic member except for Daniel Lipinski voted against the bill. Democrats argued that NIST lacked the expertise and funding necessary for audits.

The witness panel exhibited professional balance, with witnesses both supporting and opposing the proposed bill. The first witness was Salim Neino, executive officer at Kryptos Logic, an unlabeled expert who shared information on the attack and how it was stopped by Kryptos Logic. Next, the committee heard from Charles Romine, director of the Information Technology Laboratory at the National Institute of Standards and Technology. Romine was a spokesperson on behalf of NIST who gave details on NIST framework and its applications. His testimony was followed by Gregory Touhill, retired brigadier general of the U.S. Air Force and adjunct professor of cybersecurity at Carnegie Mellon University. Touhill was a "labeled expert" as a result of his service as chief information security officer under the Obama Administration. The last witness was Hugh Thompson, chief technology officer at Symantec, who was another unlabeled expert.

The hearing discourse revealed examples of inquisitive questioning and reference to earlier points. Several committee members asked for witnesses to expand or delve more deeply into topics and comment on the interest this sparked in them.

Effects

The cyber hearing displays several examples of legitimization. For example, Congresswoman Esty began her remarks by saying, "This has been very enlightening and extremely helpful," a verbal sign of an appreciation for the new vantage points and information gained in the hearing. In a later interview with me, she reflected that listening to the witnesses with opposing views speak about cyber made her think to herself, "Is that my own ideological baggage that I think this way?"

I asked one senior Democratic congressman about the hearing and he told me how it compelled him to change his vote. At the time of our interview, he noted that the cybersecurity in federal government bill would be coming to the floor for a vote the following week. He explained that he was the only Democrat to support the bill when it came to committee markup, and he recalled of the hearing "that's the sort of hearing I remember because it was a big divide between Democrats and Republicans. So, I really want to learn . . . especially to get from NIST their perspective on expanding this role and to hear from other witnesses what they thought about that and how difficult it was going to be." This hearing moved him. "It's actually a hearing that I remember something about and of wanting to actually hear what they were talking about. So, I think that . . . it convinced me enough that, okay, I could support the bill going through committee even though I had reservations about it," he explained. The congressman's recollections of how he "really wanted to learn" because this was an issue with a divergence of opinions and that the witness panel "convinced" him he should support the bill represents a powerful indication of the capacity of witness testimony to legitimize opposing perspectives.

THE SNAP HEARING

Balance Score: 0.66

On January 12, 2016, the House Agriculture Committee held the hearing, "Past, Present, and Future of SNAP: Addressing Special Populations."[39] This hearing was part of a set of hearings on SNAP over the course of several years prior to the passage of the 2018 Farm Bill. The bill represented $867 billion in government spending and is one of the major pieces of legislation that falls under the jurisdiction of the House Agriculture Committee. The bill includes important regulations pertaining to American farming as well as nutrition assistance.

SNAP is part of a wider value debate on social welfare. The question of how much the government should be involved in assisting people in need is a question of value. It transcends the raw facts on how many people need assistance and how much providing such assistance costs. Several of the interviewees, including staff and members of Congress from both parties on the committee, stressed that SNAP is an exceptionally partisan issue. Democrats are twice as likely as Republicans to have received food stamps at some point in their lives.[40] Nearly three-quarters of liberal Democrats and less than half of Republicans say the government should expand assistance to those in need.[41] This hearing was about the needs of "special populations" such as the elderly or veterans. As noted earlier, veterans affairs is a relatively bipartisan topic (even within a partisan topic). Therefore, SNAP for veterans may be a subtopic of a contentious issue with a little more potential for alignment.

The witness panel included a mix of types of experts as well as professions. The first witness, Abby Liebman, was president and CEO of Mazon (a nonprofit working on hunger issues), an unlabeled expert because she came to share expert information on hunger problems faced by veteran families. The next witness, Erika Tebbens, represented a personal storyteller coming to share her experience as a SNAP recipient and a spouse of a military veteran. She was followed by Vinsen Faris, executive director of Meals-on-Wheels of Johnson and Ellis counties in Texas, a spokesperson who came to share specialized knowledge of a particular program that helps elderly Americans receive food. Finally, the committee heard from Eric Schneidewind, president-elect of American Association of Retired Persons (AARP), a spokesperson on behalf of an organization dedicated to fighting for elderly Americans.

The hearing discourse was full of examples of deliberative speech. The chair began by asking the witnesses a series of inquisitive questions, saying she was "curious" to learn more. Adams referred to a specific statistic on veterans from Liebman's testimony and asked inquisitive questions. Conaway referred to previous points from Faris's testimony, including the specific case of a ninety-two-year-old woman in the Meals-on-Wheels program and then asked questions. Gibbs again asked for elaboration on military families' costs and other issues, and then Crawford referred directly to questions posed before him. The critical mass of committee members who asked inquisitive questions, referenced previous points made in the discussion, or included another witness renders this a clear example of deliberative hearing.

Effects

There is indication of all three effects of deliberation in this hearing. After engaging with Tebbens, Congressman Crawford asked, "Madam Chair, I ask that you might consider maybe a joint hearing with this Subcommittee and Armed Services to address nutritional issues that have been brought up in this hearing." This shows that the hearing moved him to the extent that he wanted to learn more.

Perhaps the most striking example of the effect of this hearing is personified by Republican Congressman Ted Yoho. The congressman's behavior in the hearing and statements in an interview I conducted several months after the hearing reveal signs of Young's three pathways to deliberative transformation. Congressman Yoho seemed so affected by Tebbens's experience as a veteran family on SNAP that he asked, "Why aren't we paying veterans more?" Two other people in the room that day independently recounted that they were struck by his statements. A long-time staffer on the nutrition subcommittee told me that she remembered this as an example of someone moved to reassess their own position based on testimony. In an interview with me, Liebman's deputy at Mazon, who was also there that day with his boss, echoed this view. He independently identified this same exchange as evidence that Congressman Yoho was moved by the testimony.

Their surprise may stem from Yoho's previous voting record and public statements about SNAP. In 2013, he voted to cut food stamps by $40 billion.[42] In public statements, he stressed that SNAP should be temporary and the importance of across-the-board budget cuts.[43] Yoho's behavior in the hearing may not necessarily indicate that he changed his mind, but it shows that it is plausible that he engaged with information shared by minority witnesses and gained a more comprehensive understanding of another viewpoint. In an interview with me, Congressman Yoho explained, "I think the more that you can get together and hear somebody else's perspective of why they're arguing a certain way or fighting for a certain thing kind of makes you think, you know what, I didn't think of that." The congressman's statement suggests that he appreciates the fact that others have different views and that listening to them leads him to realize new angles that he had not previously considered. The statement indicates what Young terms "understanding the partiality of your view." When I asked specifically about the SNAP veterans hearing, he explained, "That was an eye-opener for me because we've got too many people on that that are serving this country. So, what that tells me is we need to pay more and there should be some form of assistance to get these people through that." Given the congressman's question in the hearing regarding treatment of veterans, his statement would indicate that the hearing gave him a more thorough grasp of the opinions on the issue. Young writes, "through listening across difference each position can come to understand something about the ways proposals and claims affect others differently situated . . . participants gain a wider picture of the social processes in which experience is embedded."[44] Finally, when asked about the purpose of hearings in general, the congressman showed appreciation for effect three, collective problem solving. He remarked, "The Democrats were lining up on the floor, they had the same talking points, 'we will not accept one calorie taken off a plate' and 'we're over here' . . . that's what happens when you don't have interaction. Part of these are divided, there's a dichotomy up here and it's Republicans versus Democrats, or vice versa. Whereas in the committee . . . you can have a diversification of ideas, but you also have that interaction to where you see the other side of the story." His comments reaffirm his appreciation for a setting in which both sides have a right to be heard.

These examples of deliberative hearings illustrate contemporary deliberation in a nondeliberative Congress. They further substantiate the earlier exploration of the legitimization and collaboration that deliberative hearings promote.

CONCLUSION

On February 5, 2020, the Select Committee on the Modernization of Congress held the hearing "Article One: Fostering a More Deliberative Process in Congress." The impetus for the hearing was a shared understanding in the congressional reform community of the deterioration of congressional deliberation. Chair Derek Kilmer (a Democrat from Washington State) opened the hearing with the affirmation that "the framers intended for Congress to be a deliberative body." He depicted the job of Congress as giving "voice to the people we represent. It is not always easy because we are a nation of diverse views . . . the people's house embodies an amazing array of opinions and perspectives on the issues of the day, and through the process of debate and deliberation we determine policy."[45] Over the course of the hearing, all three expert witnesses touched on committees in some fashion, proposing ways to harness contemporary committees for a more deliberative legislative process.

This chapter adds to the discussion of committee deliberations by showing when and how congressional committees still act as deliberative forums today. It drew on different data to flesh out the ways in which committee culture, chairmanship, hearing topics, and chambers affect the likelihood of deliberative hearings.

In a Congress rife with partisan topics and increasingly strained relationships, hearings that meet these conditions may be less likely, but they nevertheless still take place. A Georgetown professor and expert on terror, with experience testifying on foreign affairs, told me in an interview a story of a hearing that surprised him. He recounted how a Republican congressman from Indiana "lectured me about how we need to treat Muslim communities better in the U.S., something I firmly agreed with." He used this story as an example of how terror is a bipartisan topic in which "there isn't a neat, Republicans believe X and Democrats believe Y." Committees can still discuss many such bipartisan topics.

One way to ensure that a greater percentage of hearings are dedicated to bipartisan topics is to change the rules governing how hearing are set up. The Select Committee on the Modernization of Congress recommended "bipartisan committee staff briefings and agenda-setting retreats to encourage better policy making and collaboration among Members."[46] This is one way to ensure resulting hearings pertain to topics both sides agree on rather than having them used as a partisan flex. This chapter showed that, when hearings are deliberative, these deliberations may still nurture greater understanding, legitimization, and collaboration between members.

5

COMMITTEE HEARINGS AS EDUCATIONAL PLATFORMS

"Why is Congress so dumb?" This headline opened a recent *Washington Post* opinion piece by representative Bill Pascrell, in which he chronicles the ways in which the undermining of congressional committees (and the other reforms explained in the introduction) and capacity have made it harder for Congress to specialize and gain expertise.[1] This chapter asks whether committees can still act as a space to make Congress smarter. When and how do contemporary committees serve as educational platforms? The chapter explains how partisanship, formality, types of witnesses, and the nature of the hearing topics influence the likelihood of congressional and staff learning. It then presents two illustrative examples of recent educational hearings on science, technology, engineering, and math (STEM) and genetic editing.

ARE MEMBERS OF CONGRESS LEARNING?

Many members of Congress that I interviewed emphasized how much they learn in hearings. One congresswoman on the House Science Committee explained, "I'm there to learn. They are the experts and so I tend to use my time asking questions to try to learn in helping us to sort through these difficult questions." Another first-term congressman excitedly shared, "So I'm sixty-seven and at a point you realize you've heard the same jokes again and again. I'm just amazed at how much I have learned in the thirty-nine months I've been here. It's like going to college all over again." Yet another congresswoman on the House Agriculture Committee said that she feels expert testimony adds nuance to her thinking, enabling her and her staff to delve deeper into subjects about which they might previously have known little.

A Republican senator, who served in the Senate for nearly four decades and chaired the Senate Foreign Relations Committee twice, reflected, "I'm certain I learned a great deal [in hearings] . . . [they are] an educational and illuminating experience without any doubt." These affirmations of learning may seem to come as a surprise to some. The discovery that there is indeed learning is an important contribution to the understanding of the contemporary Congress, but the more important question is, Where and how does this learning take place? The answer is explained in the next section.

WHEN ARE EDUCATIONAL HEARINGS MOST LIKELY?

PARTISANSHIP: BIPARTISAN TOPICS

First, educational hearings are more likely for bipartisan topics. Social psychology research by Sander van der Linden et al. reveals the power of agreement. His team showed in a series of experiments that the degree of expert consensus influences the extent to which people are convinced by an argument.[2] Evolutionary biology research shows that humans have, in fact, evolved to respond to consensus.[3] Van der Linden's study contends that people are motivated by "consensus cues," and evidence is less threatening when it is presented as a consensus agreement among experts. A former staffer on the Senate Finance Committee reflected:

> I think for the less contentious topics, it's less . . . gotcha moments or I'm saying this out in the open so everyone can hear my opinion. . . . For the less contentious topics you're asking, for example, I wrote a letter to the

State Department on X date and I haven't received a response. Can you please tell me the answer to this question that I've been asking for? What are you doing at the airports for X, Y, Z? They're more and more matter of fact on the noncontentious topics versus on the contentious topics, [when] you're going to get a lot more pontificating.

Her reflection underscores the idea that bipartisan topics promote learning rather than theatrics.

NATURE OF THE HEARING TOPIC: LEGISLATIVE STATUS

Educational hearings may be more likely in instances in which there is no imminent legislation because minds are not made up and because information and witnesses are more likely to be "new." One congressman on the House Science Committee commented that he was much more likely to gain a more comprehensive understanding of an issue in "nonlegislative hearings where there's not a piece of legislation already out there or that has been talked about." A Republican congressman echoed this point, explaining that "many times I haven't made up my mind and they can help me make up my mind." A staffer on the Senate Finance Committee further explained that "you can kind of tell when questions are being asked and the answer is known . . . and you can tell when members really want to hear something new and have a question on the policy."

It is logical that learning is greatest when witnesses share new information or interpretations. As one former witness explained, an expert who brings in new information or who collates information in an original way can be an especially effective teacher. In many technical areas in which members of Congress lack expertise, much of the information shared is new and often instructive. A Democratic congresswoman on the House Agriculture Committee said that new data is important because it helps her shape positions on issues where she did not previously have a clear stand. She explained, "Because I am not a farmer or a livestock owner, I don't have an opinion in a lot of instances." For this reason, the data shared resonated with her most. She also said that she has been influenced by commodities experts because it is a policy area that requires technical expertise and that she knew little about it before she came to Congress.

A Republican member of her committee agreed with this assessment, explaining that expert testimony is "much better than I can get from reading an article. It is really helpful in complex topics . . . they try their best to make it understandable." This corroborates similar work from legislative studies in other countries. In their analysis of evidence reported to legislative committees in the United Kingdom, Denmark, and the Netherlands, Helene Helboe Pedersen et al. argue that, in learning from external witnesses, committees prefer to engage "with external stakeholders who can contribute new knowledge or new perspectives."[4]

On occasion, hearings like this can even provide ideas for future legislation. Staff members of the Senate Foreign Relations Committee recounted how Ambassador Daniel Shapiro's idea in a hearing to create an escrow account for Palestinians was then incorporated into the Taylor Force Act. The staff of a Republican congresswoman on the House Science Committee told me that data explained in a hearing stressed the importance of city infrastructure and directly led to the "smart city" bill they were working on. A staff member of a senator on the Senate Foreign Relations Committee said that if their team is thinking of a new piece of legislation, they use the hearing to flesh out the ideas by seeking out expert opinions.

Hearings on "new topics" are most informative because it is so rare in the current congressional context for hearing information to be novel or fresh in any way. Indeed, as chapter 1 detailed, staff members normally interact at length with witnesses and topics prior to a hearing, and members often know a lot of what will be said ahead of time. A Democratic congressman on the House Science Committee said, "A lot of times . . . you know what a hearing's going to be about. The main issues are things that I've already thought about, talked to staff about. Sometimes things come up that are sort of outside the . . . or tangential to it that's interesting, that sort of can be illuminating. I think that's where it is more likely to have something come up and someone to say, 'Oh, that's interesting.' " She reflects that, although new information is rare or "tangential," it is instructive when it falls outside the normal issues that everyone has prepared to hear about. A senior staffer on the Senate Judiciary Committee reflected that, in his committee, "genuine fact-finding stuff is going to be pretty rare." He went on to explain, however, that "maybe the exception would be . . . the investigation of the Russia allegations or whatever it is. I think that has probably had more fact finding, probably because the witnesses are less likely to engage with staff beforehand. . . . So that might be a situation where you have more actual fact finding." This example of the investigation of collusion with Russia underlines that "fact finding" is linked to new information and witnesses who have not been groomed or grilled by the staff before the hearings.

THE KINDS OF WITNESSES TESTIFYING: UNLABELED WITNESSES

When are witnesses likely to be new? As chapter 3 described, witnesses untarnished by old connections and unburdened by clear ideological labels are defined as unlabeled witnesses. These witnesses may be more likely to be new because committee members do not associate them easily with policies or previous appointments. A Republican member of the House Science and Agriculture committees said that "for someone where we don't know where they are coming from, there is a freshness to it." He went on to explain that he learns most from people to whom he has not previously been exposed.

In addition to the "freshness" of new information from new people, other lawmakers and staff members highlighted the educational value of hearing "objective" information from experts untarnished by partisan agendas and who are not spouting the same well-known mantras. In order to present hard facts uncontaminated by value judgments, it is important to bring figures who are not publicly connected to an argument in the sphere of values. One personal staffer on the Senate Foreign Relations Committee referenced the case of labeled Iran expert Mark Dubowitz, saying, "People like Dubowitz, his organization has a clear ideology. I see someone like him as someone trying to advance a specific policy agenda and Republicans use him for those ends, whereas when you have someone from a nonpartisan think tank or university, they can often give you more objective analysis than someone like that." His evaluation of the difference between "objective analysis" and "advancing a specific agenda" shows that members of Congress may see unlabeled witnesses in a different light and therefore be more open to learning from analysis of unlabeled witnesses. A staffer on the Senate Finance Committee explained that these witnesses have a different type of engagement with members of

Congress. She described that unlabeled witnesses elicit "a lot of questions that had specific research-oriented answers. I think other witnesses might have questions, more on positions or future policies and how those would affect individuals versus more research-driven questions." This suggests that a panel of unlabeled witnesses is more likely to lead to "fact finding" and emphasis on specialization.

FORMALITY OF THE HEARING: INFORMAL HEARINGS

An informal hearing environment also has implications for learning. In an interview with me, one Republican congressman, the former subcommittee chair of the House Energy Committee, Subcommittee on Oversight and Investigations, said that the informal meetings were "informational. Members were there just to question. The idea of having it off the record was so members would not be posturing. [The idea was that] 'this person is here just to teach, so go ahead and ask questions.' . . . idea was just informational. Getting background so you can proceed to the hearing." He went on to give the example of an informal hearing on concussions that they set up after members complained that they did not even understand the language of the issue. In an interview with me, Dr. Jennifer Doudna, the scientist who developed genetic editing and testified about this topic (in a hearing detailed later in this chapter), reflected on the differences between the formalized hearing and an informal Capitol Hill briefing on the same subject. She explained that the informal briefing gave her more time to go into the details of her research and more face-to-face time with policy makers, both crucial elements in productive learning experiences. Yet another confirmation of the educational capacity of informal meetings came from a Republican congressman serving on the House Science Committee. He said that, in informal roundtables, "there is an opportunity to go deeper. There isn't the five-minute limitation or follow-up so it's a different level of learning in those meetings. . . . Maybe even not knowing the right questions to ask until you get into the discussion and start learning." His observation demonstrates how the informal element of these meetings may facilitate a different type of learning in which questions are not strategic or premeditated but rather a genuine and natural extension of the conversation.

STRUCTURE: SENATE, DESIRABILITY

In a "dumb" Congress, Senate committees may prove smarter than House committees. A senior senator and member of the Democratic leadership with experience in both chambers remarked, "When I was one of 435 in the House, I had a couple committees . . . and I could keep up with it. When I got over here [the Senate] the whole world changed." He went on to explain that, in the Senate, he was on many more committees and "I quickly realized, I can't keep up with all this." The workload clearly matters. Another longtime senator explained, "Sometimes members will come make an appearance at the beginning for the opening statement and leave even before you get to their questions . . . particularly if the committee is very active and some members say, 'I'm devoting a lot of time to this committee, but I have other things on my agenda to do.'" As explained in the previous section, engagement may be less pronounced if legislators cannot attend the hearings. Indeed, this conclusion reaffirms the narrative of senators being spread too thin that was alluded to in the introduction.

A legislative director for a senator who served for many years in both the House and Senate reflected, "Your knowledge of the issues is obviously going to be much deeper if you've been involved with a committee for a long period of time. And especially if you've been leading that committee." He went to explain that his boss is "the only member in history to chair both the House and Senate committees. . . . So his involvement on both sides of the Hill in agriculture goes back forty years. He is in a unique position where his career has sort of been defined by agriculture. So it's incredible, his depth of knowledge on agriculture. . . . I think your time with the committee or committees that have a certain jurisdiction does impact here. Hopefully impact your overall knowledge of the issues." This suggests capacity for learning might be greater in the Senate because senators have the time for the sustained engagement necessary to gain expertise.

The longer one engages with a topic, the more time there is to gain expertise. This holds true for the Senate as well as more "desirable" committees in which members are likely to invest more of their time. One Democratic congressman on the House Ways and Means Committee explained, "I would say that I'm getting better at it as time goes on. We've been in Congress for four years. I'm much better today than I was four years ago. For those people that argue for term limits, you really do learn a lot while you're doing these jobs. And I'm one of the more junior members on the committee. So I stay there and listen to my colleagues." This reflection demonstrates that legislators need time to learn. Time is, of course, a necessary but not sufficient condition for expertise. Not every senator or member of the House Ways and Means Committee will become an expert. Commitment to and propensity for learning (two highly variable and personal qualities) form the other part of the equation. Still, time matters.

This confirms similar findings from previous legislative studies. Henrik Jensen calculated a 12 percent turnover over just a five-month period in Danish parliamentary committees, a system in which committees are relatively weak and unable to specialize.[5] In their analysis of the Argentine Congress, Mark Jones et al. utilized data on committee membership between 1983 and 1985 to compare the tenure of American and Argentine politicians. They find that Argentine politicians have a much shorter half-life than American politicians.[6] As a result, they argue that Argentine politicians are less able to specialize. In the British and Indian systems, a new committee is created for nearly every new bill. This procedure stands in stark contrast to the relatively stable and permanent committees in the American Congress. Malcolm Shaw writes that "one reason that the Ways and Means Committee in the U.S. House of Representatives and the Public Accounts Committee in the British House of Commons are so important is that they have been around since 1795 and 1861, respectively."[7] Anything that limits the time members have to delve into a topic (too many committee assignments, insufficient attendance, turnover, etc.) has implications for legislative learning.

Are hearings an educational space to make Congress smarter? Some of the time. Members of Congress are most likely to learn in hearings on bipartisan topics; when there is no immediate piece of legislation under consideration; when witnesses are unlabeled and present fresh analysis of new issues; that are set up informally; and in the Senate, where members have more time to specialize and gain subject matter expertise.

STAFF EDUCATION

No less important than committee member learning are the members of the personal staff of the members of Congress (who attend more frequently than their bosses!), many of whom told me that they come to the hearings to learn, and this in turn affects their work for their respective members. This effect reaffirms previous work about the significance of staff members in the study of congressional learning. Richard Hall explains that "much of what the members do in person is prefigured by the options and information that staffers supply. . . . The study of legislative participation, then, must extend not only to the member but to the enterprise."[8] Jesse Crosson et al. echo this point in their study of congressional staff, writing that "staffers serve as a legislator's engines of policy production, as they draft bills, seek out cosponsors, meet with lobbyists and network with other key staffers."[9]

The staff members reflected on how important hearings can be in teaching them about topics. A personal staffer on the House Agriculture Committee said, "Some of these witnesses have very narrow expertise. They bring that technical expertise that I would not get somewhere else." The other staff interviews confirmed this observation, each underscoring how they learn from hearings.

The information that staffers learn affects members of Congress in several ways. First, the staffers learn in order to inform their bosses. One personal staffer on the House Science Committee said, "What matters more than what [the congressman] hears from the witnesses is what I hear from the witnesses because he is relying on me to pay closer attention because it is my job to advise him." A Democratic congressman on the House Science Committee underscored the importance of staff learning. In his opinion, staff briefings are one of the most effective learning tools because the staffers in attendance learn and shape their bosses' behavior. Both he and Doudna, the renowned expert on genetic editing and former witness, referenced a staff briefing that arose as a result of that hearing. They both spoke of the importance of this briefing, citing its ability to educate staffers, who would then inform the congressional members. A staffer on the Senate Finance Committee explained, "You are there to do your research, make sure you're prepared for everything that may come up and that the member is not surprised by anything or caught off guard by anything. . . . [You want to make sure that the member] knows what to expect and really is just looking their smartest right at the committee." Carol Weiss's in-depth study of committee staff dynamics uncovered a similar trend. She writes that "staff know that their bosses do not want to be taken by surprise. If new evidence becomes public of which she is not aware, and if that evidence is cited to support the opposition's argument, there are going to be complaints about staff work."[10] Weiss's account highlights the importance staffers place on obtaining information to inform their bosses. One of the staffers she interviewed remarked, "One of the cardinal rules of any good staff person is: Don't make your senator look like a dope."[11] Weiss's study confirms the conclusion drawn from my own interviews—staffers use hearings to learn because they need to inform their bosses.

Second, staffers sit behind their members and take notes for them during the hearing. As one staffer explained, committee members will frequently come in and out of a given hearing. Sometimes they are even on multiple committee meetings at the same time. In fact, staffers told me that every committee wants to have hearings in the mornings from Tuesday to Thursday because many members of Congress fly home for the rest of the week. Consequently, hearings often overlap. Normally, the staffers attend the hearings and take notes if their bosses cannot. A staffer on the Senate Finance Committee explained that they are there "to show a presence among both the staffers and the senators in the audience." A personal staffer on the Senate Foreign Relations Committee described how, when his boss returns to a hearing, he will sit behind him and inform him about what the witnesses said as well as what questions have been asked. Another legislative aide on the Senate Finance Committee remarked that staffers attend hearings so that "if something is said unexpectedly or that they didn't know about, they will be able to let their [congressional] member know." This information is useful to congressional members "if they've been away for votes or something so they can ask follow-up questions." A longtime senator further underscored the significance of staff involvement during a hearing, saying that "most members have pretty able staff who sit right behind them in the hearing."

Third, the staff members are responsible for preparing questions and preparatory memos for the hearings. In preparing questions and memos, they rely on a bank of prior knowledge informed by the hearings they attend. While their bosses may not attend all of the hearings and most probably do not read the memos compiled by committee staff, the personal staffers are the ones who absorb all this information. One personal staffer recounted the copious work involved in combing through the written testimony in order to prepare his boss for the hearing. On the Senate

Foreign Relations Committee, committee staffers send all of the member offices a detailed research report compiled by the Congressional Research Service (CRS) ahead of each hearing. A personal staffer explained that his boss hardly ever even sees this report. However, he relies on the report in crafting his own preparatory memo. The questions and preparatory memos have enormous potential in shaping committee members' behavior during hearings. A staffer on the House Agriculture Committee said that he believed at least half of the time his boss uses the questions he crafts for her before the hearing. The two-time chair of the Foreign Relations Committee expanded upon the point: "I want to indicate the staff plays a very important role in all this because good staff members prepare the member they serve for the hearing. They are likely to suggest a number of questions that the member might ask, where the member might not have thought of asking those questions or even what they are talking about. . . . [The] background material and preparatory sheets . . . may have triggered the member's interest." His comments affirm the significance of staff preparation and proposed questions.

Fourth, lawmakers rely on staffers to follow up about the information shared in the hearing and in some cases influence legislative negotiations. A personal staffer on the House Agriculture Committee explained that his boss is frequently struck by a statistic she hears in a hearing and asks him to investigate further and present her with more research. He said, "Every three hearings she hears a statistic and tells me to dig in deeper." Another staffer on the Senate Foreign Relations Committee explained that if his boss liked a witness, he may ask him to set up a follow-up meeting in order to learn more and then report back to him. He gave the example of a witness who testified about the human rights implications of the Authorization of the Use of Force Bill. Following the witness's testimony, the senator asked the staffer to meet with her to gather "more information and more analysis that we can then give to [the senator]." He described it as a feedback loop. Staffers also influence legislative negotiations. A senior Democratic senator who served in both the House and the Senate explained that he relies heavily on his staff to talk to other staffers "and explore whether there is room for agreement." His legislative director, seated across from us during the interview, added that she seeks common ground with other staffers and "brings the issues where no agreement is reached to the members so that they can make a final decision," thereby underscoring the power of the staff. Hearings educate the staffers and if they are the ones who strike the deals, inform their bosses, and do a lot of the work behind the scenes, then what they learn in hearings matters. This is all the more important in light of the Achilles heel discussed in chapter 1. The power of lobbyists is magnified when the inadequate substantive knowledge or specialization of the staff creates an opening for lobbyists to supply information. An educated staffer combats the power of interest groups and their lobbyists.

EXAMPLES OF EDUCATIONAL HEARINGS

Below are two examples of educational hearings in the House Science Committee that demonstrate some of the dynamics discussed above.

THE SCIENCE AND ETHICS HEARING

On June 16, 2015, the House Science Committee held the hearing titled "The Science and Ethics of Genetically Engineered Human DNA."[12] Genetic engineering of human DNA is a relatively new development. In 2012, Dr. Jennifer Doudna (who testified in this hearing) and Professor Emmanuelle Charpentier discovered the CRISPR-Cas9 method for changing the sequence of DNA and thereby altering the genome, for example, to correct mutations or to change one version of a gene to a better one. The pair won the Nobel Prize in Chemistry in 2020 for this discovery. As with other scientific and technological developments, Congress is charged with assessing how to adapt regulations to new technologies. Dr. Jeffrey Kahn told me that he thinks the impetus for the hearing was that a group in China had tried to genetically modify human embryos using research that sidestepped strict rules of scientific investigation. The research had supposedly been rejected from reputable scientific journals because of the "controversial nature of the research itself."

Congressman Bill Foster, the only PhD scientist in Congress and the person who came to the chair with the idea for the hearing, gave this hearing as an example in which "both sides behaved pretty well" because it was not a "tribal issue." This hearing remained in the sphere of facts for a number of reasons. The witnesses were brought to share specialized information about their scientific areas, and there was no clear divergence in the values they attached to it. Genetic engineering is not a particularly partisan issue. When I asked Dr. Kahn, one of the witnesses, if he felt there was more than one partisan or political perspective on the witness panel, he stressed that there were "no politics at all. And we sort of figured, and rightly, that there'll be plenty of that from the members." Doudna confirmed this assessment, saying in an interview that she felt the committee members were there to learn.

The committee heard from a series of unlabeled experts, including:

1. Dr. Victor Dzau, president, Institute of Medicine, the National Academy of Sciences
2. Dr. Jennifer Doudna, professor of biochemistry and molecular biology, University of California, Berkeley
3. Dr. Elizabeth McNally, professor of genetic medicine, Northwestern University
4. Dr. Jeffrey Kahn, professor of bioethics and public policy, Johns Hopkins University

All of the witnesses who appeared at this hearing were unlabeled experts. None were associated with a partisan cause or a particular campaign issue. The majority staffer who I interviewed took me step-by-step through the selection process:

I could say we tried to get somebody who can get sort of the big picture usually to start off. And Dzau, we chose him because he's at the Institute of Medicine. And we often have national academies. . . . Then we needed somebody who's a really strong subject matter expert. I mean not only expert but somebody who can communicate it well. In this case, it's really complicated science. Doudna is one of the actual discoverers of the technology. And she also happens to be a fantastic communicator. So then McNally was actually the minority witness. And so, she's working on the neonatal research and using gene editing for neonatal purposes and childhood diseases. So she was a minority witness but again it was part of the minority trying to fill in a hole to tell the whole story. And that's a story we wanted to tell but we knew that probably the minority wouldn't want to tell that story.

She especially stressed her desire to find an unlabeled expert, explaining that:

> We had to have an ethicist because we wanted to tell that part of the story. My biggest trouble finding an ethicist was finding one that would be (a) well respected, (b) not seen as partisan and those are really my two requirements, and (c) have some expertise in this area. And so, we came to Kahn. There were some bioethicists who've been recommended, and I looked at their bios and they have advisers in the Obama administration. I thought well, our members might see that and say, "No, I can't listen to this person because they're partisan." Same if they worked in the Bush administration, "Oh well, George W. Bush, that's partisan." So, I had to find somebody. Kahn has not worked for either administration. He was on an FDA [Food and Drug Administration] advisory committees related to it and he was available.

The detailed explanation of the staffer makes clear that the witnesses were specifically sought for their expertise rather than their brand.

Effects: Learning

When asked about the aforementioned genetics hearing, Kahn emphasized the learning that took place. He said, "I remember very clearly actually, as we talked about it with the other [witnesses] who were there, it was more inquisitive and thoughtful in many respects than I think we all expected." He went on to explain, "I think their questions, which were not just sort of one off and move on, made it seem like they were actually learning." He stressed that the tendency toward inquisitive questioning was not partisan and extended across the aisle, adding, "It wasn't like, you know, you're a friend of the Democrats, you're a friend of the Republicans. It was a little more about, you know, you are an academic, you work in a science area, I'm a friend of science, I'm going to ask you a friendly question . . . versus, you know, people like you are not to be trusted and, therefore, what should we be doing to make sure that people like you don't perform in bad ways. I think it was much more bipartisan than I expected." His assessment was confirmed by his colleague, Doudna, who sat on the same witness panel. She reflected that the hearing was driven by "information seeking" and that she was "pleasantly surprised [that the questions] were truly inquisitive." She also emphasized that she did not "detect any partisan aspect to the questioning."

Kahn said that he and the other witnesses had agreed that the worst thing that could happen was for Congress to do something "rashly and pre-emptively" in terms of regulations on genetic engineering. He remarked, "I mean I think if I had to say, how do we move the needle at all, and I think people felt like they understood more and felt more confident, you know, that the scientific community was likely to behave well." In fact, he made several references to the increased understanding of what actually goes on in genetic research. He referenced it as "education to the extent that this is not the Wild West and we don't need you to start making up laws as if it is the Wild West." His description illustrates that the hearing was educational to the extent that it educated members of the committee about research in a specialized field of science with which they were previously unfamiliar. Again, his evaluation was confirmed by Doudna. She underscored her impression that there was real interest in learning about the science and technology.

THE STEM HEARING

On July 26, 2017, the House Science Committee held the hearing titled "STEM and Computer Science Education: Preparing the 21st Century Workforce."[13] Both the staff and members on the House Science Committee underscored that STEM education is not a contentious subject in general. In fact, in the 117th Congress, senators from both sides of the aisle even came together to sponsor several different bipartisan bills to strengthen STEM education.[14] The hearings on STEM during the 116th Congress did not pertain to a specific piece of legislation; rather, they were meant to inform members about the broader issue and diffuse any possible partisan tension.

The hearing called on four witnesses:

1. Mr. James Brown, director of the STEM Education Coalition, a spokesperson for STEM
2. Mr. Pat Yongpradit, chief academic officer, Code.org, a spokesperson on behalf of his organization

3. Dr. A. Paul Alivisatos, executive vice chancellor and provost of the University of California, Berkeley, an unlabeled expert with no political association

4. Ms. Dee Mooney, executive director of Micron Technology Foundation, a spokesperson presenting specialized information based on her experience promoting STEM education at the Micron Technology Foundation

Effects: Learning

The STEM hearing provides further proof that members of Congress learn in hearings. A Democratic congressman on the House Science Committee reflected on the House Science Committee STEM hearings, saying:

> It's just interesting to me in the fact that I was a professor. . . . How do we do a better job in STEM education? And it's not really . . . most of it is not legislative. But it's interesting to hear people [talking] about what works, what doesn't work, to hear about the sort of success stories and what seems to be working. And in that way, I think, yeah, those are actually just really more informative for members who just are interested in a topic and want to learn about it.

The congressman's statements are a testament to the genuine desire to learn in the STEM hearings. Taken together, the STEM and the science and ethics hearings build on the earlier sections and provide direct evidence of instances in which hearings can act as an educational platform.

CONCLUSION—WHEN AND HOW ARE MEMBERS OF CONGRESS LEARNING?

This book began by explaining that a century of reform and displacement undermined Congress's ability to specialize. This chapter showed that contemporary congressional committees can still serve as an educational platform for members of Congress and their staff, especially in instances where hearings pertain to bipartisan topics, issues on which there is no immediate piece of legislation under consideration, informal settings, and in the Senate. In a partisan Congress, bipartisan topics may be less common than they once were, but there are still many bipartisan issues. However, in a Congress in which few pieces of legislation get passed, the fact that hearings free from a partisan vote may elicit greater learning signals that there is still space for long-term specialization in the contemporary Congress.

This finding also suggests that investing in these kinds of hearings can further increase legislative learning. As noted in the introduction, Jonathan Lewallen et al. found that the percentage of hearings about policy solutions halved between the 92nd and 111th Congress (falling from 60 percent to 30 percent).[15] Indeed, because of the changes to committees presented throughout the book, committees are already holding fewer hearings on immediate legislative issues. Instead of lamenting this change in legislative power relative to party leadership, committees can embrace their newfound role in agenda setting and overall problem definition (rather than specific policy formulation) and hold even more hearings for topics on which there is no impending vote. These hearings stand to encourage learning.

6

COMMITTEE HEARINGS AS
THEATRICAL STAGES

"Tear them up," proclaimed Senator Patrick Leahy as he tore a book of Senate Judiciary Committee procedures in front of cameras in August 2019. This represented an act of protest against Chair Lindsey Graham moving forward with a committee vote on an immigration bill in violation of a committee rule that there be a quorum present to schedule a vote. The theatrical gesture also played to the many cameras present and was indeed picked up and circulated on several news outlets.[1]

Senator Leahy's pronouncement is just one example of committee hearings used as a theatrical stage. Indeed, all official hearings (besides intelligence committee hearings) are part of the public record and (since the incorporation of television into Congress) also televised. This chapter explains when hearings may most likely be theatrical and how they stand to shape committee members, and shows two illustrative examples of theatrical hearings. It also analyzes nominations and oversight hearings separately as distinct kinds of hearings with theatrical tendencies.

"GETTING MY TELEVISION TIME":
HEARINGS AS PUBLIC SHOWS

Evidence from interviews clearly points to hearings as a space for public show and illustrates that committee members play to the cameras.

A former congressman who served in the House of Representatives for thirty years underscored this point, recalling that he would come in a few minutes before his scheduled five-minute questioning time and make a speech. He said he wanted to "get my television time." This shows that members of Congress may use hearings as publicity stunts. Those in the Senate tell the same story. In an interview with me, a senior Democratic senator admitted, "We play to the cameras. We are all sensitive to the fact that even though the chambers are empty and the galleries sparsely populated, it's going out over C-SPAN. Someone someplace suffering from insomnia is watching the speech." A staffer for a congresswoman on the House Agriculture Committee explained that "members like to clip the questions, looking for that crisp soundbite that they can use on social media platforms." As a result, hearings become staged. An academic who testified before the House Science Committee said that the hearings are "very staged and stage-managed in a way that someone has to help you know how to do that." One witness, who has experience testifying before committees, characterized hearings as "an environment that has an element of performance to it, particularly now that this is all televised."

In theatrical hearings, members may be more likely to utilize discussion time to publicize their positions on the issue at hand rather than asking inquisitive questions. If each committee member has five minutes of questioning time, members attending theatrical hearings use much of this time to get their own point across rather than question the witness. One Senate Judiciary Committee staffer reflected that "my sense is that most of the senators approach their questioning kind of in terms of positioning. Because these are public forums, an opportunity for the senator to present themselves as a leader on an issue or at least to show to the public or to the regulated community that they're interested in these issues." He went on to explain that, in his work preparing a senator, "we would use the hearing as an opportunity to sort of rate why we're here today talking about X. I actually have a bill on this issue. The hearing is a little bit about the bill. I think this is really important."

Committee members might also be more likely to ask "leading" questions, questions to which they already know the answer. One reason to ask leading questions is to make their point. A Democratic congressman on the House Ways and Means Committee explains, "My goal is often to make a point by using the witnesses, and I'll often use the minority party witness, the Republican witness, and try and make my point by asking them questions and getting them to agree on certain things." Another senior staffer on the Senate Judiciary Committee said that "the questions of the hearing are going to be either getting a friendly witness to make your points from a credible third-party neutral standpoint, or catching someone who is opposed to your view in a contradiction . . . you are try-ing to . . . have [witnesses] make admissions that add up to supporting your perspective." A staffer on the Senate Finance Committee empha-sized the importance of getting certain participants' views on the record: "I want to bring this up just so I can get things on the record and make it clear for others . . . let's talk about this and then you can tell me your answer and then at least others can hear it from the experts. . . . So he may already know the answer, but someone else is now saying the answer." As she explains, hearings are one of the major public platforms in which Congress shows its work to the American people.

WHEN ARE HEARINGS THEATRICAL?

While all hearings are public and may therefore display theatrical tenden-cies, theatrical hearings are more likely when the hearing topic garners a lot of publicity, when the witness panel includes labeled witnesses and spokespeople, and when the committees and topics are partisan.

NATURE OF THE HEARING TOPIC: PUBLICITY

It is worth staging a show only if someone is watching. Therefore, hear-ings that draw a large amount of public attention and media presence may elicit more theatrics. For example, in fall 2017, the Senate Foreign Relations Committee held a hearing on the Authorization of the Use of Force Bill.[2] Two administration witnesses, Secretary of Defense James Mattis and Secretary of State Rex Tillerson, sat at the witness stand. They were surrounded by dozens of cameras, overflowing out onto the adjacent corridor. One by one, the senators made statements, noting that they were "for the record." Across from them, in the audience, sat protestors with neon yellow jackets with the words "Free Iran." Behind the "Free Iran" protestors sat another group of protestors dressed in bright pink, representing the organization CODEPINK: Women for Peace. The rest of the space was filled with eager spectators who came to see the show. The next day, the Senate Commerce Committee had a hearing on Native American Subsistence rights. At the witness panel sat scientists and spokespeople for the Native American communities affected by this legislation. There were few people in the audience and no protestors. Although the hearing was recorded by the official congressional recording service, there was hardly any media presence. The senators asked more exploratory questions. The marked difference between these two hearings speaks for itself.

THE KINDS OF WITNESSES TESTIFYING: LABELED WITNESSES AND SPOKESPEOPLE

If the purpose of the hearing is to make a certain statement publicly, then the witnesses who come to testify will likely be people publicly associated with the perspective of interest. Labeled experts and spokespeople for causes are the most likely witness types at these hearings. One staffer explained that, if they want to tell a story, they will "pick witnesses that we think will kind of help shape it in the way that we want to shape it." A staffer on the Senate Foreign Relations Committee explained, "Part of the point of having a hearing is to articulate a policy argument to the American people. So you'll hear senators say to these witnesses, 'Can you say in simple English to the American people, why do we have thousands of soldiers deployed to a country that hates us and shouts *death to America*? or something like that." A theatrical hearing is a public display of one or multiple stories about a certain issue, and so each side chooses an advocate to make their point.

PARTISANSHIP: PARTISAN COMMITTEES AND TOPICS

Chapters 4 and 5 illustrated that in contexts of collegial relationships, or where the topic is bipartisan, deliberative or educational hearings are more likely. Conversely, there is evidence to suggest that, in partisan committees or for partisan topics, the theatrical element may be more pronounced. A former personal staffer for a member of the House Veterans Affairs Committee recollected that because of the committee's culture of bipartisanship, members were less likely to "call out witnesses" from opposing parties. He maintained that "if you compare [Veterans Affairs] to other committees . . . it was more bipartisan. I think the House Veterans Affairs Committee was more bipartisan at the time I was working than probably any other committee other than maybe like Armed Services. You know, I always joked because at the time, the Republicans, in the 113th Congress, the Republicans were the majority, right? So the Democrats are in the minority at the time. And I always joked what a crappy job, if you were like on the House Science and Technology Committee, you know, because it was such a partisan thing. This is like the time where it snowed and some representative had a snowball and he brought it into the Congress." He is referring to Senator Jim Inhofe, the Republican from Oklahoma, who scooped up a snowball from outside the Senate building and held it up during a speech in front of the chamber as proof that global warming is not real. This was a clear show of theatrics, and indeed received attention in many news networks. The staffer's juxtaposition highlights that hearings in bipartisan committees such as Veterans Affairs are less likely to be theatrical than partisan hearings on contentious issues like climate change.

The examples of hearings later in this chapter, on the Iran nuclear deal and climate change, also show the connection between partisan topics and theatricality. The nominations example demonstrates the ways in which committee culture may shape the likelihood of theatrical hearings.

HOW THEATRICAL HEARINGS STILL MATTER:
VOICING VIEWS

"Public hearings with video where it's just going to get clipped and put on social media are not useful in getting more information. They're not. And most of the time, I don't think they're also useful in informing the public because if you're just cutting things up and putting them online . . . it's not especially useful in getting more information; they serve a different purpose than informing senators or most time informing the public." This reflection of a former staffer on the Senate Judiciary Committee is representative of a larger criticism of the modern-day theatricality of hearings. As Jonathan Lewallen puts it "committee members are criticized for giving long-winded speeches as opening statements, asking 'gotcha' or leading questions, and for not knowing enough about the often-complex subjects on which they're asking questions."[3] This is doubtless a commonly held view of the theatricality discussed in this chapter. However, this book argues that even hearings that are predominantly for show stand to affect politicians in more subtle ways.

The main effect of the theatrical hearing is what I term "voicing views." Even if an argument is well known, a witness can sometimes frame it in a particularly compelling way that then gets picked up by members of Congress. It may then shape the way they speak about the issue on future occasions. One of the experts who testified claimed that hearings are a "high-profile document for the record that gets more widely circulated and more heft." She said that it is a "higher impact product compared to a blog post or a journal article." Many of the interviewees referred to the prevalence of the same voices that repeat the same arguments. An Iran expert who has testified before Congress numerous times remarked, "You'd get the same voices coming back because people know what they're going to say." This repetition affects the rhetoric and framing of that issue in Congress in subtle ways. As a senior staffer on the Senate Judiciary Committee described:

> The performance, so to speak, of the witnesses can impact, if not always, what side a legislator comes down on; it could certainly impact how they go about advancing their views or defending their side of an issue. . . . And so I think that kind of confirms that . . . even if it's not like moving the needle overall about where you, how you approach an issue, it can sometimes be like, "oh, I think we were definitely right in our instincts here because this person wasn't persuasive" or "oh, that person was more persuasive than I thought, even though I disagree with that," or something like that.

As the staffer points out, the witnesses can indeed affect "how [legislators] advance their views." A Georgetown professor who has testified before the

Senate Foreign Relations Committee explained that hearings "can inform staff thinking and argumentation as they are designing what their members should say or do. Like you are giving ammunition to people to use for what they would probably otherwise do." The professor is likely referring to the way in which members adopt the arguments of witnesses to accomplish their political goals. These comments show that the witnesses themselves regard their effect on members of Congress in this way.

Hearings can also act as an outward signal that Congress is listening to the public's views. Lewallen writes that "oversight and other non-legislative work also has value, particularly for signaling to us that members of Congress are listening and paying attention."[4] In their study of Supreme Court confirmation hearings, Supreme Court scholars Paul Collins and Lori Ringhand similarly conclude that:

> as public attention to an issue area increases, so too does discussion of that issue area in hearings . . . in addition, we find that congressional attention to an issue area results in increased discussion of that issue at the hearings. For example, when members of Congress introduce a relatively large number of legislative initiatives involving a particular topic, members of the Senate Judiciary Committee are increasingly likely to address that issue area at the hearings.[5]

These findings suggest that hearings act as a signal both for members to point out legislative directions, and to the public that Congress is listening to their views.

EXAMPLES OF THEATRICAL HEARINGS

THE IRAN NUCLEAR AGREEMENT HEARING

On July 14, 2016, the Senate Foreign Relations Committee held the hearing titled "The Iran Nuclear Agreement: One Year Later."[6] The Iran Nuclear Agreement (also known as the Joint Comprehensive Plan of Action [JCPOA]) was a deal reached between Iran and the five permanent members of the United Nations Security Council (China, the United

States, France, the United Kingdom, Russia) and Germany in July 2015. The agreement consisted of a roadmap for restricting Iran's capacity to develop nuclear weapons in exchange for lifting economic sanctions on Iran. Several committee hearings about the Iran Nuclear Agreement were held by the Senate Foreign Relations and House Foreign Affairs Committees in 2015 and 2016.

The issue of the Iran Nuclear Agreement is both partisan and theatrical. The debate about the deal, which was led by Democratic President Barack Obama, was split largely along partisan lines, with Democrats in favor and Republicans in opposition. An Iran expert and senior fellow at the Brookings Institution shared her experience testifying about Iran in Congress, recalling that it was "the kind of public manifestation of almost like a kabuki theatre that serves a political purpose." She went on to describe the general atmosphere of the Iran debate:

> Particularly over the course of the past few years, it's been a very polarized issue. It has been one [with] . . . very clearly defined poles of debate and so typically what you find is that each side is looking for the most strenuous proponent of their perspective. This was such a partisan [issue] . . . both sides really engage in a really well-orchestrated public campaign to promote either up or down on the deal. . . . I mean there is a lot of lobbying on all kinds of issues, but I don't know that you can look at any other foreign policy issue and see that same degree of orchestration of opinion . . . a lot of it is focused in this case on the Hill because of the Iran Nuclear Review Act [Iran Nuclear Agreement Review Act].

The Iran Nuclear Agreement Review Act was a bill passed by Congress in May 2015 that gave Congress the right to review the agreement before it was signed. The Iran expert's statement is a powerful testament to the contentiousness surrounding this topic.

Two labeled experts testified at the hearing. The first was Mark Dubowitz, director of the Federation for Defense of Democracy. Dubowitz is the head of a neoconservative think tank that one Iran expert described, saying that "it's a think tank, but it's a think tank with a particular perspective as opposed to others." Dubowitz also donated to Republican political campaigns.[7] Prior to the signing of the Iran Nuclear Agreement, he testified before Congress and appeared publicly on numerous occasions, always with the same mantra against the nuclear agreement. He is therefore labeled publicly as a proponent of this stance. He was followed by another labeled expert, Richard Nephew, scholar at Columbia University School for International and Public Affairs. Nephew is associated with two liberal institutions, as a fellow at the Brookings Institution and as program director for the Center on Economic Statecraft, Sanctions, and Energy Markets at the School of International and Public Affairs at Columbia University. He donated to Democratic campaigns.[8] He worked on sanctions policy in different capacities for over a decade and is publicly labeled as a supporter of the Iran Nuclear Agreement.

The hearing discourse features numerous examples of "statements not questions." Senators Jim Risch, Edward Markey, David Perdue, and Chris Coons all begin their interventions with lengthy statements of their position on the issue. Senator Coons begins by saying, "I continue to call for Congress to," a clear indication that he wants his stance to be heard. Senator Bob Menendez asks a series of yes or no leading questions of Dubowitz, all underscoring Iran's continued nuclear involvement. He also starts his testimony by saying he wants to "submit for the record" a report on Iran's behavior. This speaks to a concern for what is on the public record and a desire to prove a point.

It is clear from the video recording that the hearing draws a substantial crowd. In addition, Chair Bob Corker ends the hearing by saying, "Thank you to the folks out here from Camp Liberty." Camp Liberty was a camp under rocket attack in Iraq in 2016. The fact that Chair Corker uses the opportunity of this hearing to make a statement about an unrelated issue indicates the use of this hearing as a public platform.

Effects: Voicing Views

This effect is clearly demonstrated in the Iran hearing. A senior fellow at the Brookings Institution and Middle East expert with experience testifying before Congress estimated that Dubowitz's Iran testimony has had an impact on the way in which members of Congress frame the Iran issue. She gave him as an example of an expert who has shaped congressional discourse on the Iran debate, saying, "He will usually have one or two clear logically structured arguments that are targeted to a particular policy outcome and convey it in a compelling way, and those arguments get picked up and repeated by members of Congress." This assessment was reaffirmed by a personal staffer for a senator on the Senate Foreign Relations Committee, who attended the Iran hearings. He explained, "Dubowitz and his organization provide the intellectual firepower for what Republicans argue up here, so it helps you understand where their policies are coming from." In the July 2016 hearing, Senator Cory Gardner referenced testimony given by Dubowitz on Iranian cryptocurrencies at an earlier hearing. This reference to statements made months earlier may be a further indication that Dubowitz's voice has remained salient in the debate.

THE CLIMATE HEARING

On March 29, 2017, the House Science Committee held a hearing titled "Climate Science: Assumptions, Policy Implications, and the Scientific Method."[9] When I spoke to people involved in the House Science Committee, whether staffers or congressional members, they repeatedly identified this hearing as a prime example of a contentious and theatrical hearing. They also emphasized that climate change is a particularly divisive and partisan topic. One even said that, on the House Science Committee, "there is climate change and then there is everything else," indicating that the topic of climate change inevitably leads to a more contentious hearing. This is understandable in light of the partisanship surrounding the climate change debate in general. According to a 2016 Pew Research Center poll, 70 percent of liberal Democrats and just 15 percent of conservative Republicans trust climate scientists a lot to give accurate and full information about the causes of climate change.[10]

In the March 2017 hearing, the committee heard from four different labeled experts. Dr. Judith Curry, president of Climate Forecast Applications Network and professor emeritus at the Georgia Institute of Technology. Curry is a labeled expert. She is known to question the reliability of the science proving climate change. She has an active blog promoting her views and even testified five times before Congress prior to this hearing. As noted in chapter 1, Curry herself acknowledges that she is invited because they know her as a climate change skeptic. Curry was followed by Dr. John Christy, professor and director of the Earth System Science Center at the University of Alabama at Huntsville and Alabama's state climatologist. Christy is a labeled expert. Like Curry, he is a public figure in the debate about climate change. *The New York Times* even ran an article about him in 2014, detailing his work as a climate change skeptic. The third witness was a labeled expert with the opposing view. Dr. Michael Mann is distinguished professor of atmospheric science at Pennsylvania State University and director of the Earth System Science Center (ESSC) at Pennsylvania State University. Mann is a labeled expert known as an advocate for fighting climate change. As noted in chapter 1, the minority staff expressed that they chose him as "the loudest and most prolific person we can think of." Next on the witness stand is Dr. Roger Pielke Jr., professor of environmental studies at the University of Colorado. Pielke is another labeled expert. Like Curry, he has a public blog advertising his skepticism about climate change.

This hearing features countless examples of "statements not questions." Many of the Democratic members begin their questioning with lengthy statements about the prevalence of scientists who believe in global warming, citing specific pieces of research or data, or communicating how climate change affects their states. Several of them begin by pointing out their own credentials as scientists and engineers. Many of the Republican members start by citing data about the uncertainty regarding global warming or the bias of the world of science against those who think otherwise. Senators Johnson, Bonamici, Bera, Tonko, Rohrabacher, Higgins, Takano, LaHood, and Webster all submit documents and reports for the record. This implies that they are using the hearing to portray publicly a certain perspective. Almost all of the Democratic members direct their questions toward the minority witness (Mann) and nearly all of the Republican members direct their questions at the majority witnesses, thereby indicating that they seek confirmation of their own opinions rather than understanding of the other side.

When the committee members do pose questions to the opposing side's witness, the questions are largely "leading questions." For example, Elizabeth Esty asks the witnesses if they would agree with a series of questions. In an interview with me, Esty described the interaction as follows:

> It got very contentious. And I pressed the majority witnesses. And I said, "Well, does anyone here on the panel believe, do you believe human behavior is contributing to climate change?" And they all said yes. And

I said, "So do you think there are, are there observable changes to climate?" And they basically all voted yes. "Is human behavior contributing toward the rate of change?" And all said yes. . . . And I said, "Is it a measurable, is it a significant contribution?" And they all said yes. So this actually got written up because HuffPost or something covered it because I really kind of made them say it.

This is strong confirmation that Esty's intent in questioning was to make a point rather than ask a question. In the hearing, fellow Democratic member Bill Foster also asks witnesses similar questions, prodding them about whether they agree that funding cuts are a bad idea and climate is a problem. Similarly, Republican member Glen Clay Higgins asked the minority witness only about his affiliation with the organizations the Union of Concerned Scientists and the Climate Accountability Institute. Republican member Barry Loudermilk asked Mann the loaded question, "We could say you are a denier of natural change. Do you believe that we truly understand what creates the weather?" Again, these are not inquisitive questions. They are used to brand the witness.

The sheer number of media articles written about this hearing is clear proof of its publicity. The *Washington Post*, *Bloomberg News*, *Scientific American*, the *Huffington Post*, the *Seattle Times*, the *Guardian*, the *Verge*, the *National Review*, the Society for Environmental Journalists, and a number of other news outlets all covered this hearing. The headlines included "The Latest Theatrical House 'Science' Committee Hearing" (the *Guardian*), "Unbalanced Climate-Change Hearing Proves Pointless" (the *Washington Post*), and "Republicans Held a Fake Inquiry on Climate Change to Attack the Only Credible Scientist in the Room" (the *Verge*). These headlines attest to how public this hearing was. Indeed, one of the headlines even dubs it a theatrical hearing.

Effects: Voicing Views

The hearing further demonstrates the "voicing views" effect. When I spoke to Curry, she told me that she thought her testimony had a direct impact on an opinion piece that Congressman Lamar Smith wrote in the *Washington Post* entitled "Overheated Rhetoric on Climate Change Hurts the Economy." She asserted that "he was clearly influenced by my testimony" because "the points he was making were consistent with [the points I was making]." In fact, Smith's op-ed even referenced "recent expert testimony before the House Committee on Science, Space, and Technology" to confirm points he makes in the piece. This example again highlights how members of Congress can directly adopt the argumentation of expert witnesses.

NOMINATIONS AND OVERSIGHT HEARINGS

NOMINATIONS HEARINGS

"Judicial nominations hearings are kind of their own creature," a seasoned staffer on the Senate Judiciary Committee concluded. For this reason, this book handles them as a unique subset of hearings, separate from legislative hearings. The publicity that contemporary nominations hearings garner and the partisanship they stir make them candidates for theatricality.

The Constitution sets out that the president "shall nominate, and by and with the Advice and Consent of the Senate, shall appoint Ambassadors, other public Ministers and Consuls, Judges of the Supreme Court, and all other Officers of the United States, whose Appointments are not herein otherwise provided for . . ." (Article II, section 2). Since the creation of the Senate Judiciary Committee in 1816, nominations are referred to the committee rather than the entire chamber. However, the practice of holding public hearings as part of the nominations process is relatively recent. In 1916, Louis Brandeis was the first nominee to have a hearing, and it did not even involve testimony. In 1939, Felix Frankfurter was the first nominee to be questioned in an open hearing. In 1981, Sandra Day O'Connor became the first nominee whose hearings were televised. As noted earlier, television provides an opportunity for political theater. *Time* magazine reported of the O'Connor hearings that "the rambling inquiries directed at O'Connor often seemed designed less to elucidate her judicial philosophy and qualifications than to give the questioner an opportunity to state one of his own pet political positions."[11]

The advent of televised hearings and the aforementioned congressional dynamics led to a rise in the number of hearings and the length of the hearings. A staffer on the Senate Judiciary nominations unit explained that in the 1970s and 1980s (indeed into the 1990s), nominations hearings looked very different. Typically, one hearing included seven to nine circuit court nominees and lasted about half an hour. "They basically came in and did the introductions, asked them more basic, surface level stuff and then were done. . . . That was back before, when most of those people were confirmed either by voice vote or a ninety-plus vote," he said. The staffer went on to explain that modern-day nominations hearings serve an almost entirely theatrical purpose, saying, "Senators will be asking questions that are designed either for fundraising purposes or to be clipped and put out on social media to build their social media platform or to play specifically to their base. And it's not trying to understand how the person would function as a judge." When I asked if hearings for the purpose of such "question clipping" extended to different kinds of nominations hearings (both Supreme Court and lower court nominations), he determined that "there is almost no other purpose. There are some senators who will ask questions related to what [the nominee is] going to be doing, but there are about three on each side." He portrayed the purpose of these hearings as follows: "people will just be able to see it and watch." This characterization suggests that theatricality is a primary, if not the sole, purpose of nominations hearings. One personal staffer for a senator who serves on both the Finance and Senate Judiciary committees compared legislative hearings in general to nominations hearings in the Senate Judiciary Committee, saying that the former had more "substantive questions" and in "nominations hearings . . . those are more questions where you want to have the witness or the nominee more confirm or deny something verbally." In their extensive study of Supreme Court nominations, Collins and Ringhand argue that one of the primary functions of nominations hearings is as public forums. They show, through a large data set of nominations hearings, that "questions senators ask closely follow changes in public attention to the relevant issues of the day."[12] Indeed, nominations hearings may be particularly prone to theatricality and used to shape public image rather than pointing inward at the institutions and nominees they check.

On the Senate Judiciary Committee, nominations hearings are also set up in a different way from the standard process described in chapter 1. Unlike the standard procedure described in chapter 1, whereby the minority is allotted one witness, judicial nominations hearings usually feature only the nominees. A former staffer said that, in his time on the committee under various chairs, he can only recall the minority inviting witnesses for higher-status nominations hearings like the attorney general or a Supreme Court justice. In these instances, the two sides would reach a deal on the specific number of witnesses for that hearing and, as the staffer described, from the minority's perspective, "there's a messaging aspect of it that they're trying to get certain messages up. And so they want a certain number of witnesses to cover each of those parts of the messaging." This "messaging" is further testament to the use of nominations as a public stage.

In addition, nominations are handled by separate staff units (on either side) dedicated almost entirely to nominations. Staff shared that this unit is known to have less collegial relations than other subcommittee staffs. One staffer reflected that "judicial nominations are always fraught. There's a very, very long history of bad blood between both sides on the issue of judicial nominations, so I think that at least at the staff level, there's less of a culture of working together across the aisle on judicial nominations." Indeed, Alvin Chang's analysis of cabinet confirmation votes shows that cabinet confirmations are passing by slimmer margins than they had several decades ago, suggesting increasingly partisan votes.[13]

KAVANAUGH NOMINATION HEARINGS

A notable example of remarkably theatrical nominations hearings were the infamous 2018 Brett Kavanaugh Supreme Court nomination hearings. According to NBC News, 20.4 million people watched the hearings. Video recordings show committee rooms packed with spectators, cameras, and protestors. Kavanaugh was labeled in several ways when the confirmation hearings began. His writings and public rulings demonstrated his conservative viewpoints, and he was, of course, appointed by a Republican president. The already partisan confirmation became all the more divisive after the revelation of a letter from Dr. Christine Blasey Ford accusing Kavanaugh of sexually assaulting her. The committee then postponed the vote to allow Ford and Kavanaugh to testify in another public hearing. The following day, the committee voted to confirm Kavanaugh.

A staffer's reflections in an interview point to the theatricality as both the result of the contentious topic and fueling further partisanship on the committee. He recalled that before the letter from Ford was revealed, "it was definitely less rancorous." He went on to describe how the rancor permanently changed the committee dynamics. He explained that "both sides of that were very unhappy coming out of it and did not think the other side was acting appropriately. . . . So there were a lot of bad feelings about that. . . . The Democrats on the committee were not happy about the fact that we went forward with the hearing and we went forward with the votes." The extreme contentiousness that this caused between staff and senators is "still there to some degree and I'm not sure if it will go away." When I asked in what ways this contentiousness is manifested, he said that:

> I think that you saw the circuit court level, for some of the nominations, more willingness to ignore or make nominations to the circuit courts earlier than you normally would have. . . . If a senator is objecting to a nomination and saying either that someone is too ideological or there's some type of bias, a lot of the senators on the committee and also the staffers not did not believe those were actually in good faith. . . . If you hadn't had Kavanaugh and you'd had a more functional and a working relationship . . . there are a lot of senators who would have been more uncomfortable with going forward with some of those nominees . . . they would have been seen as legitimate objections as opposed to an attempt to just obfuscate until you have the next election. . . . You'll also see some of it in the hearings where . . . if you'll have complaints about how a process was run or something, some of the [Democratic] senators now are more willing to kind of push back against the Republican senators, [who are also] more willing to push back against some of the Democratic senators . . . they're more willing to criticize some of the other senators on the committee for not having a legitimate complaint or for not applying the rules in the same way that they claim to want them applied in in some other setting.

Indeed, no fewer than one in four circuit court judges is now a Trump appointee.[14] This is in part a result of the 103 vacancies Trump inherited upon assuming office, but the staffer's reflections suggest that this is also partly a consequence of the partisan tension caused by the Kavanaugh hearings. As the staffer explained, whereas minority party opinions might have held greater weight in earlier Congresses, nowadays nominations can be pushed through even amidst criticisms. The Kavanaugh hearings reflect the publicity and partisanship of contemporary nominations hearings and the resulting tendency toward theatricality.

OVERSIGHT HEARINGS

One of the core functions of committees is oversight of executive agencies. In fact, Lewallen argues that oversight has become an increasingly important committee function. He explains that as the executive branch and its agencies grew, demand for oversight grew, writing, "Congress has faced increased demand for oversight from both developments in the executive branch after World War II and the legislative branch's own actions (and inactions)."[15] Oversight hearings during periods of divided government may be predisposed toward theatrics. Lee Drutman and Timothy M. LaPira explain: "Programs and executive agencies that are functioning well may face undue interference in the guise of oversight, and political motivated oversight and budget cutting may abuse the power of the purse more than it is constitutionally intended to check and balance the execution of power."[16]

A former staffer of a member of the House Veterans Affairs Committee explained, "Particularly if it was a failure on behalf of someone who was in the VA, right, if there's an administration official that was supposed to do X, Y, and Z, and he didn't do X, Y, and Z and this case has come up again. And it was basically like, what the hell are you doing? You were supposed to fix this. And now it's a big issue and it's embarrassing for everyone. So there's aggressiveness, too. . . . I've seen them definitely go after [witnesses]." Some political scientists argue that there is an increase in the degree of oversight conducted by committees in periods of divided government.[17]

Interviewees point to a change in the kinds of oversight hearings as well. A staffer on the Senate Judiciary Committee commented:

> You're going to have more oversight hearings. . . . If the opposing party is in the White House and it's going to be on a different set of subjects,

there were hearings, some degree on some of the immigration stuff under Senator Graham. But they are a lot less frequent. They're going to be more limited in scope. A lot of times the number of witnesses you have, it will be much lower. . . . If you're just having the administration people come in and talk about something from an oversight perspective, you don't have witnesses who are going to provide more anecdotal accounts.

The aforementioned staffer on the Senate Judiciary Committee went on to explain that oversight hearings in this context therefore serve a purely theatrical purpose, saying that "[senators] . . . want to build a profile. . . . It's not about coming up with new legislative solutions because if you want to do that, you would call the people at DOJ that are working on the issue and you would talk to them about it. It's more about building public awareness on something or building your own public profile on it."

An example of such a theatrical oversight hearing is the Integrated Risk Information System (IRIS) program hearing. The IRIS program is the arm of the Environmental Protection Agency (EPA) that assesses health effects of exposure to environmental contaminants. The chemical industry therefore has an incentive to push back against some of the assessments of the chemicals they produce. The minority staffer for the Subcommittee on Energy and Environment described this hearing as an "assault" that was "clearly not an actual examination of the IRIS program." He explained how in "the IRIS hearing, it was pretty straightforward given not just how they've treated the EPA, but the IRIS program specifically. . . . We know that the way they've treated the IRIS program in the past is very industry friendly and we assume that what they would do is they would bring in people critical of the program. . . . We know who the people in the chemical industry who are particularly critical are." He went on to explain that the minority witness, Thomas Burke of Johns Hopkins University, was someone they knew could combat the industry perspective. This example demonstrates that beneath the veneer of an oversight hearing lies a motivation to condemn publicly an executive agency run by the opposing party. Indeed, other staffers across the different committees noted that such oversight hearings with members of executive agencies are often a show of force, a public muscle-flexing exercise rather than a purely investigative endeavor.

Over four decades ago, shortly after the introduction of television cameras into committee hearings, Michael Robinson and Kevin Appel studied the impact of television coverage and noted the "specter of Congress shifting its incentive structure even farther away from legislation and legislative hearings and moving more towards media-dominated, investigative hearings."[18] Indeed, the data presented in this chapter suggests that investigative oversight and nominations hearings, dominated by media and partisanship, may be particularly theatrical.

CONCLUSION

This chapter opened with a dramatic scene of Senator Leahy playing to the cameras in a committee hearing. As a public forum, hearings increasingly serve as a stage for politicians to convey a message to constituents. Indeed, over 1,500 correspondents from news media on Capitol Hill cover Congress every day.[19] This chapter demonstrated that theatrics might be even more pronounced when hearing topics or witnesses draw crowds, when witnesses are clearly labeled, and when committee dynamics and topics are contentious. Nominations and oversight hearings may also be particularly prone to theatrics. In the face of broad criticism that theatrics render hearings entirely superficial, however, this chapter argued that they may still shape congressional rhetoric and argumentation on important issues.

There is evidence to suggest that the scope of these findings may extend beyond American committees. For several decades, public hearings have been held in Italy, Germany, Canada, the United Kingdom, Japan, France, Belgium, Sweden, and countless other major democracies. Even in the 1990s, scholars of legislative committees Ingvar Mattson and Kaare Strøm noted that the number of public hearings was on the rise.[20] The COVID-19 pandemic has accelerated livestreaming of hearings and further broadened public access. The global reach of public hearings suggests the same propensity for theatricality might hold true in other countries as well.

Stephen Marc Solomon writes of public hearings in the German Bundestag: "Public hearings are supposed to generate publicity and inform the public. In practice this means that they must create an audience to fulfill their intended function."[21] David Wilson, clerk of the New Zealand House of Representatives, remarked that when New Zealand's parliament discussed introducing television into committee hearings, there was a concern that "people might play for the cameras" and so it might "change the behavior of members or the public who appeared before them."[22]

Playing to the cameras might change behavior in similar ways in different legislatures. On the one hand, theatrics may inhibit learning and deliberation. The work of Jürg Steiner et al. about legislative deliberation showed the constraints that publicity places on deliberation conducted in major European legislatures, suggesting that this extends beyond the halls of Congress.[23] In their comparative analysis of committee systems, Mattson and Strøm similarly contend that there is a relationship between strong legislative committees and private hearings in European parliaments.[24] A longtime staffer in the French National Assembly similarly complained that the media attention that committees receive inhibits deliberation. She said, "It's also their own fault you know, the MPs [members of parliament]. Always tweeting everything, sometimes the meeting is not over yet that they all tweeted stuff. . . . How do you want them to discuss after that? It's already on record!"[25] In a study of Chilean Senate committees, Weston Agor conducted interviews with staff members and senators about committee norms and work. He writes that Chilean Senate committees, when "there is no public gallery or press recording every comment . . . dialogue is free and open, resembling more a club get-together than a formal committee meeting."[26] This characterization emphasizes not only the effect of nonpublic hearings but also the marked informal and collegial feel, similar to American informal hearings. A staffer interviewed in the study said, "If senators know what they are saying will not go out of the room, they work a lot better together."[27]

Still, committee hearings may form the agenda-setting space in which witnesses can shape congressional rhetoric and members can make their positions clear to the public. Legislative scholars Sven Siefken and Hilmar Rommetvedt write in their comparative analysis of committees: "Committees can also serve as a rehearsal or testing for the plenary meeting. Here, positions are pointedly made into arguments, ideas, rhetoric and narratives are tested."[28]

Studies in other country contexts suggest that the book's discussion of the theatricality resulting from legislatures being public-facing institutions may be inherent in democratic legislatures and especially pronounced as cameras are present in more proceedings. Legislatures must balance their duty to uphold transparency and provide a public forum, on the one hand, with the inhibitory effects of public access on legislative deliberation, on the other.

One way to address this democratic dilemma is to remove some of the cameras. It would be difficult to stop televising all hearings because there is a strong argument for cameras increasing transparency, accountability, and public access to Congress. Certainly, my research would not have been possible were it not for public records of hearings. A senior Democratic senator took this stand, saying, "I would err in favor of more public access to what we do, even though I do believe there is a theatrical aspect to the floor and at the meetings." His comment illustrates the theatrical consequence of cameras and the trade-off between public access and genuine discussion.

Committees can cut down on the number of televised hearings, however, without eliminating them completely. They now televise every single hearing, and instead they could televise only a portion while still giving the public access. Committees could also hold more hearings that are not televised at all. Even if television cameras are removed, hearing transcripts are still public record. The only committee in which all hearings are off the record is the Intelligence Committee, and this may be one of the reasons it is known to be a bipartisan committee. A senior Democratic member of the Intelligence Committee reflected, "[The] Intelligence Committee is kind of a different animal because most of our hearings are classified closed session. . . . The committee has historically been very nonpartisan." Similarly, off the record meetings could create an environment where posturing is less necessary, and connection is more accessible

7

COMMITTEES AS SPACES FOR
PERSONAL CONNECTION

" **I** 'm really good friends with my Republican counterpart. I love
that dude. He and I could cut a deal tomorrow that would be
a good deal and get a farm bill," reflected a Democratic staffer
on the Senate Agriculture Committee.[1] This book began by comparing
Congress to a living organism. Congress represents a conglomeration
of the people who walk its halls and engage in its committee rooms. As
political psychologist Philip Tetlock explains, "Politics is ultimately the
product of the thoughts, feelings, and actions of human beings."[2] This
chapter first describes how hearings serve as spaces for personal connection between members and witnesses by encouraging empathy. It then
illuminates when and how contemporary committees can foster bipartisan social interactions.

HOW CAN HEARINGS SERVE AS SPACES FOR
PERSONAL CONNECTION?

EMPATHIZING WITH WITNESSES

First, committee testimony may lead members of Congress to connect
with witnesses, in particular those witnesses they can relate to personally.

For example, in my conversations with committee members, one congresswoman took more interest in female witnesses, another congressman connected to those witnesses who attended the same universities as he had, and a third congressman paid close attention to local farmers from his district in Northern California. One Democratic congresswoman on the House Science Committee told a story about how, when she invited a witness from her district, she tried to "humanize" her witness before the Republican chair by introducing her as a classmate of his daughter's at Yale. She explained that if she could make him relate to her as someone who was like his daughter, maybe he would afford her the same respect and listen as intently as he would to his own daughter.

This is consistent with work in social psychology that identifies empathy as a key indicator of the results of social interactions in group settings. C. D. Batson et al. found that encouraging empathy toward members of stigmatized groups (a woman with acquired immune deficiency syndrome [AIDS] or a homeless man) improved attitudes toward that group in general.[3] Similarly, personal storytellers and personal connections may induce more empathy toward the speaker or group. This empathy may then affect attitudes toward that group. Suzanne Keen breaks down the notion of empathy further based on the height of the "empathy wall" one needs to overcome. She distinguishes between bounded empathy, which appeals to fellow members of one's group with shared experiences; broadcast empathy, which traverses a higher wall by appealing to an even larger, more diverse group; and ambassadorial empathy, which overcomes the highest wall by communicating to those with completely different experiences.[4] This categorization suggests that it may be easiest to evoke empathy in people who share common experiences, further reinforcing the aforementioned partiality of committee members toward those witnesses with whom they could personally identify.

WHEN IS EMPATHIZING WITH WITNESSES MOST LIKELY?

The Kinds of Witnesses Testifying: Personal Storytellers

Members were moved by testimony from personal storytellers who shared personal experiences during a hearing. I ended almost every interview by asking senators and representatives to recall a story of a witness who they found particularly influential. Almost every interviewee cited a witness who came to tell their personal story. They told me of the mother of the sex-trafficking victim, the Women's National Basketball Association (WNBA) star on food stamps, the North Korean defectors who escaped horrors to tell about their trauma, the journalist who lived with members of the Islamic State of Iraq and Syria (ISIS), the farmers who talk about their livelihoods, and the list continues. The fact that, upon reflecting, many of the members of Congress cited interlocutors who were personal storytellers is a testament to the distinct effect of this type of testimony. The reflection of a staffer on the Senate Finance Committee underscores this point. She said, "I think witnesses that have personal stories are always impactful. There was a Senate Finance Committee witness, a mother whose son had diabetes, and it was very hard for her to afford the insulin. And I think that that really resonated with a lot of members of why it is such an important issue and they could kind of see that reflected across a lot of Americans. But having a mother sit there and talk about worrying about whether or not she could get her son the right amount of insulin for the month, I think was really important." Her comment illustrates the power of the personal. Similarly, a Democratic congressman on the House Ways and Means Committee described that:

> The thing that I remember the most is John Lewis, who was the chair of my oversight committee. Every time a witness came before us and it was a particularly emotional person or a topic that came up, he would really focus on that person and thank them for having come forward. . . . It was really just very genuine and very sincere. . . . I make a point now that he's gone, if I hear a particularly compelling person speak of a health care issue or a single mom who is battling a disease and has no money and trying to raise their family, we hear these types of things often. I make a point of really taking the time to try and thank that person for their testimony and in honor of him. [He is] really who [is] in my mind, when I'm when I'm doing that.

This emotional recollection is a testament to the power of humanity in interactions.

Members even incorporate personal stories of their constituents into their statements, a further indication that they have picked up on the power of personal stories. A former staffer of a Texas congressman on the House Veterans Affairs Committee recollected how his boss:

> Did a really good job of connecting it to the district because he had so many veterans in his district and because Fort Bliss was in his district. He was able to take stories, like personal stories, [and] weave them into whatever he was doing that was very El Paso–centric. Whereas with certain members, it was just "this is affecting veterans in general as just a giant mass of individuals." . . . He did a very good job of always connecting it to the district and he'd always have something, whether it was a constituent affairs case that came into our office that highlighted that certain issue that he could pull from or like a VSO [veterans service organization] that visited our office.

Formality of the Hearing: Informal Hearings

Informal hearings in particular hold the potential to stimulate personal connections with witnesses. One congresswoman who attended a House Agriculture Committee listening tour contrasted her experience on the tour with a formal hearing, saying, "I found in the listening tour the questions are really just questions, versus the hearings that are sound bites." Her perception highlights the potential difference between formal and publicized hearings versus interactions that are away from the cameras and from regimented speaking times of formal committee hearings. A Republican congressman on the House Agriculture Committee described the difference between the formal hearings in the committee and the listening tour, saying the formal hearing "is very regimented. You get five minutes to ask questions, to try to get a response and so you're limited. And you're limited in how many people can participate. The listening sessions . . . was neat because there's 200 to 300 people in a room that could go up to a microphone and they would just ask questions, so we could hear from them what was of interest for the next farm bill. So we had a lot more input. I think it was a lot more open." A Democratic congressman on the House Agriculture Committee further emphasized this difference. He recalled that the listening tour was less formal or structured, and consequently there was more of a chance to hear from the average farmer. This type of listening, he stressed, is informative in a very different way from the formal hearings. A Democratic congresswoman on the House Agriculture Committee said of the people who spoke in the listening tour: "They aren't experts. They are actually people in the community farming or insurance for farmers businesses. They are actually people practicing, not experts from think tanks. There isn't the ability to stage it as much because pretty much anyone in the community can speak for a certain time. It isn't as if the chair is getting three people providing data or information the way he likes and then providing one or two for minority staff position." Her statement highlights the more personal and authentic climate of the listening tour. In the House Science Committee, another congressman said similar things about the roundtables. He explained, "The roundtables are good in that you get much more of a give and take. The lack of formality I think is very helpful. So, in that way, they can be very valuable." These comments demonstrate how informal hearings may lead to a more open and personable interaction between committee members and witnesses.

This confirms previous legislative research from other countries. In Serbia, the nineteen parliamentary committees have held forty hearings outside parliament. The chair of Subotica City Association for People with Autism reflected that when a parliamentary committee held a hearing in her town and she was able to speak directly to politicians, "only then I realized they are people just like us. We just need to present them the problems we are coping with." She reflected that field hearings in her city allowed her organization to emphasize issues faced by people living with disabilities and their families. She said, "I believe it was very useful for them as well . . . as they were able to see the real life and hear about essential problems."[5] In Georgia, the deputy speaker of parliament similarly explained that the lack of a strict agenda in field hearings allows members to listen more openly, saying, "I will listen to all of them, will listen to the local population. . . . We went out in the street, literally walking down the street, and asking people about this stuff. It's . . . not like an 'agenda,' you just hear the people or some concerns and then you realize right away what is the best way to proceed. That was very useful."[6] The power of getting out of parliament and hearing and seeing someone's reality firsthand is universal.

ENCOURAGING BIPARTISANSHIP:
COMMITTEE COLLECTIVE

Committees are also bipartisan institutions in a hyperpolarized Congress. Laurel Harbridge writes that "committees, in particular, are often known for fostering bipartisanship, and both the leadership and staff play important roles building cross-party collaboration."[7]

As bipartisan institutions, committees require members of both parties to come together in the same space and connect to each other. Social psychologists have identified the tendency to view those who agree with us as a coherent in-group and those who disagree as a homogeneous out-group.[8] Diane Mackie's work on attitude polarization also showed that group attitudes shift toward the position of the in-group (those with shared beliefs).[9] There is a vast literature on in-group versus out-group relations in social psychology showing that the in-group versus out-group binary leads to delegitimization of the out-group and negative perceptions of them as untrustworthy, uncooperative, and other negative stereotypes.[10] Research further shows that the most effective means of overcoming this bias is through exposure to the other. In the Nigerian National Assembly, Benjamin Ekeyi writes that committees similarly "provide the 'informal collegial environment' that facilitates interparty compromises on small matters."[11] Kerry Kawakami et al. showed that people who were trained to make counterstereotypic gender associations were less likely to display gender stereotyping when choosing job candidates.[12] Nilanjana Dasgupta et al. further illustrated that exposure to counterstereotypic exemplars decreases bias.[13] This suggests that being in the same hearing every week and sharing experiences may similarly reduce polarization among members.

Second, committees encourage collective problem solving. Political theorist Iris Marion Young argues that a group engaged in collective problem solving and understanding that others have a right to challenge the group's claims "requires such expressed claims to appeal across difference, to presume a lack of understanding to be bridged."[14] Young's analysis underlines the importance of a sense of collective effort in changing the social experience.

Social psychology research further shows that collective cooperation and superordinate goals are key social components to overcoming

158 COMMITTEES AS SPACES FOR PERSONAL CONNECTION

intergroup conflict.[15] In Samuel Gaertner et al.'s 1999 experiment, partisan groups deliberated about ways to reduce the federal budget deficit. The research showed that interaction across groups, both through open discussion and through exchange of information about each group's preferences, led to an atmosphere of collective decision making.[16]

The interviews illustrated that even in today's polarized Congress, the experience of being on a committee and attending hearings can shape bipartisan interaction. While not all of the members knew each other well or attended all the hearings, I heard many stories of how committee membership facilitated bipartisan relationships between members. A Democratic congressman on the House Science Committee told me that when Chair Smith began his tenure as chair, he decided to approach him and get to know him and his legislative interests better. As a result, they have formed a friendship and have been able to collaborate on matters of interest, a development with implications for the hearings themselves. For example, the chair and the congressman agreed that the congressman would withdraw an amendment that he had proposed provided that Smith agreed to hold a hearing on the topic. The congressman credited his relationship with Smith for his success on the committee. There was also the story of the two congresswomen, a Republican and a Democrat, who sit on two committees together (Science and Transportation) and as a result they are cosponsoring each other's bills.

In the Senate, a two-time chair of the Senate Foreign Relations Committee, a Republican senator from Indiana, spoke of how the committee led to a friendship with then Democratic senator Barack Obama. He recalled that Obama was a junior senator on the Senate Foreign Relations Committee while he was chair. He said, "Very frequently when the committee met and there were lots of things going on, members disappeared and Barack Obama and I as chair were the only members left. . . . One time, I congratulated Barack on being there until the end and raising his questions. And he reciprocated by saying, 'I know you go to Russia every August; I'd like to go with you this year,' which he did. We had a remarkable trip together." The two maintained a friendship across party lines for years, up until the passing of the Republican senator in 2019. In a statement on his passing, Obama praised him as "someone who wasn't a Republican or Democrat first, but a problem-solver . . . an example of the impact a public servant can make by eschewing partisan divisiveness to instead focus on common ground."[17]

A personal staffer of Senator Diane Feinstein told another story of how her relationship with Senator Lindsey Graham led to cosponsorship of a bill to grant stay to immigrants who would otherwise be deported and die of a life-threatening condition; immigration is usually a contentious issue. In an even more recent instance, sources credited Senate Energy Committee Chair Lisa Murkowsky, a Republican from Alaska, and ranking member Maria Cantwell, a Democrat from Washington State, with working closely and collegially together to gain bipartisan support for energy reform in 2016.[18]

In the current climate of polarization and the breakdown of bipartisan coalitions, these stories may in fact prove to be isolated incidents rather than indicators of larger change. However, numerous scholars argue that it is partly loss of personal relationships that are to blame for the decline in bipartisanship. This work is largely anecdotal, based on the stories that members of Congress have told, and researchers have relayed how Capitol Hill has changed over the past several decades.

My interviews reaffirm the importance of personal relationships, and many of the interviewees referred directly to the degradation in relations that Thomas Mann and Norman Ornstein describe in *The Broken Branch*.[19] A Republican member of the committee echoed this same point, saying of the House Agriculture Committee listening tour, "You know what else was neat about it? You have Republicans and Democrats coming together, members of Congress. . . . The neat part was, we're there with Republicans and Democrats and we just were creating that camaraderie that you don't have up here that they got rid of when Newt Gingrich told everybody to go home." As detailed in the introduction, in 1995, Newt Gingrich, then Speaker of the House, encouraged freshman Republican representatives not to bring their families with them to Washington. Before that time, most congresspeople brought their families and were likely to send their children to the same schools, have spouses who knew and were friendly with one another, and attend the same social gatherings. Many scholars have pointed to 1995 as a watershed moment in the disintegration of cross-party relationships. A personal staffer for the ranking member of the House Science Committee, who has worked in different roles in the House for nearly three decades, recalled an especially vitriolic anecdote. He said that, in 1995, he was working for a freshman Democratic congressman who asked for a television in his office. Although he had been in his office requesting the television for months, Republicans would not give him the television until the last possible moment. It was "out of spite" the staffer recalled.

WHEN IS BIPARTISAN PERSONAL CONNECTION MOST LIKELY?

In this context, when might committees still serve as spaces for bipartisan social interaction? The partisanship of committees, the formality of hearings, and the chamber (House or Senate) all affect the likelihood of bipartisan social connection.

Partisanship: Bipartisan Committees

As noted in chapter 1, relations between committee leaders, members, and staff members vary based on the partisanship of the specific committee and subcommittee. Some committees are more partisan than others. Chapter 1 revealed that this has direct implications for the interactions between members and therefore for personal connection. A congressman who formerly served on the traditionally bipartisan Armed Services Committee similarly remarked, "So Armed Services, which is a bipartisan committee, most of the time, it wasn't as much recently, but it historically has been. I went out of my way to demonstrate bipartisanship." This reflection shows how bipartisan committee culture prompts bipartisan behavior on the part of members.

Formality of the Hearing: Informal Hearings

Couched in the historical context of the breakdown of social relations and the declining opportunities for informal interactions, the informal hearings create an environment that allows members to cultivate relationships with one another. A Democratic congresswoman on the House Agriculture Committee said of the listening tour, "I think that really brings members closer together because it isn't really us talking. It's us listening and asking questions. Not asking questions that are really statements. Members can ask questions that are really just trying to drive a point in that they want to get done." She concluded that in the listening tour, "members are much more willing to listen." This description of informal settings encouraging a "willingness to listen" echoes Jürg Steiner et al.'s finding that nonpublic discourse displayed much higher levels of justification and respect.[20] A former staffer on the House Senate Commerce Committee reinforced this point, recollecting that congressional delegation (codel) trips that bring together members of Congress and their families build comradery. Indeed, one of the recommendations of the Select Committee on the Modernization of Congress is to institutionalize codel trips as a way to encourage these interactions.

One key component of informal hearings is the structure. As referenced in chapter 1, whereas formal hearings place Democrats and Republicans on opposite sides of the room in assigned seating, informal hearings frequently bring them together around one table or one microphone. Although the technicalities of structure and seating charts may seem inconsequential, they can be yet another indicator of a friendly setting rather than a rigid space. The importance of seating was emphasized in an interview with a Democratic congressman of the House Ways and Means Committee. He referenced another congressman on the committee, saying, "We're very lucky that we're sitting right next to each other. I mean, you know, we were good friends and really helps pass the time." By sitting together and getting to know one another, they can pass the time as friends.

Social psychologist Jonathan Haidt identifies the lack of cross-party friendships as part of the reason behind the partisan battles in Washington. Jason Grumet, president of the Bipartisan Policy Center, told the Select Committee on Modernization that "the culture of collaboration that once steeled American democracy against division has eroded. Long gone are the days when Republican and Democratic families attended the same social events, when their kids went to school together, or when they took substantive bipartisan trips to form a common understanding of challenging issues and one another."[21] Grumet is referring to the fact that while senators and representatives used to live in Washington, today they live in their home states and commute to work in Washington. As a result, the de facto schedule runs from Tuesday morning to Thursday afternoon every week, known as the Tuesday to Thursday Club. Consequently, committees almost always schedule their hearings Tuesday morning or afternoon, Wednesday morning or afternoon, or Thursday morning. This change in working schedules began in the 1990s, with Gingrich's sweeping changes and the advent of accessible low-cost plane travel. The spouses and children of representatives now live permanently in their home states rather than in Washington. Representatives may not want to spend half of every month away from them. The endless need to campaign locally and fundraise is yet another incentive for politicians to spend more time away from Washington and from each other.

Other work in social psychology has further demonstrated the importance of shared activities that create intimacy to reduce prejudice against out-groups.[22] By the same reasoning, committees' capacity to connect in the listening tours, roundtables, and other informal gatherings could cultivate the positive social interactions necessary to build trust and change intuition and behavior. There are signs that even members themselves have picked up on the importance of such gatherings. One Democratic congresswoman on the House Science Committee told me of an interesting tradition, the "bipartisan buddy dinner" system set up by a group of representatives. These dinners are for members only (no staff and no media), and each member has to invite a "buddy" from across the aisle to attend with them. She was in fact invited to a dinner by the Republican chair of her committee and has since been a participant. These dinners have a similar effect, creating personal friendships between members. On the other side of the aisle, a personal staffer for a Republican member of the House Agriculture Committee spoke about the office's monthly coffee dates with Democratic members. He said that, every month, they invite a different Democratic member for an informal coffee and discussion. This is a deliberate tradition meant to foster social relations across the aisle. When I asked where they meet the members they decide to invite, he said that they often meet at the notorious weekly prayer breakfasts. These bipartisan Christian prayer meetings are yet another opportunity for members of Congress to meet people across the aisle.

Structure: Senate

Friendships take time to build. Senators serve longer terms on average and therefore relationships can build over time. The aforementioned example of Obama's friendship with a longtime Republican senator resulted from years of shared experiences on their committee. In Weston Agor's study of Chilean Senate committees, he notes that committees featuring high levels of continuity of members lead to more collegial relations. One interviewee told Agor, "The real Senate work is done here in committees . . . this is where you get to know each other, and prove your ability."[23] Another senator in Agor's study remarked, "There is still partisanship, but a lower degree of it. It's easier to overcome in committees. . . . One thing I've observed with some experience here is that the longer you stay, the more you tend to identify with a solution. A new senator arrives with strong partisan feelings; he isn't attached to the committee work. After a few years, he becomes less partisan, more mature; he begins to reason, and the committee becomes a meeting of friends."[24] He went on to describe that "attachment to committee work" dilutes partisan sentiment and encourages friendly interactions. Agor explains that, in personal conversations, committee members use first names and the familiar Spanish *tu* instead of the more formal *usted*. The senator's comments point to the importance of time in building comradery.

In addition, senators have a much harder time than their counterparts in the House of Representatives in passing legislation without working across the aisle. Political scientists James Curry and Frances Lee write that "the majority party tends more often to need minority party help to pass the most important laws. . . . Compared with the House, Senate majorities more frequently need minority party support to enact laws."[25] Sarah Binder and Steven S. Smith similarly point out, in their study of majority-minority relations in the House, that the minority has greater power in the Senate as a result of the filibuster and other procedures.[26] In the House, Binder and Smith maintain that rules such as the Hastert rule empower the majority. These structural differences were mentioned in chapter 4 on deliberation. They also stand to affect cross-party friendships by promoting a culture of working across the aisle.

In an interview with me, a two-time Republican chair of the Senate Foreign Relations Committee said of his relationships with ranking members, "I had very good relationships with Joe Biden during the period of time that he served and with [John] Kerry. I think in both cases there was both a mutual feeling of trust and beyond that of friendship and this was tremendously important in getting the job done. . . . [The] rest of [the] world looks to this committee as representing American sentiment.

It can't be nine to eight. It's got to be seventeen to zero. There has to be a united front. We've got to work very hard to make this come about. And that [feeling] was shared by both Kerry and Biden." The senator's words indicate a shared sense of committee responsibility that crossed party lines in the Senate Foreign Relations Committee.

The same chair told a story of working with ranking member John Kerry on arms control legislation. He said that he had "to work very closely with John Kerry knowing that the leadership in my own party was going to oppose this." The senator's story points to the significance of bipartisan relationships in empowering committee leaders relative to their party leaders.

CONCLUSION

Richard Fenno began his landmark book *Congressmen in Committees* with this assertion: "This book rests on a simple assumption and conveys a simple theme. The assumption is that congressional committees matter."[27] Nearly half a century later and following countless displacements and changes to procedure, this book reaffirms Fenno's claim. Committees still matter in Congress.

Committees serve as a deliberative forum in which members can engage with a variety of perspectives on an issue. They provide an educational platform for members and staffers to learn about specialized issues. They act as a theatrical stage for politicians to convey messages to constituents and for ardent advocates to provide rhetorical ammunition to committee members in framing a policy debate. They represent a space for personal connection between members themselves as well as with witnesses who represent different facets of American society. Personal connection matters because "politics is ultimately the product of the thoughts, feelings, and actions of human beings."[28] This chapter has shed light on when and how contemporary committees may serve as spaces for personal connection, both between members and witnesses and among the committee members themselves.

Given the current state of committee procedure described in chapter 1, the preceding chapters have explored when committees are most likely to serve these different functions in the contemporary Congress. Chapters 5–7 explained how chamber, partisanship (of committee and hearing topic), committee desirability, formality of the hearing, the nature of the hearing topic (legislative status of issue and publicity), and the kinds of witnesses testifying all shape the resulting hearing. It also drew on extensive interview evidence to suggest how these different kinds of hearings might affect members of Congress today. Taken together, it provides a snapshot of how and when congressional committees matter.

RETHINKING HEARINGS

In concluding chapters 4–7, this book will close by looking forward. This book has demonstrated that, although almost all hearings follow a very strict schedule, agenda, and format, variations on formal hearings hold great promise.

One way to solve the scheduling problem and encourage personal connection would be to hold more field hearings outside Washington. Committees already hold such hearings on occasion. They travel to a different state to speak to local stakeholders or visit a particular facility. Examples include House Agriculture Committee field hearings with farmers in different states, and a Senate Commerce Committee field hearing on cybersecurity at Dakota State University. At the beginning of each session, committee staffers could take stock of where in the country members live and schedule one field hearing a month that is a convenient distance for at least some of the members. The locations would change every month to account for the different home regions of members. Rather than traveling all the way to Washington, they can travel a shorter distance for a hearing. Chapter 7 explained that hearings outside Washington can amplify local and personal accounts from stakeholders. Committees do not pay for witnesses to travel to Washington, so if the committee travels to the witnesses, it may hear from a wider array of voices. Given the current state of resentment and mistrust toward Washington, such interactions may also serve to improve American faith in institutions.

The final report of the Select Committee on the Modernization of Congress states that "currently, there are no areas in the U.S. Capitol Complex where Members can gather to privately collaborate or socialize. Often, the only opportunity for Members to discuss policies in private is with their own party caucuses, or in their own party's cloak room. Bipartisan discussions cannot occur there. The Committee recommends Congress establish bipartisan, biennial retreats at the beginning of each Congress. These retreats should be not only bipartisan but also include Members' families."[29] As explained in this chapter, trips outside Washington may actually prove more effective than Washington hearings for bonding members and drawing attention to local voices. Outside the echo chambers of Washington party politics, members are freer to socialize and see different sides of one another. A Democratic congressman on the House Science Committee joked that, on one uniquely isolated educational expedition, he was in a submarine under the North Pole with a prominent Republican congressman and they had lots of time to bond and talk.

Another way to break the mold of formal hearings is to introduce digital solutions. A crucial way in which American society has evolved over the past century is the rapid uptake of technological advancement in every facet of professional life. In the age of the internet and modern technology, much of today's business world has already retooled so that it is not so location-specific. Many companies hold phone or video meetings in which an employee from India and an employee from California can join and discuss their work as if they were not separated by oceans and time zones. Although congressional committees have yet to catch up, the COVID-19 pandemic acted as a catalyst for committees to start holding virtual hearings. As remote working became standard around the country, virtual hearings allowed members to join, regardless of their location. Both chambers have adopted a hybrid model, with hearings that include some members in person and others joining virtually.

When I asked the digital director for a Democratic senator if these virtual hearings will remain once the pandemic ends, she reflected, "I think people have appreciated being able to be virtual right now and that that infrastructure has been built out." The fact that the pandemic showed virtual hearings are possible and led to the development of infrastructure makes it more likely for them to continue. Verónica Seguel, chief lawyer of the Access to Information and Transparency Unit in the Chilean Parliament, argued that the digital procedures introduced during the COVID-19 pandemic will outlast the pandemic, saying, "We show[ed] them that it can be done. . . . They are in the office in Santiago, and they connect in a virtual way at a distance with the commission so they can talk with them. . . . I think that in the future they will be less reluctant to have this distance."[30] The Select Committee on the Modernization of Congress (which also held virtual meetings) recommended that Congress "identify changes made to House operations due to the COVID-19 pandemic and determine what—if any—additional changes should be made."[31] Video hearings are one such change that could be institutionalized as regular practice.

Committees may have been founded at a time when people would ride in their horse-drawn carriages to attend hearings, but they live in and must adjust to today's world by maintaining COVID-19 hybrid practices. With video hearings, witnesses could testify, and members could all join and ask questions as they do in regular hearings. The only difference would be that members would be free to spend that week in their districts and tune in for a few hours rather than flying in for several days. Elisabete Azevedo-Harman, legislative oversight and openness specialist at the United Nations Development Programme (UNDP), reflected that, in large African countries like Angola and Mozambique, digital hearings allowed politicians to be "more present in their own constituency . . . and to be more available to the local population there." She went on to explain the following:

> They have these buildings in all the provinces that they call Delegations of the National Assembly, so it's like a local office . . . but no one was really using them because [members of parliament] were in the capital . . . they saw that it was important to have these buildings in the provinces and this was an important change. . . . It's very costly to bring an MP for a committee meeting from one island that needs to take three airplanes to arrive to the capital. . . . You managed to fundraise to have all the equipment to do the meetings before, on Skype or whatever. And they didn't, they refused all the time, with COVID they started to [use this technology]. So, I think it's a huge result, a positive result.[32]

Her explanation suggests that the flexibility that virtual hearings introduce into parliamentary working calendars holds for other countries as well and allows parliamentarians to balance more easily two core parts of their job—legislating in the capital and being present in the district.

A former witness who represents a major veterans service organization and who testified six times before the House Veterans Affairs Committee virtually during 2020 reflected on the difference between virtual and traditional hearings:

> It almost creates this more informal type feeling than you might get out of a traditional testimony where you sit there in your suit, and you sweat. And then, of course, there's the less formality when it comes to answering questions. . . . One hearing I was on, someone was obviously drinking a glass of wine, or they were drinking something in a wine glass. You could hear the glass clinking. And so, they took a sip. And it just, it's really been interesting to even to see where they're logging in from. You get this personal view into their life. You don't normally get to see their pictures on the wall. You see their office setting or whatever, which is something you would never get in a traditional hearing format.

In addition, the timing of hearings allows for greater engagement. The same witness reflected that "when we talk about virtual hearings, that's how difficult scheduling them is and how much longer they take and how much longer the members are engaged because normally they come in, they ask the question, and they leave. They'll stay for the opening and then leave this there. For the most part, they're required to stay in attendance the whole time. And so, you have them listening to you for a two-hour block versus the ten, fifteen minutes they would normally be there."

An added benefit of such hearings is that witnesses would not need to travel to Washington. As mentioned in chapter 1, committees do not pay for witnesses to travel, and so sparing them the burden of traveling across the country may attract witnesses who would not otherwise have taken the time. As with the field hearings, Washington could hear more of America's voices.

Traditionally, there is little variation between hearings. They almost all take place in person, in Washington, DC, with strict guidelines dictating interactions with witnesses. When more informal committee hearings, such as briefings, roundtables, field hearings, and listening tours outside the capital do take place, evidence suggests that they may increase opportunities for personal connection, cross-party collaboration, and learning.

They also increase accessibility of hearings for overburdened legislators and open them up to a larger swath of the American public. When the COVID-19 pandemic hit and much of the working world shifted online, Congress showed that digital hearings are another workable solution to increase the accessibility and personability of hearings. In an evolving branch, committees can and should bend to match congressional development.

8

NEITHER DEAD NOR OSSIFIED

Congress Today

Institutions must advance and keep pace with the times. We may as well require a man to wear still the coat that fitted him when a boy as civilized society to remain ever under the regimen of their barbarous ancestors.

—THOMAS JEFFERSON[1]

Esq: "How would you improve it?"
Baldwin: "By beginning it."

—"JAMES BALDWIN: HOW TO COOL IT," INTERVIEW
WITH *ESQUIRE* MAGAZINE, 1968[2]

CONGRESS HAS NOT DIED!

If you read and try to stay informed, you probably think Congress is dead. On the one hand, journalistic accounts tend toward what is most salacious. Congress is embroiled in scandal and paralyzed by partisan rancor. On the other hand, academic political scientists zero in on what can be counted. Congress is passing fewer laws and spending less time on legislative work. When they do hold hearings, committee hearings are less likely to be legislative hearings. Jonathan Lewallen describes, for example, how "most committees in both chambers show relatively consistent downward trends in legislative hearings—that is, the vast majority of committees are devoting relatively more of their hearing activity to oversight today than they did 38 years ago."[3]

What is missed in these accounts is all of the grey matter in between. This book argued that when you look under the legislative hood at the stories that shape Congress, the reality of Congress is much more complicated and nuanced. This book showed how committees work, shedding light on the mechanics of hearing setup, the actors involved in the process, the kinds of witnesses Congress hears, and how it listens. An analysis of committees, how they work, and when they work in the contemporary Congress reveals the parts of the legislative machinery that still function.

It showed that when the culture of the committee and the working relationship between majority and minority staff (and chair and ranking member) remain collegial or the hearing topics are bipartisan, hearings are more likely to be used as deliberative forums, educational platforms, and spaces for personal connection between members. Senate committees may also have a greater propensity than House committees for deliberation, personal connection, and learning because of structural and cultural differences. Television cameras promote theatricality and superficiality, whereas informal settings may elicit greater learning and more personal connection. As a result, an external observer might understandably overestimate the number of theatrical hearings. They are the ones reported on, whereas informal get-togethers are, by nature, less likely to garner media attention.

Committee hearings still serve as spaces to hear a range of public voices. The witness testimony shared in committee hearings is diverse, analytical, and informative. It draws on the professional expertise, opinions, and personal background of many Americans and is shaped by their experiences and communication styles. Certain types of witnesses may affect committee members in distinct ways. Personal storytellers encourage the empathy and relatability that form a base for personal connection. Witnesses untarnished by labels that stem from their affiliations are more likely to inspire open listening and inquisitive questioning on the part of members.

In addition, committees still serve as agenda-setting and agenda-shaping platforms. They are stages for members to signal their priorities and positions to one another as well as the public. Witnesses can shape the rhetoric and argumentation of members. Education about issues may eventually shape resulting legislation. Exposure to different views may lead to the legitimization and collaboration necessary to overcome partisan gridlock.

When you zoom out and explore the legislative process as a whole instead of just the vote counts, Congress appears full of working parts. Although it is broken by procedural, partisan, and other constraints, as Thomas Mann and Norman Ornstein argue, parts of the committee process still work.[4] As the congressman in the introduction to this book recommended, when you zoom in and take a close look at the stories that shape senators and representatives and their work, a complex tapestry of relationships, informal norms, and hopeful stories of learning and legislating emerges. This does not mean that Congress today is not broken, impotent, and embroiled in conflict, but the intention is to present a more accurate and more nuanced picture.

CONGRESS IS A CAST OF CHANGING CHARACTERS

This book opened with the assertion that Congress is in a state of evolution. As American society changes, so does Congress. The book has shown how informal norms can trump formal rules, how personal tendencies and interests can shape hearings, and how committees vary based on the individuals who inhabit them at any given point. The book has even illustrated how a single election and a single person—like Newt Gingrich in 1995—can change the entire institution. Beyond Gingrich or Nancy Pelosi, countless other personalities shape Congress. When chairs and ranking members form collegial relationships, their committees may more likely be a space for learning, deliberation, and collaboration. When staffers get along, they can collaborate informally on hearings regardless of the formal rules. Individual members, with their personal interests, experiences, and motivations, interact with witnesses and approach committee work in unique ways. The book showed that congressional committees act as "creatively syncretic" organizations, "composed of an indeterminate number of features, which are decomposable and recombinable in unpredictable ways. . . . Action within institutions is always potentially creative, that is, actors draw on a wide variety of cultural and institutional resources to create novel combinations."[5] Congress has not died, and it has also not ossified. It continues to represent a conglomeration of the legislators and staff members who walk its halls. This has implications that extend beyond American borders and say something about the essence of elected representatives and democratic legislatures. Legislators are, first and foremost, humans. And legislatures are shaped by the humanity of these legislators.

THE COMMITTEE SYSTEM CAN BE REFORMED TO STRENGTHEN CONGRESS

Chapters 1–7 provide recommendations for congressional reforms emerging from the research. Implementing these reforms can ensure that committee hearings make full use of their modern potential. Bipartisan agenda-setting meetings and active promotion of nonlegislative hearings could increase the number of educational and deliberative hearings. Hiring of professional policy staffers with adequate pay and professional advisory boards not beholden to chairs would strengthen the quality of information and information processing in committees. Procedural changes to promote more women and minority members to chairmanship positions would broaden the range of American voices that committees hear from as well as the depth with which they listen. Repairing the hiring pipeline and pay schemes through the newly minted Office of Diversity and Inclusion could go a long way in creating a more representative group of committee staffers and reshape resulting witness panels and committee work. Adapting hearings to modern circumstances by increasing the use of hearings outside Washington, DC, as well as video hearings would boost bipartisanship, learning, and the representational value of hearings.

Despite their devolution, committees still matter. They simply need to modernize to adapt to their purpose in a modern Congress. In their study of institutions, Frank Baumgartner and Bryan D. Jones identify "the tension between the desire for clarity and clear organizational rules and procedures, and that of finding the proper fit with the environment and the problems the organization seeks to resolve."[6] In his comprehensive study of how congressional committee jurisdictions are formed and maintained, David King explains that "legislative entrepreneurs breathe life into legislatures and help governments embrace new problems."[7] Legislative entrepreneurship can readapt committee procedures to properly fit the contemporary environment.

CONGRESS IS NOT UNIQUE

In legislative studies, committees are everywhere. Even though they are not facsimiles of one another, committees around the world share similar goals and procedures. The comparisons to other committee systems introduced throughout the book underline the scope of this book's findings. There is a universal friction between the role of democratic parliaments as transparent and public-facing institutions and as places where legislators can focus on deliberating and passing legislation. This tension will become increasingly salient as more parliamentary work becomes publicly accessible through television, social media, and other media. In addition, it matters who has the power in legislatures. When the allocation of power within the legislature is not representative, legislation may not represent the interests of all citizens equally and therefore may undermine democratic values. Legislatures also frequently inhabit a shared ecosystem with the executive branch and other centers of power. Their power as a branch of government rests on the capacity of members (and their support staff) to make informed decisions.

This book also revealed several important conclusions about the nature of being an elected representative. Legislators are humans first, and thus they are susceptible to the same forces that guide all people. They are touched by personal stories and shaped by their own personal backgrounds. The same dynamics that social psychology identifies in guiding people in groups affects groups in different legislatures. Legislatures comprise many individual legislators, each with his or her own unique characteristics. Consequently, the evolving informal norms and individual tendencies of legislators who inhabit committees at any given time are of great consequence to legislative outcomes.

These themes discussed in the book appear to hold true beyond American borders, highlighting its significance to legislative studies more broadly. As Gerhard Loewenberg, Peverill Squire, and D. Roderick Kiewiet point out, "Scholars have rarely investigated whether their findings are generalizable to legislative institutions outside the United States."[8] The initial comparisons point to directions for future research.

CONGRESS HAS THE POWER TO REPRESENT THE AMERICAN PEOPLE

Congress also represents the American people. It is known as the people's branch because its members are elected to represent the people's wishes. Congress must hold its own against the executive branch and other powerful players (such as lobbyists) in order to advance this goal. Over the past several decades, Congress has been losing power. And it appears that it has acquiesced to its marginalization. In his work entitled "How Congress Fell Behind the Executive Branch," Phillip Wallach tracks two centuries of push-and-pull power dynamics between Congress and the executive.[9] The 1946 passage of the Legislative Reorganization Act represents an attempt by Congress to reassert itself vis-à-vis an executive office that expanded its power during World War II.[10] Wallach shows that other high points of congressional power followed the same pattern, with Congress coming together to reassert itself against an executive that has usurped power. In an increasingly divided Congress, coming together as a branch proves increasingly difficult. For example, Kenneth Schultz argues that, in a divided Congress, it is "more difficult to get bipartisan support for ambitious or risky undertakings, particularly the use of military force and the conclusion of treaties."[11] Indeed, even though Congress has the constitutional right to declare war, it has not done so since the Korean War. The recent proposals to amend the Authorization of Use of Military Force, which was passed in the aftermath of the 9/11 attacks and expanded the president's power, represent an attempt to reign in executive power; however, Congress remains largely indolent in the field of foreign affairs. In addition, Wallach shows how the staff size and degree of specialization of the executive increased as congressional staff size and capacity shrunk.

As explained in chapter 1, a legislature dependent on the executive for specialized information is a weak legislature.

In addition to the expanding power of the executive, Congress must reckon with other centers of political power. Lobbyists have also become increasingly enmeshed in congressional affairs. Chapter 1 highlighted the ways in which lobbyists shape the congressional hearing process. They can be the witnesses, the staffers, or the script writers of many hearings. In addition, the valuable information they supply gives them power in a Congress crippled by lack of expertise and staff capacity. In his study of lobbying, Lee Drutman tells the story thus:

> Prior to the 1970s, few corporations had their own lobbyists. . . . When corporations first became politically engaged in the 1970s, their approach to lobbying was largely reactive . . . but as the labor movement weakened and government became much more pro-industry, companies continued to invest in politics. . . . The increasing complexity of policy also makes it more difficult for generally inexperienced government staffers to maintain an informed understanding. . . . This puts those who can afford to hire the most experienced and policy literate lobbyists—generally large companies—at the center of the policymaking process.[12]

Drutman's account portrays a Congress that has steadily lost power relative to powerful interest groups and their lobbyists. This book has provided recommendations for ways in which Congress can regain its capacity to specialize and come together, both essential to regaining its power as a branch and therefore its position as representative of the American people.

This book has also shown the importance of identity and shared experience. When committee chairs and their staffs select witnesses, they are inclined to choose people from their districts, from their networks, or those who represent their views. When members can relate to witnesses based on shared experience, witness testimony is all the more effective. Therefore, it is of great consequence who chairs and staffs committees and which witnesses come to testify. In a country formed of a sundry tapestry of different races, religious groups, ethnicities, and gender identities, committee leadership and witness selection should reflect the diversity of the American public. Chapter 7 suggested reforms to ensure that

Congress represents the voices of all Americans, rather than a select and privileged few.

Congress has the power to represent the American people. *Inside Congressional Committees: Function and Dysfunction in the Legislative Process* told countless stories of senators and representatives, activists and professors, who are working to advance what they think will make the country better. In 1946, Representative Mike Monroney, a Democrat from Oklahoma, said that "the representative system is the best guardian of the people's liberty in the world. It can only be able to guard liberty where it is strong enough and well organized enough to carry the load that present-day problems place upon them."[13] With an understanding of what works and when and what can be improved, Congress can continue to strengthen itself as a guardian of the American people, properly fit to tackle present-day problems.

APPENDIX A

DETAILS ON INTERVIEW SAMPLE

I used purposive nonrandom sampling for my interviews, actively constructing the sample rather than relying on random selection. Layna Mosley defines purposive sampling as "a form of non-random sampling that involves selecting elements of a population according to specific characteristics deemed relevant to the analysis."[1] As Gary King, Robert O. Keohane, and Sidney Verba explain, "When we are able to focus on only a small number of observations, we should rarely resort to random selection of observations. Usually selection must be done in an intentional fashion."[2] I aimed for a sample frame that is representative in the sense that it includes both political parties and diverse geographic districts, different types of witnesses, and different committees and types of subject matter. There were three main categories of interviewees: members of committees, committee staffers, and witnesses who have testified before committees. I chose to keep interviewee identities anonymous. As Mosley states, participants may be less forthcoming if they do not believe their responses are anonymous.[3]

The data unavoidably suffered a degree of response bias. Notably, Republican members were much less responsive than Democrats. One possible reason for this is that Republicans represented a majority of both chambers at the time that I conducted my interviews. The opposition party may have a more natural interest in speaking to researchers and the press to lament the situation, whereas the party in power may fear implicating itself. Nevertheless, my sample included a Republican senator, six Republican representatives who sit on the House Science and House Agriculture committees (including two members who have been on both committees), twelve Republican staff, and six witnesses invited to testify by the Republican party. Second, senators were difficult to reach. My experience was in line with that of other scholars of American politics who also rarely get access to sitting senators. Nevertheless, I interviewed one Republican and one Democratic senator. In total, I interviewed sixty-five people, including two senators, seventeen representatives, twenty-one committee staffers, eleven personal staffers, eleven witnesses, and three people who work as lobbyists or for other external organizations. The sample included both Republican and Democratic staffers on every committee, witnesses who appeared before every committee, and committee members from both parties.

The committee staff sample was diverse in several important ways. It included both full committee and subcommittee staff. The respondents ranged in seniority. Several of the staffers I interviewed had worked on their committees for over a decade and were able to speak to the difference in committee procedures under different chairs and ranking members. Most important, I spoke to both sides of committees; hearing from minority and majority staff was crucially important because they are hired separately and function largely independently. Therefore, both groups had to be interviewed in order to paint a full picture of the committee procedures. In addition, I spoke to several staffers who served on committees outside my sample to get a sense of the generality of my findings. I spoke to staffers on the Senate Health, Education, Labor, and Pensions Committee, and the House Energy and Commerce Committee.

The personal staffer interviews were important for several reasons. First, they are used as proxies for members. This helps account for response bias in the Senate. I spoke to six personal staffers for senators, and they were able to speak about their bosses' work. Using staffers as proxies is a technique that has been used by other academics seeking access to information about elites. Melani Cammett explains that proxy interviews can shed light on aspects of the situation that elites may be reluctant to address.[4] Proxy interviews have also been used by academics studying the American Congress. Richard Hall explains that "the actor in congressional decision making is no longer the member but his enterprise, an organization of 20 to 120 agendas for which the member serves as principal."[5] In fact, in his own research, Hall chose to focus exclusively on staff interviews in studying members of Congress in committees, a testament to the power of staff interviews. He interviewed more than two hundred professional committee and subcommittee staffers and largely based his conclusions on these in-depth interviews.

Another important reason I use staff interviews is to account for social desirability bias, or the tendency of respondents to answer questions in a way that will be viewed positively by others. Social desirability bias may lead respondents to overreport good behavior and underreport bad behavior. The responses of the personal staffers who work for members of Congress may be less biased in this way because they are not shaped by reelection concerns. Committee staff interviews (particularly those with the minority staff) accomplished the same goal. While majority staff may have an interest in overemphasizing the positive ways in which they run the committee, the minority staff are not biased in this way.

I interviewed several actors who do not fall into the three major categories. These interviews shed light on other significant aspects of hearing procedures. I spoke to a lobbyist for the auto industry about the involvement of lobbyists in the hearing process. I also interviewed congressional relations staffers at a leading neoconservative think tank and at the National Science Foundation. These staffers explained their involvement in positioning their witnesses to testify and preparing them for testimony, as well as their relationship with the committee staff.

LIST OF INTERVIEWEES

Below is a comprehensive list of the people interviewed in the study. They are divided into categories (representatives, senators, committee staffers, personal staffers, witnesses, and other relevant actors) and numbered in chronological order of the date the interview was conducted. For each participant, the date, location, method of interview, and other relevant information about the participant is also listed.

REPRESENTATIVES

- Congressperson 1: In-person interview conducted on March 28, 2016. Washington, DC. Democratic congresswoman from Northern California and a member of the House Committee on Energy and Commerce. She has served in Congress for nearly thirty years.

- Congressperson 2: In-person interview conducted on October 3, 2017. Washington, DC. Democratic congressman from Virginia and the senior member of the Science Committee.
- Congressperson 3: In-person interview conducted on October 12, 2017. Washington, DC. Senior Democratic congressman from Southern California. The congressman is the senior member of the House Intelligence Committee and has previously served on the House Foreign Affairs Committee.
- Congressperson 4: In-person interview conducted on October 12, 2017. Washington, DC. Democratic congresswoman from Connecticut and a member of the House Science Committee.
- Congressperson 5: In-person interview conducted on October 24, 2017. Washington, DC. Democratic congresswoman from the Virgin Islands and a nonvoting member of the House Agriculture Committee.
- Congressperson 6: In-person interview conducted on October 25, 2017. Washington, DC. Junior Democratic congressman from Northern California and a member of the House Agriculture Committee.
- Congressperson 7: In-person interview conducted on October 26, 2017. Washington, DC. Former Republican congressman from California (served for twelve years).
- Congressperson 8: In-person interview conducted on November 1, 2017. Washington, DC. Democratic congressman from Illinois. The congressman is a member of the Science Committee and senior member of the Research and Technology Subcommittee.
- Congressperson 9: In-person interview conducted on November 3, 2018. Washington, DC. Republican congressman from Florida and a member of the House Agriculture Committee.
- Congressperson 10: Interview conducted via email during November 2017. Republican congressman from Kansas. The congressman is a member of the House Agriculture and House Science committees.
- Congressperson 11: In-person interview conducted on March 9, 2018. Oxford, UK. Former Republican congressman from Pennsylvania (served for fourteen years) and former chair of the House Energy and Commerce Committee.
- Congressperson 12: In-person interview conducted on March 9, 2018. Oxford, UK. Former Democratic congressman from Washington State (served for twenty-eight years) and former chair of the House Ethics Committee.

- Congressperson 13: Interview conducted via email during June 2018. Republican congressman from Virginia and former chair of the House Agriculture Committee.
- Congressperson 14: In-person interview conducted on July 14, 2018. Washington, DC. Republican congressman from Illinois. The congressman is a member of the House Science Committee and a former member of the House Agriculture Committee.
- Congressperson 15: In-person interview conducted on July 24, 2018. Washington, DC. Democratic congresswoman from Texas. The congresswoman is the senior member of the House Science Committee.
- Congressperson 16: In-person interview conducted on July 25, 2018. Washington, DC. Democratic congressman from Illinois. The congressman is a member of the House Science Committee and the only PhD scientist in the House of Representatives.
- Congressperson 17: Zoom interview conducted on November 9, 2020. Democratic congressman from New York. The congressman is a member of the House Ways and Means Committee.

SENATORS

- Senator 1: In-person interview conducted on July 17, 2018. Washington, DC. Senior senator who served on the House Science, House Agriculture, and Senate Foreign Relations committees. He served in the House of Representatives for over a decade and has served in the Senate for more than two decades.
- Senator 2: In-person interview conducted on July 19, 2018. Washington, DC. Former Republican senator from Indiana who served in the Senate for over thirty years. The senator was chair of the Senate Foreign Relations Committee twice.

COMMITTEE STAFFERS

- Committee staffer 1: In-person interview conducted on October 2, 2017. Washington, DC. Republican staff director for the House Science Committee Subcommittee on Research and Technology.

- Committee staffer 2: In-person interview conducted on October 6, 2017. Washington, DC. Senior Democratic staffer on the Senate Foreign Relations Committee. The Democratic staff on this committee is organized by regional expertise, and this staffer specializes in the Middle East.
- Committee staffer 3: In-person interview conducted on October 13, 2017. Washington, DC. Democratic staff director on the House Science Committee Subcommittee for Research and Technology. The staffer is a PhD scientist and has served on the committee for nearly two decades (both in the majority and in the minority).
- Committee staffer 4: In-person interview conducted on October 13, 2017. Washington, DC. Democratic staffer on the House Science Committee Subcommittee for Energy and Environment.
- Committee staffer 5: In-person interview conducted on October 13, 2017. Washington, DC. Deputy Democratic staff director for the Senate Commerce Committee.
- Committee staffer 6: In-person interview conducted on October 13, 2017. Washington, DC. Democratic subcommittee staffer on the Senate Commerce Committee Subcommittee on Aviation.
- Committee staffer 7: In-person interview conducted on October 24, 2017. Washington, DC. Democratic staff director on the House Agriculture Committee Nutrition Subcommittee.
- Committee staffer 8: In-person interview conducted on October 24, 2017. Washington, DC. Democratic staffer on the House Agriculture Committee Biotechnology Subcommittee.
- Committee staffer 9: In-person interview conducted on November 2, 2017. Washington, DC. Senior Republican staffer for a senator on the Senate Foreign Relations Committee and a former Middle East staffer on the Senate Foreign Relations Committee.
- Committee staffer 10: In-person interview conducted on November 3, 2017. Washington, DC. Former personal staffer for a member of the Senate Foreign Relations Committee. The staffer worked for the senator when he was Subcommittee Chair of the African Affairs Subcommittee. (On the Senate Foreign Relations Committee, personal staff of subcommittee chairs play a big role in organizing subcommittee hearings.)
- Committee staffer 11: Phone interview conducted on November 7, 2017. Former Republican chief of staff and general counsel for the House Energy and Commerce Committee.

- Committee staffer 12: In-person interview conducted on November 8, 2017. Washington, DC. Former Republican staffer on the House Agriculture Committee. While on the committee, the staffer specialized in nutrition issues.
- Committee staffer 13: In-person interview conducted on June 12, 2018. Oxford, UK. Former staffer on the House Energy and Commerce Committee.
- Committee staffer 14: In-person interview conducted on July 11, 2018. Washington, DC. Democratic staffer on the Senate Health, Education, Labor, Pension Committee.
- Committee staffer 15: In-person interview conducted on July 19, 2018. Washington, DC. Republican staffer on the House Ways and Means Committee.
- Committee staffer 16: Zoom interview conducted on November 11, 2020. Staffer on the Senate Judiciary Committee.
- Committee staffer 17: Zoom interview conducted on November 18, 2020. Former Republican staffer on the Senate Judiciary Committee.
- Committee staffer 18: Zoom interview conducted on November 23, 2020. Staffer serves on the Senate Judiciary Antitrust Subcommittee as an antitrust expert seconded from the Department of Justice.
- Committee staffer 19: Zoom interview conducted on November 30, 2020. Republican staffer on the Senate Finance Committee.
- Committee staffer 20: Zoom interview conducted on December 3, 2020. Former Democratic staffer serving as international trade counsel and foreign policy adviser on the Senate Finance Committee.
- Committee staffer 21: Zoom interview conducted on December 30, 2020. Former Republican staffer on the Senate Judiciary Committee nominations unit.

PERSONAL STAFFERS

- Personal staffer 1: In-person interview conducted on October 17, 2017. Washington, DC. Personal staffer for a Democratic congressperson from Illinois who serves on the Science Committee.
- Personal staffer 2: In-person interview conducted on October 23, 2017. Washington, DC. Personal staffer for a Republican congressperson

who serves as a member of the Science Committee as chair of the Subcommittee for Research and Technology.

- Personal staffer 3: In-person interview conducted on November 1, 2017. Washington, DC. Personal staffer for a Republican congressperson from Illinois who serves on the Science Committee.
- Personal staffer 4: In-person interview conducted on November 7, 2017. Washington, DC. Personal staffer for a senior Democratic senator on the Senate Foreign Relations Committee. The staffer is charged with the foreign policy portfolio and committee work of the senator. (This personal staffer was interviewed together with personal staffer 5 and shares a similar role.)
- Personal staffer 5: In-person interview conducted on November 7, 2017. Washington, DC. Personal staffer for a senator from New Hampshire who serves on the Senate Foreign Relations Committee. The staffer is charged with the senator's foreign policy portfolio. (This personal staffer was interviewed together with personal staffer 4 and shares a similar role.)
- Personal staffer 6: In-person interview conducted on November 9, 2017. Washington, DC. Personal staffer for a senator from New Hampshire who serves on the Senate Foreign Relations Committee. The staffer is charged with the senator's foreign policy portfolio.
- Personal staffer 7: In-person interview conducted on July 10, 2018. Washington, DC. Personal staffer for a Democratic congresswoman who serves on the Agriculture Committee.
- Personal staffer 8: In-person interview conducted on July 16, 2018. Washington, DC. Personal staffer for a Democratic senator on the Senate Foreign Relations Committee.
- Personal staffer 9: Zoom interview conducted on November 25, 2020. Legislative director for a Republic senator on the Senate Finance Committee.
- Personal staffer 10: Zoom interview conducted on January 6, 2021. Digital director for a Democratic senator on the Senate Commerce and Senate Judiciary committees.
- Personal staffer 11: Zoom interview conducted on February 23, 2021. Former personal staffer for a Democratic congressman from Texas who served on the Veterans Affairs Committee.

WITNESSES

- Witness 1: In-person interview conducted on October 4, 2017. Washington, DC. The witness is an Iran expert and senior fellow at the Brookings Institution who has testified about foreign affairs issues before both chambers of Congress.
- Witness 2: In-person interview conducted on October 9, 2017. New York, NY. The witness is a scientist and the former director of the National Institutes of Health and the National Cancer Institute. He has many years of experience testifying before Congress on biological science issues.
- Witness 3: In-person interview conducted on October 19, 2017. Washington, DC. The witness is a Middle East expert and senior fellow at the Brookings Institution. Previously, she served as deputy assistant secretary of state for Near Eastern Affairs and coordinated U.S. policy in the Middle East during the Arab uprisings. She has testified before several congressional committees, including the Senate Foreign Relations Committee.
- Witness 4: In-person interview conducted on October 19, 2017. Washington, DC. The witness is a professor at Georgetown University and senior fellow at the Brookings Institution. He is a terrorism expert who has testified before several congressional committees, including the Senate Foreign Relations Committee.
- Witness 5: In-person interview conducted on October 25, 2017. Washington, DC. The witness is vice president of Mazon, a nonprofit hunger relief organization. He and his employer both testified before the House Agriculture Committee about the Supplemental Nutrition Assistance Program (SNAP).
- Witness 6: In-person interview conducted on October 27, 2017. Washington, DC. The witness is a professor of bioethics and public policy and director of the Johns Hopkins Bioethics Institute. He has testified before Congress several times, including at a House Science Committee hearing on genetic editing.
- Witness 7: In-person interview conducted on November 3, 2017. Washington, DC. The witness testified before the Senate Commerce Committee as general counsel of the Internet Association (an association

of technology companies, including Google, Facebook, Amazon, and others).

- Witness 8: Phone interview conducted on May 23, 2018. The witness is the president of the Climate Forecast Applications Network and professor emeritus at the Georgia Institute of Technology. She testified before the House Science Committee several times about climate change.
- Witness 9: Phone interview conducted on June 13, 2018. The witness is a professor of biochemistry at the University of California, Berkeley, and a genetic editing expert. She testified about genetic editing before the House Science Committee.
- Witness 10: In-person interview conducted on February 25, 2021. The witness is the former Israeli ambassador to the United States and an academic historian of the Middle East. He testified before the Senate Foreign Relations and House Foreign Affairs committees on different occasions.
- Witness 11: Zoom interview conducted on March 2, 2021. The witness represents a prominent veterans service organization and has testified six times before the House Veterans Affairs Committee.

OTHER RELEVANT ACTORS

- Interviewee 1: In-person interview conducted on October 16, 2017. Washington, DC. Interviewee is the senior legislative affairs specialist for the National Science Foundation. She also previously worked for the House Science Committee for ten years.
- Interviewee 2: In-person interview conducted on November 1, 2017. Washington, DC. Interviewee is a congressional relations staffer at a prominent neoconservative think tank. Experts from this think tank testify regularly before Congress.
- Interviewee 3: In-person interview conducted on July 12, 2018. Washington, DC. Interviewee is a senior executive at a leading auto lobby. He was formerly a senior Republican staffer on the Senate Commerce Committee.

APPENDIX B

DESIRABILITY AND PARTISANSHIP RANKINGS

The table lists the eight sample committees in order of desirability and partisanship.

Committee[1]	Desirability	Partisanship
House Ways and Means	High	Medium
Senate Finance	High	Medium
Senate Foreign Relations	High	High/medium[2]
Senate Judiciary	Medium	High
Senate Commerce	Medium	Medium
House Agriculture	Medium/low	Medium
House Science	Medium/low	Medium
House Veterans Affairs	Low	Low

[1]The table illustrates that the sample represents a range of committee desirability and partisanship.
[2]Deering and Smith classified it as high in 1997, but my interviews suggest it is less partisan in the contemporary Congress.
Source: Based on the work of Christopher Deering and Steven Smith, *Committees in Congress* (Washington, DC: CQ Press, 1997) and Tim Groseclose and Charles Stewart III, "The Value of Committee Seats in the House, 1947–91," *American Journal of Political Science* 42, no. 2 (1998): 453–74.

.

APPENDIX C

BALANCE SCORE DATA SET BY TERM

Number of hearings per Congress (party control of each chamber)

Committee (total pieces of testimony)	112th Congress (S-D, H-R)[1]	113th Congress (S-D, H-R)	114th Congress (S-R, H-R)	115th Congress (S-R, H-R)	116th Congress (S-R, H-R)
Agriculture (120)			35		
Science (86)		20	23		
Commerce (246)			56		
Foreign Relations (22)	24	47	85		
Judiciary (130)			25		
Finance (93)			27		
Ways and Means (81)		24	17	34	13
Veterans Affairs (6)			11		13
Total	24	91	280	35	26

S-D = Democratic control of the Senate, H-R = Republican control of the House, and S-R = Republican control of the Senate.
Source: https://www.congress.gov/.

NOTES

INTRODUCTION

1. Ronald Pestritto, *Woodrow Wilson: The Essential Political Writings* (Lanham, MD: Lexington Books, 2005), 121.

2. Stephen Skowronek and Karen Orren, "Pathways to the Present: Political Development in America," in *The Oxford Handbook of American Political Development*, ed. Richard Valelly, Suzanne Mettler, and Robert Lieberman (Oxford: Oxford University Press, 2016), 29.

3. Keith T. Poole and Howard Rosenthal, *Ideology and Congress* (Piscataway, NJ: Transaction, 2007).

4. American Political Science Association, "Taskforce on Congressional Reform Report," October 2019, https://www.apsanet.org/Portals/54/APSA%20RPCI%20Congressional%20Reform%20Report.pdf?ver=2020-01-09-094944-627.

5. George Connor and Bruce Oppenheimer, "Deliberation: An Untimed Value in a Timed Game," in *Congress Reconsidered*, 5th ed., ed. Lawrence Dodd and Bruce Oppenheimer (Washington, DC: CQ Press, 1993).

6. John David Lees and Malcolm Shaw, *Committees in Legislatures: A Comparative Analysis* (Durham, NC: Duke University Press, 1979), 29.

7. Nelson W. Polsby, "The Institutionalization of the US House of Representatives," *American Political Science Review* 62, no. 1 (1968): 144–68.

8. Thomas Hamilton, *Men and Manners in America* (Edinburgh: W. Blackwood, 1843).

9. Bryan D. Jones, Frank R. Baumgartner, and Jeffery C. Talbert, "The Destruction of Issue Monopolies in Congress," *American Political Science Review* 87, no. 3 (1993): 657–71.

10. Jones et al., "The Destruction of Issue Monopolies in Congress," 661.

11. National Archives, "Progressive Reform: Speaker Cannon," https://www.archives.gov/exhibits/treasures_of_congress/text/page16_text.html.

12. Eric Schickler and Ruth Bloch Rubin, "Congress and American Political Development," in *The Oxford Handbook of American Political Development*, ed. Richard Valelly, Suzanne Mettler, and Robert Lieberman (Oxford: Oxford University Press, 2016).

13. Richard Fenno, *Congressmen in Committees* (Boston: Little Brown, 1973).

14. Nelson W. Polsby, *How Congress Evolves: Social Bases of Institutional Change* (Oxford: Oxford University Press, 2004), 126.

15. This story is taken from the 2018 *Atlantic* article, "The Man Who Broke Politics." In it, McKay Coppins explains in great detail Gingrich's past and the ramifications of his political career. McKay Coppins, "The Man Who Broke Politics," *The Atlantic*, October 17, 2018, https://www.theatlantic.com/magazine/archive/2018/11/newt-gingrich-says-youre-welcome/570832/.

16. Polsby, *How Congress Evolves*, 142.

17. Brookings Institution, *Vital Statistics on Congress* (Washington, DC: Brookings Institution, 2021), https://www.brookings.edu/multi-chapter-report/vital-statistics-on-congress/.

18. The graph is taken from the Brookings Institution's *Vital Statistics on Congress* report. The full data set can be accessed at https://www.brookings.edu/multi-chapter-report/vital-statistics-on-congress/.

19. Lee Drutman and Timothy M. LaPira, "Capacity for What? Legislative Capacity Regimes in Congress and the Possibilities for Reform," in *Congress Overwhelmed: The Decline in Congressional Capacity and Prospects for Reform*, ed. Timothy M. LaPira, Lee Drutman, and Kevin R. Kosar (Chicago: University of Chicago Press, 2020), 31.

20. Molly Reynolds, "The Decline in Congressional Capacity," in *Congress Overwhelmed: The Decline in Congressional Capacity and Prospects for Reform*, ed. Timothy M. LaPira, Lee Drutman, and Kevin R. Kosar (Chicago: University of Chicago Press, 2020).

21. Polsby, *How Congress Evolves*, 119.

22. Polsby, *How Congress Evolves*, 125.

23. Desmond S. King and Rogers M. Smith, "Racial Orders in American Political Development," *American Political Science Review* 99, no. 1 (2005): 75–92.

24. Polsby, "The Institutionalization of the US House of Representatives."

25. John A. Lawrence, *The Class of '74: Congress After Watergate and the Roots of Partisanship* (Baltimore, MD: Johns Hopkins University Press, 2018), 8.

26. Jonathan Haidt, *The Righteous Mind: Why Good People Are Divided by Politics and Religion* (London: Penguin, 2013), 363.

27. Schickler and Rubin, "Congress and American Political Development," 266.

28. Connor and Oppenheimer, "Deliberation."

29. Brookings Institution, *Vital Statistics on Congress*.

30. Thomas Mann and Norman Ornstein, *The Broken Branch: How Congress Is Failing America and How to Get it Back on Track* (Oxford: Oxford University Press, 2006), 83.

31. Brookings Institution, *Vital Statistics on Congress*.

32. Sarah Binder and Steven S. Smith, *Politics or Principle? Filibustering in the United States Senate* (Washington, DC: Brookings Institution, 1997), 2.

33. Brookings Institution, *Vital Statistics on Congress*.

34. Binder and Smith, *Politics or Principle?*, 15.

35. Mann and Ornstein, *The Broken Branch*, 80.

36. Sarah Eckman, *Video Broadcasting of Congressional Procedure* (Washington, DC: Congressional Research Service, 2017).

37. Polsby, *How Congress Evolves*, 127.

38. American Political Science Association, "Taskforce on Congressional Reform Report," 42.

39. Jonathan Lewallen, *Committees and the Decline of Lawmaking in Congress* (Ann Arbor: University of Michigan Press, 2020); James Curry and Frances Lee, *The Limits of Party: Congress and Lawmaking in a Polarized Era* (Chicago: University of Chicago Press, 2020).

40. Lewallen, *Committees and the Decline of Lawmaking*, 24.

41. Richard Hall, *Participation in Congress* (New Haven, CT: Yale University Press, 1996), 6.

42. Polsby, "The Institutionalization of the US House of Representatives."

43. Fenno, *Congressmen in Committees*.

44. Kenneth Shepsle, *The Giant Jigsaw Puzzle* (Chicago: University of Chicago Press, 1978).

45. Keith Krehbiel, *Information and Legislative Organization* (Ann Arbor: University of Michigan Press, 1992).

46. Hall, *Participation in Congress*.

47. Schickler and Rubin, "Congress and American Political Development," 276.

48. Joseph Bessette, *The Mild Voice of Reason: Deliberative Democracy and American National Government* (Chicago: University of Chicago Press, 1997), 43.

49. Arthur Maass, *Congress and the Common Good* (New York: Harper Collins, 1983).

50. Bessette, *The Mild Voice of Reason*, 156.

51. Polsby, "The Institutionalization of the US House of Representatives."

52. Krehbiel, *Information and Legislative Organization*; Frank Baumgartner and Bryan D. Jones, *The Politics of Information: Problem Definition and the Course of Public Policy in America* (Chicago: University of Chicago Press, 2015).

53. Laura Perna et al., "The Role and Contribution of Academic Researchers in Congressional Hearings: A Critical Discourse Analysis," *American Educational Research Journal* 56, no. 1 (2019): 111–45.

54. Emma Simson, "An Exploratory Study of Congress's Explicit Use of High Quality Social Research in Congressional Proceedings" (MSc thesis, University of Oxford, 2010).

55. Sarah Binder, *Stalemate: Causes and Consequences of Legislative Gridlock* (Washington, DC: Brookings Institution, 2003), 128.

56. Bessette, *The Mild Voice of Reason*, 152.

57. Paul Pierson, "The Costs of Marginalization: Qualitative Methods in the Study of American Politics," *Comparative Political Studies* 40, no. 2 (2007): 149.

58. Lawrence Evans, "Congressional Committees," in *The Oxford Handbook of the American Congress*, ed. George C. Edwards III, Frances E. Lee, and Eric Schickler (Oxford: Oxford University Press, 2011).

59. John H. Aldrich and David W. Rohde, "Congressional Committees in a Continuing Partisan Era," in *Congress Reconsidered*, 9th ed., ed. Lawrence Dodd and Bruce Oppenheimer (Washington DC: CQ Press, 2009).

60. Emma Roller and Stephanie Stamm, "Here Are America's Most Wanted (House Committee Chairs)," *The Atlantic*, June 5, 2014, https://www.theatlantic.com/politics/archive/2014/06/here-are-americas-most-wanted-house-committee-chairmen/455682/.

61. In each chamber, each party has panels that decide committee assignments by secret ballot (the Democratic and Republican Steering Committees, the Republican Committee on Committees for Senate Republicans, and the Steering and Outreach Committees for Senate Democrats). After approval by the party caucuses, the lists are voted on by the House and Senate.

62. Roller and Stamm, "Here Are America's Most Wanted (House Committee Chairs)."

63. Fenno, *Congressmen in Committees*; Shepsle, *The Giant Jigsaw Puzzle*; Gary Cox and Matthew Mccubbins, *Legislative Leviathan: Party Government in the House* (Cambridge: Cambridge University Press, 2007).

64. Shepsle, *The Giant Jigsaw Puzzle*; Lee Drutman, *The Business of America Is Lobbying* (Oxford: Oxford University Press, 2015).

65. Charles Stewart III and Tim Groseclose, "The Value of Committee Seats in the United States Senate, 1947–91," *American Journal of Political Science* 43, no. 3 (1999): 963–73; Tim Groseclose and Charles Stewart III, "The Value of Committee Seats in the House, 1947–91," *American Journal of Political Science* 42, no. 2 (1998): 453–74.

66. Christopher Deering and Steven Smith, *Committees in Congress* (Washington, DC: CQ Press, 1997); Poole and Rosenthal, *Ideology and Congress*.

67. Christopher Deering and Steven Smith define committee conflict as "the degree to which concerned outsiders see their interests as competing or compatible with each other" (*Committees in Congress*, p. 93). They base their own categorization on interviews with members and staff.

68. Maya Kornberg et al., *2022 Global Parliamentary Report* (Geneva: Inter-Parliamentary Union and United Nations Development Program, 2022).

69. Lawrence Longley and Roger Davidson, *The New Roles of Parliamentary Committees* (London: Frank Cass, 1998), 2.

1. SETTING UP A HEARING

1. Kevin M. Leyden, "Interest Group Resources and Testimony at Congressional Hearings," *Legislative Studies Quarterly* 20, no. 3 (1995): 433.

2. Lewis Froman and Paul A. Freund, *The Congressional Process: Strategies, Rules, and Procedures* (Boston: Little, Brown, 1967).

3. Jonathan Lewallen et al., "Congressional Dysfunction: An Information Processing Perspective," *Regulation and Governance* 10, no. 2 (2016): 179–90.

4. Jonathan Lewallen, *Committees and the Decline of Lawmaking in Congress* (Ann Arbor: University of Michigan Press, 2020).

5. Thomas Mann and Norman Ornstein, *The Broken Branch: How Congress Is Failing America and How to Get It Back on Track* (Oxford: Oxford University Press, 2006); Nelson W. Polsby, *How Congress Evolves: Social Bases of Institutional Change* (Oxford: Oxford University Press, 2004).

6. United States Congress House of Representatives Committee on House Administration, *Rules of the Committee on House Administration 117th Congress* (Washington, DC: U.S. Government Printing Office, 2021).

7. This book uses gender neutral pronouns (to the extent possible) to reference chairs. As a result of systemic discrimination, women are underrepresented in Congress, and even more dramatically underrepresented in congressional leadership. According to a Congressional Research Service Report, in the 250 years of congressional history, only twenty-six women have chaired House committees, and only fifteen have chaired Senate committees. Though most chairs identify as male, the choice of pronoun reflects the importance of gender equity in congressional leadership. Congressional Research Service, "Women in Congress: Statistics and Brief Overview" (Washington, DC: Congressional Research Service, 2022), https://sgp.fas.org/crs/misc/R43244.pdf.

8. David Whiteman, *Communication in Congress: Members, Staff, and the Search for Information* (Lawrence: University Press of Kansas, 1995).

9. Jack R. Van Der Slik and Thomas C. Stenger, "Citizen Witnesses Before Congressional Committees," *Political Science Quarterly* 92, no. 3 (1977): 471.

10. Inter-Parliamentary Union, "Women in Politics: 2021," January 1, 2021, https://www.ipu.org/women-in-politics-2021.

11. Catherine Bolzendahl, "Opportunities and Expectations: The Gendered Organization of Legislative Committees in Germany, Sweden, and the United States," *Gender & Society* 28, no. 6 (2014): 847–76.

12. Bolzendahl, "Opportunities and Expectations," 849.

13. Congressional Research Service, "Women in Congress."

14. Bolzendahl, "Opportunities and Expectations," 852.

15. In 1978, Nancy Kassebaum of Kansas was elected to the Senate, making her the first woman in American history to be elected to the Senate without her husband having served.

16. Senate Historical Office, "Making Room for Women in the Senate," *United States Senate*, March 1, 2022, https://www.senate.gov/artandhistory/senate-stories/making-room-for-women-in-the-senate.htm.

17. Victor Ray, "A Theory of Racialized Organizations," *American Sociological Review* 84, no. 1 (2019): 32.

18. Alexander Furnas et al., "The Congressional Capacity Survey: Who Staff Are, How They Got There, What They Do, and Where They May Go," in *Congress Overwhelmed: The Decline in Congressional Capacity and Prospects for Reform*, ed. Timothy M. LaPira, Lee Drutman, and Kevin R. Kosar (Chicago: University of Chicago Press, 2020), 79.

19. Elsie L. Scott, Karra W. McCray, Donald Bell, and Spencer Overton, "Racial Diversity Among Top U.S. House Staff," *Joint Center for Political and Economic Studies*, 2020.

20. Furnas et al., "The Congressional Capacity Survey," 77.

21. Audrey Henson, "Diversity on Capitol Hill Starts with Paying Interns," *Vox*, January 8, 2019, https://www.vox.com/first-person/2018/12/26/18147165/internship-interns-unpaid-congress-alexandria-ocasio-cortez.

22. Susan Franceschet and Jennifer M. Piscopo, "Gender Quotas and Women's Substantive Representation: Lessons from Argentina," *Politics & Gender* 4, no. 3 (2008): 393.

23. Christine Nittrouer, "Gender Disparities in Colloquium Speakers at Top Universities," *Proceedings of the National Academy of Sciences* 115, no. 1 (2018): 104–8.

24. Maya Kornberg et al., 2022 *Global Parliamentary Report* (Geneva: Inter-Parliamentary Union and United Nations Development Program, 2022).

25. Beth Leech, "Lobbying and Influence," in *The Oxford Handbook of American Political Parties and Interest Groups*, ed. Sandy Maisel and Jeffrey Berry (Oxford: Oxford University Press, 2010).

26. Lee Drutman, *The Business of America Is Lobbying* (Oxford: Oxford University Press, 2015), 219.

27. Leyden, "Interest Group Resources," 434.

28. Drutman, *The Business of America Is Lobbying*, 221.

29. Leyden, "Interest Group Resources," 438.

30. Van Der Slik and Stenger, "Citizen Witnesses Before Congressional Committees," 471.

31. Christine DeGregorio, *Networks of Champions: Leadership, Access, and Advocacy in the U.S. House of Representatives* (Ann Arbor: University of Michigan Press, 1997), 107.

32. Kevin Esterling, *The Political Economy of Expertise: Information and Efficiency in American National Politics* (Ann Arbor: University of Michigan Press, 2009).

33. Drutman, *The Business of America Is Lobbying*, 194.

34. Drutman, *The Business of America Is Lobbying*, 139.

35. Whiteman, *Communication in Congress*; Furnas et al., "The Congressional Capacity Survey."

36. Jesse M. Crosson, Geoffrey M. Lorenz, Craig Volden, and Alan E. Wiseman, "How Experienced Legislative Staff Contribute to Effective Lawmaking," in *Congress Overwhelmed: The Decline in Congressional Capacity and Prospects for Reform*, ed. Timothy M. LaPira, Lee Drutman, and Kevin R. Kosar (Chicago: University of Chicago Press, 2020).

37. Crosson et al., "How Experienced Legislative Staff," 212.

38. Crosson et al., "How Experienced Legislative Staff," 212.

39. Emma Newburger, "There's a Gender Pay Gap for Congressional Staffers—and It's Worse Among Republicans," *CNBC*, January 16, 2019, https://www.cnbc.com/2019/01/15/a-12-percent-average-gender-pay-gap-exists-in-congress-and-is-worse-among-republicans-new-study-finds.html.

40. Furnas et al., "The Congressional Capacity Survey."

41. Furnas et al., "The Congressional Capacity Survey," 78.

42. Van Der Slik and Stenger, "Citizen Witnesses Before Congressional Committees."

43. Leyden, "Interest Group Resources."

44. Richard Hall, *Participation in Congress* (New Haven, CT: Yale University Press, 1996).

45. Lewallen et al., "Congressional Dysfunction."

46. Sven T. Siefken and Hilmar Rommetvedt, *Parliamentary Committees in the Policy Process* (London: Routledge, 2022), 17.

47. Claire Bloquet, "Twenty Years of Attempts at Reforming Committees: A Tale of Reforms Missing the Mark at the French National Assembly," in *Parliamentary Committees in the Policy Process*, ed. Sven T. Siefken and Hilmar Rommetvedt (London: Routledge, 2022), 136.

48. Ali Sawi, "Assess—to Assist: A Preliminary Analysis of Committees in Arab Parliaments," in *Parliamentary Committees in the Policy Process*, ed. Sven T. Siefken and Hilmar Rommetvedt (London: Routledge, 2022).

49. Reuven Hazan, "Political Reform and the Committee System in Israel: Structural and Functional Adaptation," in *The New Role of Parliamentary Committees*, ed. Lawrence Longley and Roger Davidson (London: Frank Cass, 1998), 180.

50. Sawi, "Assess—to Assist," 69.

51. Furnas et al., "The Congressional Capacity Survey," 123.

52. Nelson W. Polsby, *Congressional Behavior* (New York: Random House, 1971), 12.

53. Crosson et al., "How Experienced Legislative Staff," 224.

54. "The Select Committee on the Modernization of Congress: Final Report," October 2020, https://modernizecongress.house.gov/download/final-modernization-committee-report.

55. "The Select Committee on the Modernization of Congress."

56. "The Select Committee on the Modernization of Congress."

57. "The Select Committee on the Modernization of Congress."

58. Bridget Bowman, "House Members Are More Diverse, but Does the Same Go for Staff?," *Roll Call*, January 25, 2019, https://rollcall.com/2019/01/25/house-members-are-more-diverse-but-does-the-same-go-for-staff/.

59. Henson, "Diversity on Capitol Hill Starts with Paying Interns."

60. William Cummings, "Ocasio-Cortez Decries Congressional Pay, Vows to Give Interns 'at Least' $15 an Hour," *USA Today*, December 6, 2018, https://www.usatoday.com/story/news/politics/2018/12/06/alexandria-ocasio-cortez-interns/2224892002/.

2. WHO ARE THE WITNESSES?

1. Marc K. Landy, Marc J. Roberts, and Stephen R. Thomas, *The Environmental Protection Agency: Asking the Wrong Questions* (Oxford: Oxford University Press, 1990).

2. Jonathan Lewallen et al., "Congressional Dysfunction: An Information Processing Perspective," *Regulation and Governance* 10, no. 2 (2016): 179–90; Kevin Esterling, *The Political Economy of Expertise: Information and Efficiency in American National Politics* (Ann Arbor: University of Michigan Press, 2009).

3. Jonathan Lewallen, *Committees and the Decline of Lawmaking in Congress* (Ann Arbor: University of Michigan Press, 2020).

4. Yla R. Tausczik and James W. Pennebaker, "The Psychological Meaning of Words: LIWC and Computerized Text Analysis Methods," *Journal of Language and Social Psychology* 29, no. 1 (2010): 24–54.

5. Pamela C. Corley and Justin Wedeking, "The (Dis)Advantage of Certainty: The Importance of Certainty in Language," *Law & Society Review* 48, no. 1 (2014): 35–62; Jaime E. Settle et al., "From Posting to Voting: The Effects of Political Competition on Online Political Engagement," *Political Science Research and Methods* 4, no. 2 (2016): 361–78.

6. Kenneth Benoit et al., "Crowd-Sourced Text Analysis: Reproducible and Agile Production of Political Data," *American Political Science Review* 110, no. 2 (2016): 278–95; Michael Laver and John Garry, "Estimating Policy Positions from Political Texts," *American Journal of Political Science* 44, no. 3 (2000): 619–34.

7. Kevin Quinn et al., "How to Analyze Political Attention with Minimal Assumptions and Costs," *American Journal of Political Science* 54, no. 1 (2010): 209–28.

8. James W. Pennebaker et al., *The Development and Psychometric Properties of LIWC 2015* (Austin: University of Texas, 2015).

9. Kate Faasse et al., "A Comparison of Language Use in Pro- and Anti-Vaccination Comments in Response to a High Profile Facebook Post," *Vaccine* 34, no. 47 (2016): 5808–14.

10. Robert Moore et al., "Exploring the Relationship Between Clout and Cognitive Processing in MOOC Discussion Forums," *British Journal of Educational Technology* 52, no. 1 (2021): 482–97.

11. Ewa Kacewicz et al., "Pronoun Use Reflects Standings in Social Hierarchies," *Journal of Language and Social Psychology* 33, no. 2 (2014): 125–43.

12. Meina Zhu et al., "Exploring Presence in Online Learning Through Three Forms of Computer-Mediated Discourse Analysis," *Distance Education* 40, no. 2 (2019): 205–25.

13. Bridianne O'dea et al., "A Linguistic Analysis of Suicide-Related Twitter Posts," *Crisis: The Journal of Crisis Intervention and Suicide Prevention* 38, no. 5 (2017): 319.

14. Ryan Owens and Justin P. Wedeking, "Justices and Legal Clarity: Analyzing the Complexity of US Supreme Court Opinions," *Law & Society Review* 45, no. 4 (2011): 1027–61.

15. Alex Stevens, "Telling Policy Stories: An Ethnographic Study of the Use of Evidence in Policymaking in the UK," *Journal of Social Policy* 40, no. 2 (2011): 243.

16. Adnan Hyder et al., "National Policy-Makers Speak Out: Are Researchers Giving Them What They Need?," *Health Policy and Planning* 26, no. 1 (2011): 73–82.

17. Carol Weiss, "Congressional Committees as Users of Analysis," *Journal of Policy Analysis* 8, no. 3 (1989); David Whiteman, *Communication in Congress: Members, Staff, and the Search for Information* (Lawrence: University Press of Kansas, 1995).

18. Bryan Sexton and Robert L. Helmreich, "Analyzing Cockpit Communications: The Links Between Language, Performance, Error, and Workload," *Human Performance in Extreme Environments* 5, no. 1 (2000): 63–68; Steven Blader and Ya-Ru Chen, "Differentiating the Effects of Status and Power: A Justice Perspective," *Journal of Personality and Social Psychology* 102, no. 5 (2012): 994.

19. William Marcellino, "Talk Like a Marine: USMC Linguistic Acculturation and Civil–Military Argument," *Discourse Studies* 16, no. 3 (2014): 385–405.

20. Marcellino, "Talk Like a Marine," 401.

21. Minqing Hu and Bing Liu, "Mining and Summarizing Customer Reviews," Proceedings of the Tenth ACM SIGKDD International Conference on Knowledge Discovery and Data Mining, ACM, 2004.

22. Jack R. Van Der Slik and Thomas C. Stenger, "Citizen Witnesses Before Congressional Committees," *Political Science Quarterly* 92, no. 3 (1977): 473.

23. Kathryn Oliver et al., "A Systematic Review of Barriers to and Facilitators of the Use of Evidence by Policymakers," *BMC Health Services Research* 14, no. 1 (2014).

3. WITNESS TYPOLOGY

1. Richard Fenno, *Congressmen in Committees* (Boston: Little, Brown, 1973).

2. Daniel Maliniak, Ryan Powers, and Barbara F. Walter, "The Gender Citation Gap in International Relations," *International Organization* 67, no. 4 (2013): 889–922.

3. Lin Bian, Sarah-Jane Leslie, and Andrei Cimpian, "Evidence of Bias Against Girls and Women in Contexts That Emphasize Intellectual Ability," *American Psychologist* 73, no. 9 (2018): 1139.

4. Lyn Kathlene, "Power and Influence in State Legislative Policymaking: The Interaction of Gender and Position in Committee Hearing Debates," *American Political Science Review* 88, no. 3 (1994): 560–76.

5. Costas Cavounidis and Kevin Lang, "Discrimination and Worker Evaluation," Working Paper No. w21612, National Bureau of Economic Research, 2015.

6. Marianne Bertrand and Sendhil Mullainathan, "Are Emily and Greg More Employable Than Lakisha and Jamal? A Field Experiment on Labor Market Discrimination," *American Economic Review* 94, no. 4 (2004): 991–1013.

7. Laura Perna et al., "The Role and Contribution of Academic Researchers in Congressional Hearings: A Critical Discourse Analysis," *American Educational Research Journal* 56, no. 1 (2019): 114.

8. This exchange is taken from an article about the hearing published by *The Hill*. Anna Primosch, "Hoops Star Defends Food Stamps Program," *The Hill*, October 27, 2015, https://thehill.com/regulation/258241-hoops-star-defends-food-stamp-program.

9. Allen Schick, "Informed Legislation: Policy Research Versus Ordinary Knowledge," in *Knowledge, Power and Congress*, ed. William Robinson and Clay Wellborn (Washington, DC: CQ Press, 1991), 99–119.

10. Carolyn Hughes Touhy, "Epics, Anecdotes, and the Bounds of Solidarity: Policy Narratives of the Welfare State" (Policy Narratives, Populism and the Institutions of Liberal Democracy: Challenge and Response Conference, University College London, February 11–12, 2019), 5.

11. Lisa Gring-Pemble, "'Are We Going to Now Govern by Anecdote?' Rhetorical Constructions of Welfare Recipients in Congressional Hearings, Debates, and Legislation, 1992–1996," *Quarterly Journal of Speech* 87, no. 4 (2001): 341–65.

12. Touhy, "Epics, Anecdotes, and the Bounds of Solidarity," 15.

4. HOW CONGRESS LISTENS: THE DIFFERENT HEARING TYPES

1. Quoted in Woodrow Wilson, *Congressional Government: A Study in American Politics* (Boston: Houghton Mifflin, 1885).

2. Quoted in Colby Itkowitz, "Hating Congress? That's Always Been in Vogue," *Washington Post*, August 9, 2014.

3. Wilson, *Congressional Government*, para. 82.

4. "The Select Committee on the Modernization of Congress: Final Report," October 2020, https://modernizecongress.house.gov/download/final-modernization-committee-report.

5. Kenneth Shepsle, *The Giant Jigsaw Puzzle* (Chicago: University of Chicago Press, 1978).

6. Congressional Research Service, "Congressional Careers: Service Tenure and Patterns of Member Service, 1789–2021," Washington, DC: Congressional Research Service, January 5, 2021, https://sgp.fas.org/crs/misc/R41545.pdf, 3.

7. James Curry and Frances Lee, *The Limits of Party: Congress and Lawmaking in a Polarized Era* (Chicago: University of Chicago Press, 2020); Sarah Binder, *Minority Rights,*

Majority Rule: Partisanship and the Development of Congress (Cambridge: Cambridge University Press, 1997).

8. Jonathan Lewallen, *Committees and the Decline of Lawmaking in Congress* (Ann Arbor: University of Michigan Press, 2020).

9. Christine Smith et al., "Minority and Majority Influence in Freely Interacting Groups: Qualitative Versus Quantitative Differences," *British Journal of Social Psychology* 35, no. 1 (1996): 137–49.

10. Richard Hall, *Participation in Congress* (New Haven, CT: Yale University Press, 1996), 27.

11. Itkowitz, "Hating Congress?"

12. Joshua Cohen, "Democracy and Liberty," in *Deliberative Democracy*, ed. Jon Elster (Cambridge: Cambridge University Press, 1998).

13. John S. Dryzek and Valerie Braithwaite, "On the Prospects for Democratic Deliberation: Values Analysis Applied to Australian Politics," *Political Psychology* 21, no. 2 (2000): 242.

14. Jürgen Habermas, *The Theory of Communicative Action, Volume I* (Boston: Beacon, 1984).

15. Lee Drutman and Timothy M. LaPira, "Capacity for What? Legislative Capacity Regimes in Congress and the Possibilities for Reform," in *Congress Overwhelmed: The Decline in Congressional Capacity and Prospects for Reform*, ed. Timothy M. LaPira, Lee Drutman, and Kevin R. Kosar (Chicago: University of Chicago Press, 2020), 16.

16. Habermas, *The Theory of Communicative Action*.

17. John Stuart Mill, *Considerations on Representative Government* (London: Parker, Son, & Bourn, 1861).

18. Edward L. Lascher Jr., "Assessing Legislative Deliberation: A Preface to Empirical Analysis," *Legislative Studies Quarterly* 21, no. 4 (1996): 509.

19. Keith Poole and Howard Rosenthal, *Ideology and Congress* (Piscataway, NJ: Transaction, 2007).

20. Christopher Deering and Steven Smith, *Committees in Congress* (Washington, DC: CQ Press, 1997).

21. Jürg Steiner et al., *Deliberative Politics in Action: Analyzing Parliamentary Discourse* (Cambridge: Cambridge University Press, 2004), 131.

22. Steiner et al., *Deliberative Politics in Action*, 125.

23. Steiner et al., *Deliberative Politics in Action*, 126.

24. Anthony Greenwald and Mahzarin Banaji, "Implicit Social Cognition: Attitudes, Self-Esteem, and Stereotypes," *Psychological Review* 102, no. 1 (1995): 4–27.

25. Matthew Levendusky, *How Partisan Media Polarize America* (Chicago: University of Chicago Press, 2013).

26. Cass Sunstein, *Going to Extremes: How Like Minds Unite and Divide* (Oxford: Oxford University Press, 2009).

27. Philip Tetlock, "Identifying Victims of Groupthink from Public Statements of Decision Makers," *Journal of Personality and Social Psychology* 37, no. 8 (1979): 1314.

28. Irving Janis, *Victims of Groupthink: A Psychological Study of Foreign-Policy Decisions and Fiascoes* (Boston: Houghton Mifflin, 1972).

29. Tetlock, "Identifying Victims of Groupthink."

30. Christopher Hsee et al., "Preference Reversals Between Joint and Separate Evaluations of Options: A Review and Theoretical Analysis," *Psychological Bulletin* 125, no. 4 (1999): 576.

31. Sunstein, *Going to Extremes*.

32. Iris Marion Young, "Communication and the Other: Beyond Deliberative Democracy," in *Democracy and Difference*, ed. Seyla Benhabib (Princeton, NJ: Princeton University Press, 1996), 128.

33. Jason Barabas, "How Deliberation Affects Policy Opinions," *American Political Science Review* 98, no. 4 (2004): 687–701.

34. Michael Rush, "Committees in the Canadian House of Commons," in *Committees in Legislatures: A Comparative Analysis*, ed. John David Lees and Malcolm Shaw (Durham, NC: Duke University Press, 1979), 228.

35. Young, "Communication and the Other," 128.

36. Paul Quirk and William Bendix, "Deliberation in Congress," in *The Oxford Handbook of the American Congress*, ed. George C. Edwards III, Frances E. Lee, and Eric Schickler (Oxford: Oxford University Press, 2011), 553.

37. Lascher, "Assessing Legislative Deliberation," 509.

38. *Bolstering the Government's Cybersecurity: Lessons Learned from WannaCry*, House of Representatives, 116th Congress, June 15, 2017.

39. *Past, Present, and Future of SNAP: Addressing Special Population*, House of Representatives, 116th Congress, January 12, 2016.

40. Rich Morin, "The Politics and Demographics of Food Stamp Recipients," Washington, DC: Pew Research Center, July 12, 2013.

41. Carroll Doherty, Jocelyn Kiley, and Nida Asheer, "In a Politically Polarized Era, Sharp Divides in Both Partisan Coalitions," Washington, DC: Pew Research Center, December 17, 2019.

42. Statistic taken from voting record for HR3102, accessible at http://clerk.house.gov/evs/2013/roll476.xml.

43. Peta-Gay Sheerwood and Stephanie Denardo, "Congressman Yoho Speaks About Food Stamp Program," *WUFT News*, September 24, 2013, https://www.wuft.org/news/2013/09/24/yoho-3/.

44. Young, "Communication and the Other," 128.

45. *Article One: Fostering a More Deliberative Process in Congress*, House of Representatives, 116th Congress, February 5, 2020.

46. "The Select Committee on the Modernization of Congress."

5. COMMITTEE HEARINGS AS EDUCATIONAL PLATFORMS

1. Bill Pascrell Jr., "Why Is Congress So Dumb?," *Washington Post*, January 11, 2019.

2. Sander L. van der Linden et al., "The Scientific Consensus on Climate Change as a Gateway Belief: Experimental Evidence," *PloS One* 10, no. 2 (2015).

3. Larissa Conradt and Timothy Roper, "Consensus Decision Making in Animals," *Trends in Ecology & Evolution* 20, no. 8 (2005): 449–56.

4.   Helene Helboe Pedersen, Darren Halpin, and Anne Rasmussen, "Who Gives Evidence to Parliamentary Committees? A Comparative Investigation of Parliamentary Committees and Their Constituencies," *Journal of Legislative Studies* 21, no. 3 (2015): 411.

5.   Henrik Jensen, *Partigrupperne i Folketinget* (Jurist-og Økonomforbundets Forlag, 2002).

6.   Mark P. Jones et al., "Amateur Legislators—Professional Politicians: The Consequences of Party-Centered Electoral Rules in a Federal System," *American Journal of Political Science* 46, no. 3 (2002): 656–69.

7.   Malcolm Shaw, "Parliamentary Committees: A Global Perspective," in *The New Roles of Parliamentary Committees*, ed. Lawrence Longley and Roger Davidson (London: Frank Cass, 1998), 238.

8.   Richard Hall, *Participation in Congress* (New Haven, CT: Yale University Press, 1996), 28.

9.   Jesse Crosson, Geoffrey M. Lorenz, Craig Volden, and Alan E. Wiseman, "How Experienced Legislative Staff Contribute to Effective Lawmaking," in *Congress Overwhelmed: The Decline in Congressional Capacity and Prospects for Reform*, ed. Timothy M. LaPira, Lee Drutman, and Kevin R. Kosar (Chicago: University of Chicago Press, 2020), 287.

10.   Carol Weiss, "Congressional Committees as Users of Analysis," *Journal of Policy Analysis* 8, no. 3 (1989): 418.

11.   Weiss, "Congressional Committees as Users of Analysis," 418.

12.   *The Science and Ethics of Genetically Engineered Human DNA*, House of Representatives, 116th Congress, June 16, 2015.

13.   *STEM and Computer Science Education: Preparing the 21st Century Workforce*, House of Representatives, 116th Congress, July 26, 2017.

14.   The Mathematical and Statistical Education Modeling Act was introduced by Senators Maggie Hassan (D-NH) and Marsha Blackburn (R-TN). The Rural STEM Education Act was introduced by Senators Roger Wicker (R-MS), Jacky Rosen (D-NV), John Cornyn (R-TX), and Maggie Hassan (D-NH).

15.   Jonathan Lewallen et al., "Congressional Dysfunction: An Information Processing Perspective," *Regulation and Governance* 10, no. 2 (2016): 179–90.

6. COMMITTEE HEARINGS AS THEATRICAL STAGES

1.   Thomas McKinless, "Leahy Tears Up Committee Rule Book After Graham Pushes Immigration Vote," *RollCall*, August 1, 2019.

2.   *The Authorizations for the Use of Military Force: Administration Perspective*, 116th Congress, Senate, October 30, 2017.

3.   Jonathan Lewallen, *Committees and the Decline of Lawmaking in Congress* (Ann Arbor: University of Michigan Press, 2020), 125.

4.   Lewallen, *Committees and the Decline of Lawmaking*, 120.

5.   Paul M. Collins and Lori A. Ringhand, *Supreme Court Confirmation Hearings and Constitutional Change* (Cambridge: Cambridge University Press, 2013), 86.

6.   *The Iran Nuclear Agreement: One Year Later*, Senate, 116th Congress, July 14, 2016.

7.   As evidenced by data from the Federal Election Commission, https://www.fec.gov/.

8.   As evidenced by data from the Federal Election Commission, https://www.fec.gov/.

9. *Climate Science: Assumptions, Policy Implications, and the Scientific Method*, House of Representatives, 116th Congress, March 29, 2017.

10. Carry Funk and Brian Kennedy, "The Politics of Climate," Washington, DC: Pew Research Center, October 4, 2016.

11. Olivia Waxman, "Supreme Court Confirmation Hearings Weren't Always Such a Spectacle: There's a Reason That Changed," *Time Magazine*, September 6, 2018.

12. Collins and Ringhand, *Supreme Court Confirmation Hearings*, 101.

13. Alvin Chang, "Partisanship of Cabinet Confirmations is Rising, but Trump's Picks are Still Different," *Vox*, February 7, 2017.

14. Colby Itkowitz, "1 in 4 Circuit Court Judges is Now a Trump Appointee," *Washington Post*, December 22, 2019.

15. Lewallen, *Committees and the Decline of Lawmaking*, 84.

16. Lee Drutman and Timothy M. LaPira, "Capacity for What? Legislative Capacity Regimes in Congress and the Possibilities for Reform," in *Congress Overwhelmed: The Decline in Congressional Capacity and Prospects for Reform*, ed. Timothy M. LaPira, Lee Drutman, and Kevin R. Kosar (Chicago: University of Chicago Press, 2020), 17.

17. Joel Aberbach, *Keeping a Watchful Eye: The Politics of Congressional Oversight* (Washington, DC: Brookings Institution Press, 2001); Seymour Scher, "Conditions for Legislative Control," *Journal of Politics* 25, no. 3 (1963): 526–51; David Parker and Matthew Dull, "Divided We Quarrel: The Politics of Congressional Investigations, 1947–2004," *Legislative Studies Quarterly* 34, no. 3 (2009): 319–45.

18. Michael Robinson and Kevin Appel, "Network News Coverage of Congress," *Political Science Quarterly* 94, no. 3 (1979): 417.

19. "The Select Committee on the Modernization of Congress: Final Report," October 2020, https://modernizecongress.house.gov/download/final-modernization-committee-report.

20. Ingvar Mattson and Kaare Strøm, "Parliamentary Committees," in *Parliaments and Majority Rule in Western Europe*, ed. H. Döring (Frankfurt: Campus Mannheim, 1995), 249–307.

21. Stephen Marc Solomon, "Listen Carefully: Public Hearings in the German Bundestag" (PhD diss., University of Mannheim, 2015), 20.

22. Maya Kornberg et al., *2022 Global Parliamentary Report* (Geneva: Inter-Parliamentary Union and United Nations Development Program, 2022).

23. Jürg Steiner et al., *Deliberative Politics in Action: Analyzing Parliamentary Discourse* (Cambridge: Cambridge University Press, 2004).

24. Mattson and Strøm, "Parliamentary Committees."

25. Claire Bloquet, "Twenty Years of Attempts at Reforming Committees: A Tale of Reforms Missing the Mark at the French National Assembly," in *Parliamentary Committees in the Policy Process*, ed. Sven T. Siefken and Hilmar Rommetvedt (London: Routledge, 2022), 136.

26. Weston Agor, "Autonomy of Standing Committees in the Chilean Senate," *Journal of Latin American Studies* 2, no. 1 (1970): 43.

27. Agor, "Autonomy of Standing Committees," 43.

28. Sven T. Siefken and Hilmar Rommetvedt, *Parliamentary Committees in the Policy Process* (London: Routledge, 2022), 42.

7. COMMITTEES AS SPACES FOR PERSONAL CONNECTION

1. Ross Baker, *Is Bipartisanship Dead? A Report From the Senate* (Abingdon: Routledge, 2015).
2. Philip E. Tetlock, "Social Psychology and World Politics," in *The Handbook of Social Psychology*, ed. D. Gilbert, S. Fiske, and G. Lindzey (New York, McGraw Hill, 1998), 868.
3. C. D. Batson et al., "Empathy and Attitudes: Can Feeling for a Member of a Stigmatized Group Improve Feelings Toward the Group?," *Journal of Personality and Social Psychology* 72, no. 1 (1997): 105–18.
4. Suzanne Keen, "Empathetic Hardy: Bounded, Ambassadorial, and Broadcast Strategies of Narrative Empathy," *Poetics Today* 32, no. 2 (2011): 349–89.
5. United Nations Development Programme (UNDP), 2017. *Sednice van sedišta odbora Narodne Skupštine*, www.youtube.com/watch?v=Q5iHJg1E46I.
6. This interview was conducted by Maya Kornberg as part of the research for the 2022 Global Parliamentary Report, a joint publication of the IPU and UNDP. Maya Kornberg et al., *2022 Global Parliamentary Report* (Geneva: Inter-Parliamentary Union and United Nations Development Program, 2022).
7. Laurel Harbridge, *Is Bipartisanship Dead? Policy Agreement and Agenda-Setting in the House of Representatives* (Cambridge: Cambridge University Press, 2015), 332.
8. Ronnie Janoff-Bulman and Amelie Werther, "The Social Psychology of Respect: Implications for Delegitimization and Reconciliation," in *The Social Psychology of Intergroup Reconciliation*, ed. Arie Nadler, Thomas Malloy, and Jeffrey Fisher (Oxford: Oxford University Press, 2008), 145–70.
9. Diane Mackie and Joel Cooper, "Attitude Polarization: Effects of Group Membership," *Journal of Personality and Social Psychology* 46, no. 3 (1984): 575–85.
10. Ananthi Al Ramiah and Miles Hewstone, "Discrimination Conditions, Consequences, and Cures," in *The Oxford Handbook of Political Psychology*, ed. Leonie Huddy, David O. Sears, and Jack S. Levy (Oxford: Oxford University Press, 2013); Mazafer Sherif, *Group Conflict and Cooperation: Their Social Psychology* (Abingdon: Routledge & Kegan Paul, 1967).
11. Benjamin Ekeyi, "Exploring the Gap Between Theory and Practice in Law-Making and Oversight by Committees of the Nigerian National Assembly," in *Parliamentary Committees in the Policy Process*, ed. Sven T. Siefken and Hilmar Rommetvedt (London: Routledge, 2022), 274.
12. Kerry Kawakami et al., "Kicking the Habit: Effects of Nonstereotypic Association Training and Correction Processes on Hiring Decisions," *Journal of Experimental Social Psychology* 41, no. 1 (2005): 68–75.
13. Nilanjana Dasgupta and Luis M. Rivera, "From Automatic Anti-Gay Prejudice to Behavior: The Moderating Role of Conscious Beliefs About Gender and Behavioral Control," *Journal of Personality and Social Psychology* 91, no. 2 (2006): 268–80.
14. Iris Marion Young, "Communication and the Other: Beyond Deliberative Democracy," in *Democracy and Difference*, ed. Seyla Benhabib (Princeton, NJ: Princeton University Press, 1996), 128.
15. Samuel L. Gaertner et al., "How Does Cooperation Reduce Intergroup Bias?," *Journal of Personality and Social Psychology* 59, no. 4 (1990): 692–704; Thomas F. Pettigrew and

Linda R. Tropp, "A Meta-Analytic Test of Intergroup Contact Theory," *Journal of Personality and Social Psychology* 90, no. 5 (2006): 751–83.

16. Samuel L. Gaertner et al., "Reducing Intergroup Bias: Elements of Intergroup Cooperation," *Journal of Personality and Social Psychology* 76, no. 3 (1999): 388.

17. Maureen Groppe, "Here's Why Barack Obama Is Praising Late Former Sen. Richard Lugar," *USA Today*, April 28, 2019.

18. Harbridge, *Is Bipartisanship Dead?*, 332.

19. Thomas E. Mann and Norman J. Ornstein, *The Broken Branch: How Congress Is Failing America and How to Get it Back on Track* (Oxford: Oxford University Press, 2006).

20. Jürg Steiner et al., *Deliberative Politics in Action: Analyzing Parliamentary Discourse* (Cambridge: Cambridge University Press, 2004).

21. *Promoting Civility and Building a More Collaborative Congress*, House of Representatives, 116th Congress, September 26, 2019.

22. Rhiannon Turner, Miles Hewstone, and Alberto Voci, "Reducing Explicit and Implicit Outgroup Prejudice via Direct and Extended Contact: The Mediating Role of Self-Disclosure and Intergroup Anxiety," *Journal of Personality and Social Psychology* 93, no. 3 (2007): 369.

23. Weston Agor, "Autonomy of Standing Committees in the Chilean Senate," *Journal of Latin American Studies* 2, no. 1 (1970): 44.

24. Agor, "Autonomy of Standing Committees," 43.

25. James Curry and Frances Lee, *The Limits of Party: Congress and Lawmaking in a Polarized Era* (Chicago: University of Chicago Press, 2020), 29.

26. Sarah Binder and Steven S. Smith, *Politics or Principle? Filibustering in the United States Senate* (Washington, DC: Brookings Institution Press, 1997).

27. Richard Fenno, *Congressmen in Committees* (Boston: Little Brown, 1973).

28. Tetlock, "Social Psychology and World Politics," 868.

29. "The Select Committee on the Modernization of Congress: Final Report," October 2020, https://modernizecongress.house.gov/download/final-modernization-committee-report.

30. This interview was conducted as part of the research led by Maya Kornberg for the 2022 Global Parliamentary Report, a joint publication of the IPU and UNDP. Kornberg et al., *2022 Global Parliamentary Report.*

31. "The Select Committee on the Modernization of Congress."

32. This interview was conducted as part of the research led by Maya Kornberg for the 2022 Global Parliamentary Report, a joint publication of the IPU and UNDP. Kornberg et al., *2022 Global Parliamentary Report.*

8. NEITHER DEAD NOR OSSIFIED: CONGRESS TODAY

1. Beth Orren and Stephen Skowronek, *The Search for American Political Development* (Cambridge: Cambridge University Press, 2004), 78.

2. "James Baldwin: How to Cool It," *Esquire Magazine*, July 1968, https://www.esquire.com/news-politics/a23960/james-baldwin-cool-it/.

3. Jonathan Lewallen, *Committees and the Decline of Lawmaking in Congress* (Ann Arbor: University of Michigan Press, 2020), 38.

4. Thomas E. Mann and Norman J. Ornstein, *The Broken Branch: How Congress Is Failing America and How to Get It Back on Track* (Oxford: Oxford University Press, 2006).

5. Gerald Berk and Dennis Galvan, "How People Experience and Change Institutions: A Field Guide to Creative Syncretism," *Theory and Society* 38, no. 6 (2009): 543.

6. Frank Baumgartner and Bryan D. Jones, *The Politics of Information: Problem Definition and the Course of Public Policy in America* (Chicago: University of Chicago Press, 2015), 20.

7. David C. King, *Turf Wars: How Congressional Committees Claim Jurisdiction* (Chicago: University of Chicago Press, 1997).

8. Gerhard Loewenberg, Peverill Squire, and D. Roderick Kiewiet, eds., *Legislatures: Comparative Perspectives on Representative Assemblies* (Ann Arbor: University of Michigan Press, 2002), 3.

9. Phillip Wallach, "How Congress Fell Behind the Executive Branch," in *Congress Overwhelmed: The Decline in Congressional Capacity and Prospects for Reform*, ed. Timothy M. LaPira, Lee Drutman, and Kevin R. Kosar (Chicago: University of Chicago Press, 2020).

10. US Capitol Visitor Center Legislative Highlights, *Legislative Reorganization Act of 1946*, https://www.visitthecapitol.gov/exhibitions/legislative-highlights/legislative -reorganization-act-1946-august-2-1946.

11. Kenneth Schultz, "Perils of Polarization for US Foreign Policy," *Washington Quarterly* 40, no. 4 (2017): 9.

12. Lee Drutman, *The Business of America Is Lobbying* (Oxford: Oxford University Press, 2015), 218.

13. Wallach, "How Congress Fell Behind the Executive Branch," 64.

APPENDIX A. DETAILS ON INTERVIEW SAMPLE

1. Layna Mosley, ed., *Interview Research in Political Science* (Ithaca, NY: Cornell University Press, 2013), 41.

2. Gary King, Robert O. Keohane, and Sidney Verba, *Designing Social Inquiry: Scientific Inference in Qualitative Research* (Princeton, NJ: Princeton University Press, 1994), 139.

3. Mosley, *Interview Research in Political Science*.

4. Melani Cammett, "Using Proxy Interviewing to Address Sensitive Topics," in *Interview Research in Political Science*, ed. Layna Mosley (Ithaca, NY: Cornell University Press, 2013).

5. Richard Hall, *Participation in Congress* (New Haven, CT: Yale University Press, 1996), 28.

BIBLIOGRAPHY

Aberbach, Joel D. *Keeping a Watchful Eye: The Politics of Congressional Oversight*. Washington, DC: Brookings Institution Press, 2001.

Ackerman, Bruce, and James Fishkin. *Deliberation Day*. New Haven, CT: Yale University Press, 2004.

Adler, Scott. *Why Congressional Reforms Fail: Reelection and the House Committee System*. Chicago: University of Chicago Press, 2002.

Adler, E. Scott, and John D. Wilkerson. *Congress and the Politics of Problem Solving*. Cambridge: Cambridge University Press, 2013.

Agor, Weston H. "Autonomy of Standing Committees in the Chilean Senate." *Journal of Latin American Studies* 2, no. 1 (1970): 29–50.

Aldrich, John H., and David W. Rohde. "Congressional Committees in a Continuing Partisan Era." In *Congress Reconsidered*, 9th ed., ed. Lawrence Dodd and Bruce Oppenheimer, 217–40. Washington, DC: CQ Press, 2009.

Aldrich, John H., and Kenneth A. Shepsle. "Explaining Institutional Change: Soaking, Poking, and Modeling in the US Congress." In *Congress on Display, Congress at Work*, vol. 31, ed. William Bianco. Ann Arbor: University of Michigan Press, 2000.

Al Ramiah, Ananthi, and Miles Hewstone. "Discrimination Conditions, Consequences, and Cures." In *The Oxford Handbook of Political Psychology*, ed. Leonie Huddy, David O. Sears, and Jack S. Levy, 890–922. Oxford: Oxford University Press, 2013.

——. "Intergroup Contact as a Tool for Reducing, Resolving, and Preventing Intergroup Conflict: Evidence, Limitations, and Potential." *American Psychologist* 68, no. 7 (2013): 527–42.

Arendt, Hannah. *The Human Condition*. Chicago: University of Chicago Press, 1958.

Baker, Ross. *Is Bipartisanship Dead? A Report from the Senate*. Abingdon: Routledge, 2015.

Barabas, Jason. "How Deliberation Affects Policy Opinions." *American Political Science Review* 98, no. 4 (2004): 687–701.

Batson, C. D., et al. "Empathy and Attitudes: Can Feeling for a Member of a Stigmatized Group Improve Feelings Toward the Group?" *Journal of Personality and Social Psychology* 72, no. 1 (1997): 105–18.

Baumgartner, Frank R., and Bryan D. Jones. *The Politics of Information: Problem Definition and the Course of Public Policy in America.* Chicago: University of Chicago Press, 2015.

Beach, Derek, and Rasmus Pederson. *Process Tracing Methods: Foundations and Guidelines.* Ann Arbor: University of Michigan Press, 2013.

Benoit, Kenneth, et al. "Crowd-Sourced Text Analysis: Reproducible and Agile Production of Political Data." *American Political Science Review* 110, no. 2 (2016): 278–95.

Berk, Gerald, and Dennis Galvan. "How People Experience and Change Institutions: A Field Guide to Creative Syncretism." *Theory and Society* 38, no. 6 (2009): 543–80.

Berry, Christopher R., and Anthony Fowler. "Cardinals or Clerics? Congressional Committees and the Distribution of Pork." *American Journal of Political Science* 60, no. 3 (2016): 692–708.

Bertrand, Marianne, and Sendhil Mullainathan. "Are Emily and Greg More Employable Than Lakisha and Jamal? A Field Experiment on Labor Market Discrimination." *American Economic Review* 94, no. 4 (2004): 991–1013.

Bessette, Joseph M. *The Mild Voice of Reason: Deliberative Democracy and American National Government.* Chicago: University of Chicago Press, 1997.

Bian, Lin, Sarah-Jane Leslie, and Andrei Cimpian. "Evidence of Bias Against Girls and Women in Contexts That Emphasize Intellectual Ability." *American Psychologist* 73, no. 9 (2018): 1139.

Binder, Sarah. *Minority Rights, Majority Rule: Partisanship and the Development of Congress.* Cambridge: Cambridge University Press, 1997.

——. *Stalemate: Causes and Consequences of Legislative Gridlock.* Washington, DC: Brookings Institution Press, 2003.

Binder, Sarah, and Steven S. Smith. *Politics or Principle? Filibustering in the United States Senate.* Washington, DC: Brookings Institution Press, 1997.

Blader, Steven L., and Ya-Ru Chen. "Differentiating the Effects of Status and Power: A Justice Perspective." *Journal of Personality and Social Psychology* 102, no. 5 (2012): 994.

Blair, I. V., et al. "Imagining Stereotypes Away: The Moderation of Implicit Stereotypes Through Mental Imagery." *Journal of Personality and Social Psychology* 81, no. 5 (2001): 828–41.

Bloquet, Claire. "Twenty Years of Attempts at Reforming Committees: A Tale of Reforms Missing the Mark at the French National Assembly." In *Parliamentary Committees in the Policy Process*, ed. Sven T. Siefken and Hilmar Rommetvedt, 98–115. London: Routledge, 2022.

Bolzendahl, Catherine. "Opportunities and Expectations: The Gendered Organization of Legislative Committees in Germany, Sweden, and the United States." *Gender & Society* 28, no. 6 (2014): 847–76.

Bonica, Adam. "Avenues of Influence: on the Political Expenditures of Corporations and Their Directors and Executives." *Business and Politics* 18, no. 4 (2016): 367–94.

Bonica, Adam, Chen Jowei, and Johnson Tim. "Senate Gate-Keeping, Presidential Staffing of 'Inferior Offices' and the Ideological Composition of Appointments to the Public Bureaucracy." *Quarterly Journal of Political Science* 10, no. 1 (2015): 5–40.

Bowman, Bridget. "House Members Are More Diverse, But Does the Same Go for Staff?" *Roll Call*, January 25, 2019.

Brauer, Markus, and Charles M. Judd. "Group Polarization and Repeated Attitude Expressions: A New Take on an Old Topic." *European Review of Social Psychology* 7, no. 1 (1996): 173–207.

Brauer, Markus, Charles M. Judd, and Melissa D. Gliner. "The Effects of Repeated Expressions on Attitude Polarization During Group Discussions." *Journal of Personality and Social Psychology* 68, no. 6 (1995): 1014–29.

Brookings Institution. "Vital Statistics on Congress: Chapter 6—Legislative Productivity in Congress and Workload." https://www.brookings.edu/wpcontent/uploads/2016/06/Vital-Statistics -Chapter-6-Legislative-Productivity-in-Congress-and-Workload_UPDATE.pdf.

Cairney, Paul. *The Politics of Evidence-Based Policymaking.* London: Palgrave Macmillan, 2016.

Cammett, Melani. "Using Proxy Interviewing to Address Sensitive Topics." In *Interview Research in Political Science*, ed. Layna Mosley, 125–43. Ithaca, NY: Cornell University Press, 2013.

Carey, John. "Parties, Coalitions, and the Chilean Congress in the 1990s." In *Legislative Politics in Latin America*, ed. Scott Morgenstern and Nacif Benito, 222–53. Cambridge: Cambridge University Press, 2002.

Carpini, Michael X. Delli, Fay Lomax Cook, and Lawrence R. Jacobs. "Public Deliberation, Discursive Participation, and Citizen Engagement: A Review of the Empirical Literature." *Annual Review of Political Science* 7 (2004): 315–44.

Carson, Donald W., and James W. Johnson. *Mo: The Life and Times of Morris K. Udall.* Tucson: University of Arizona Press, 2004.

Cavounidis, Costas, and Kevin Lang. "Discrimination and Worker Evaluation." Working Paper No. w21612. National Bureau of Economic Research, Cambridge, MA, 2015.

Chang, Alvin. "Partisanship of Cabinet Confirmations Is Rising, but Trump's Picks Are Still Different." *Vox*, February 7, 2017.

Cohen, Joshua. "Democracy and Liberty." In *Deliberative Democracy*, ed. Jon Elster, 185–231. Cambridge: Cambridge University Press, 1998.

Collins, Paul M., and Lori A. Ringhand. *Supreme Court Confirmation Hearings and Constitutional Change.* Cambridge: Cambridge University Press, 2013.

Congressional Management Foundation. *Life in Congress: A Member Perspective.* Washington, DC: Congressional Management Foundation, 2013.

Congressional Research Service. "Congressional Careers: Service Tenure and Patterns of Member Service, 1789–2021." Washington, DC: Congressional Research Service, January 5, 2021.

——. "Women in Congress: Statistics and Brief Overview." Washington, DC: Congressional Research Service, July 7, 2022.

Connor, George, and Bruce Oppenheimer. "Deliberation: An Untimed Value in a Timed Game." In *Congress Reconsidered*, 5th ed., ed. Lawrence Dodd and Bruce Oppenheimer, 315–30. Washington, DC: CQ Press, 1993.

Conradt, Larissa, and Timothy J. Roper. "Consensus Decision Making in Animals." *Trends in Ecology & Evolution* 20, no. 8 (2005): 449–56.

Contandriopoulos, Damien, et al. "Knowledge Exchange Processes in Organizations and Policy Arenas: A Narrative Systematic Review of the Literature." *Milbank Quarterly* 88, no. 4 (2010): 444–83.

Cooper, Joseph. *The Origins of the Standing Committees and the Development of the Modern House.* Houston: Rice University Press, 1971.

Coppins, McKay. "The Man Who Broke Politics." *The Atlantic*, October 17, 2018.

Corley, Pamela C., and Justin Wedeking. "The (Dis)Advantage of Certainty: The Importance of Certainty in Language." *Law & Society Review* 48, no. 1 (2014): 35–62.

Cox, Gary, and Matthew Mccubbins. *Legislative Leviathan: Party Government in the House.* Cambridge: Cambridge University Press, 2007.

Crosson, Jesse M., Geoffrey M. Lorenz, Craig Volden, and Alan E. Wiseman. "How Experienced Legislative Staff Contribute to Effective Lawmaking." In *Congress Overwhelmed: The Decline in Congressional Capacity and Prospects for Reform*, ed. Timothy M. LaPira, Lee Drutman, and Kevin R. Kosar, 209–24. Chicago: University of Chicago Press, 2020.

Curry, James M., and Frances E. Lee. *The Limits of Party: Congress and Lawmaking in a Polarized Era.* Chicago: University of Chicago Press, 2020.

Dasgupta, Nilanjana, and Luis M. Rivera, "From Automatic Anti-Gay Prejudice to Behavior: The Moderating Role of Conscious Beliefs About Gender and Behavioral Control." *Journal of Personality and Social Psychology* 91, no. 2 (2006): 268–80.

Davidson, Roger H., et al. *Congress and Its Members.* Washington, DC: CQ Press, 2013.

Deering, Christopher, and Steven Smith. *Committees in Congress.* Washington, DC: CQ Press, 1997.

DeGregorio, Christine. *Networks of Champions: Leadership, Access, and Advocacy in the U.S. House of Representatives.* Ann Arbor: University of Michigan Press, 1997.

Dodd, Lawrence C., and Scot Schraufnagel. "Party Polarization and Policy Productivity in Congress: From Harding to Obama." In *Congress Reconsidered*, 10th ed., ed. Lawrence Dodd and Bruce Oppenheimer, 437–64. Washington, DC: CQ Press, 2013.

D'Onofrio, Francesco. "Committees in the Italian Parliament." In *Committees in Legislatures: A Comparative Analysis*, ed. John D. Lees and Malcolm Shaw, 61–101. Durham, NC: Duke University Press, 1979.

Drutman, Lee. *The Business of America Is Lobbying: How Corporations Became Politicized and Politics Became More Corporate.* Oxford: Oxford University Press, 2015.

Dryzek, John, and Valerie Braithwaite. "On the Prospects for Democratic Deliberation: Values Analysis Applied to Australian Politics." *Political Psychology* 21, no. 2 (2000): 241–66.

Eckman, Sarah. "Video Broadcasting of Congressional Proceedings." Washington, DC: Congressional Research Service, 2017.

Ekeyi, Benjamin. "Exploring the Gap Between Theory and Practice in Law-Making and Oversight by Committees of the Nigerian National Assembly." In *Parliamentary Committees in the Policy Process*, ed. Sven T. Siefken and Hilmar Rommetvedt, 206–23. London: Routledge, 2022.

Elster, Jon. *Deliberative Democracy.* Cambridge: Cambridge University Press, 1998.

Esterling, Kevin. *The Political Economy of Expertise: Information and Efficiency in American National Politics.* Ann Arbor: University of Michigan Press, 2009.

Evans, Lawrence. "Congressional Committees." In *The Oxford Handbook of the American Congress*, ed. George C. Edwards III, Frances E. Lee, and Eric Schickler, 396–425. Oxford: Oxford University Press, 2011.

Faasse, Kate, Casey J. Chatman, and Leslie R. Martin. "A Comparison of Language Use in Pro- and Anti-Vaccination Comments in Response to a High Profile Facebook Post." *Vaccine* 34, no. 47 (2016): 5808–14.

Fenno, Richard. *Congressmen in Committees.* Boston: Little, Brown, 1973.

——. *Home Style: Representatives in Their Districts.* Boston: Little, Brown, 1978.

——. *The Power of the Purse: Appropriations Politics in Congress.* Boston: Little, Brown, 1966.

Fiorina, Morris. *Culture War? The Myth of a Polarized America.* New York: Pearson Education, 2006.

Fiorina, Morris P., and David W. Rohde. *Home Style and Washington Work: Studies of Congressional Politics.* Ann Arbor: University of Michigan Press, 1991.

Fishkin, James S. "Consulting the Public Through Deliberative Polling." *Journal of Policy Analysis and Management* 22, no. 1 (2003): 128–33.

Fishkin, James S., and Robert C. Luskin. "Bringing Deliberation to the Democratic Dialogue." In *The Poll with a Human Face: The National Issues Convention Experiment in Political Communication,* ed. Maxwell McCombs and Amy Reynolds. Abingdon: Routledge, 1999.

Franceschet, Susan, and Jennifer M. Piscopo. "Gender Quotas and Women's Substantive Representation: Lessons from Argentina." *Politics & Gender* 4, no. 3 (2008): 393.

Froman, Lewis Acrelius, and Paul A. Freund. *The Congressional Process: Strategies, Rules, and Procedures.* Boston: Little, Brown, 1967.

Furnas, Alexander, Lee Drutman, Alexander Hertel-Fernandez, Timothy LaPira, and Kevin Kosar. "The Congressional Capacity Survey: Who Staff Are, How They Got There, What They Do, and Where They May Go." In *Congress Overwhelmed: The Decline in Congressional Capacity and Prospects for Reform,* ed. Timothy M. LaPira, Lee Drutman, and Kevin R. Kosar. Chicago: University of Chicago Press, 2020.

Gaertner, Samuel L., et al. "How Does Cooperation Reduce Intergroup Bias?" *Journal of Personality and Social Psychology* 59, no. 4 (1990): 692–704.

Gaertner, Samuel L., John F. Dovidio, Mary C. Rust, Jason A. Nier, Brenda S. Banker, Christine M. Ward, Gary R. Mottola, and Missy Houlette. "Reducing Intergroup Bias: Elements of Intergroup Cooperation." *Journal of Personality and Social Psychology* 76, no. 3 (1999): 388.

Gertzog, Irwin N. *Congressional Women: Their Recruitment, Integration, and Behavior.* Westport, CT: Greenwood Publishing, 1995.

Goodwin, George. "Subcommittees: The Miniature Legislatures of Congress." *American Political Science Review* 56, no. 3 (1962): 596–604.

Granstaff, Bill. *Losing Our Democratic Spirit: Congressional Deliberation and the Dictatorship of Propaganda.* Westport, CT: Greenwood Publishing, 1999.

Green, Donald P., and Ian Shapiro. *Pathologies of Rational Choice Theory: A Critique of Applications in Political Science.* New Haven, CT: Yale University Press, 1994.

Greenwald, Anthony, and Mahzarin Banaji. "Implicit Social Cognition: Attitudes, Self-Esteem, and Stereotypes." *Psychological Review* 102, no. 1 (1995): 4–27.

Grimmer, Justin. "We Are All Social Scientists Now: How Big Data, Machine Learning, and Causal Inference Work Together." *PS: Political Science & Politics* 48, no. 1 (2015): 80–3.

Grimmer, Justin, and Brandon M. Stewart. "Text as Data: The Promise and Pitfalls of Automatic Content Analysis Methods for Political Texts." *Political Analysis* 21, no. 3 (2013): 267–97.

Grimmer, Justin, and Eleanor Neff Powell. "Congressmen in Exile: The Politics and Consequences of Involuntary Committee Removal." *Journal of Politics* 75, no. 4 (2013): 907–20.

Gring-Pemble, Lisa M. "'Are We Going to Now Govern by Anecdote?' Rhetorical Constructions of Welfare Recipients in Congressional Hearings, Debates, and Legislation, 1992–1996." *Quarterly Journal of Speech* 87, no. 4 (2001): 341–65.

Groseclose, Tim, and Jeffrey Milyo. "A Measure of Media Bias." *Quarterly Journal of Economics* 120, no. 4 (2005): 1191–237.

Groseclose, Tim, and Charles Stewart III. "The Value of Committee Seats in the House, 1947–91." *American Journal of Political Science* 42, no. 2 (1998): 453–74.

Gruenfeld, Deborah H. "Status, Ideology, and Integrative Complexity on the US Supreme Court: Rethinking the Politics of Political Decision Making." *Journal of Personality and Social Psychology* 68, no. 1 (1995): 5–20.

Gruenfeld, Deborah H., Paul V. Martorana, and Elliott T. Fan. "What Do Groups Learn from Their Worldliest Members? Direct and Indirect Influence in Dynamic Teams." *Organizational Behavior and Human Decision Processes* 82, no. 1 (2000): 45–59.

Gruenfeld, Deborah H., Melissa C. Thomas-Hunt, and Peter H. Kim. "Cognitive Flexibility, Communication Strategy, and Integrative Complexity in Groups: Public Versus Private Reactions to Majority and Minority Status." *Journal of Experimental Social Psychology* 34, no. 2 (1998): 202–26.

Gutmann, Amy, and Dennis F. Thompson. *Democracy and Disagreement.* Cambridge, MA: Harvard University Press, 1998.

Habermas, Jürgen. *The Theory of Communicative Action, Volume I.* Boston: Beacon, 1984.

Haidt, Jonathan. *The Righteous Mind: Why Good People Are Divided by Politics and Religion.* London: Penguin, 2013.

Hall, Andrew B. "What Happens When Extremists Win Primaries?" *American Political Science Review* 109, no. 1 (2015): 18–42.

Hall, Richard L. *Participation in Congress.* New Haven, CT: Yale University Press, 1996.

Hall, Richard L., and Bernard Grofman. "The Committee Assignment Process and the Conditional Nature of Committee Bias." *American Political Science Review* 84, no. 4 (1990): 1149–66.

Hamilton, Thomas. *Men and Manners in America.* Edinburgh: W. Blackwood, 1843.

Hammer, Dean, and Aaron Wildavsky. "The Open-Ended, Semi-Structured Interview: An (Almost) Operational Guide." In *Craftways: On the Organization of Scholarly Work,* ed. Aaron Wildavsky, 57–101. Piscataway, NJ: Transaction, 1993.

Harbridge, Laurel. *Is Bipartisanship Dead? Policy Agreement and Agenda-Setting in the House of Representatives.* Cambridge: Cambridge University Press, 2015.

Haskins, Ron. "Congress Writes a Law: Research and Welfare Reform." *Journal of Policy Analysis and Management* 10, no. 4 (1991): 616–32.

Hazan, Reuven. "Political Reform and the Committee System in Israel: Structural and Functional Adaptation." In *The New Role of Parliamentary Committees,* ed. Lawrence Longley and Roger Davidson, 163–87. London: Frank Cass, 1998.

Heath, Roseanna Michelle, Leslie A. Schwindt-Bayer, and Michelle M. Taylor-Robinson. "Women on the Sidelines: Women's Representation on Committees in Latin American Legislatures." *American Journal of Political Science* 49, no. 2 (2005): 420–36.

Henson, Audrey. "Diversity on Capitol Hill Starts with Paying Interns." *Vox,* January 8, 2019.

Higgins, E. T. "Self-Discrepancy: A Theory Relating Self and Affect." *Psychological Review* 94, no. 3 (1987): 319–40.

Hsee, Christopher, et al. "Preference Reversals Between Joint and Separate Evaluations of Options: A Review and Theoretical Analysis." *Psychological Bulletin* 125, no. 4 (1999): 576.

Hu, Minqing, and Bing Liu. "Mining and Summarizing Customer Reviews." *Proceedings of the Tenth ACM SIGKDD International Conference on Knowledge Discovery and Data Mining*. Seattle, WA: ACM, 2004.

Hyder, Adnan, et al. "National Policy-Makers Speak Out: Are Researchers Giving Them What They Need?" *Health Policy and Planning* 26, no. 1 (2011): 73–82.

Inter-Parliamentary Union. *Women in Parliament: 1995–2020*. Geneva: Inter-Parliamentary Union, March 8, 2020.

Itkowitz, Colby. "Hating Congress? That's Always Been in Vogue." *Washington Post*, August 9, 2014.

Janis, Irving L. *Victims of Groupthink: A Psychological Study of Foreign-Policy Decisions and Fiascoes*. Boston: Houghton Mifflin, 1972.

Janoff-Bulman, Ronnie, and Amelie Werther. "The Social Psychology of Respect: Implications for Delegitimization and Reconciliation." In *The Social Psychology of Intergroup Reconciliation*, ed. Arie Nadler, Thomas Malloy, and Jeffrey Fisher, 145–70. Oxford: Oxford University Press, 2008.

Jensen, Henrik. *Partigrupperne i Folketinget*. Jurist-og Økonomforbundets Forlag, 2002.

Jewell, Malcolm Edwin, and Samuel Charles Patterson. *The Legislative Process in the United States*. New York: Random House, 1977.

Jones, Bryan D., Frank R. Baumgartner, and Jeffery C. Talbert. "The Destruction of Issue Monopolies in Congress." *American Political Science Review* 87, no. 3 (1993): 657–71.

Jones, Mark P., Sebastian Saiegh, Pablo T. Spiller, and Mariano Tommasi. "Amateur Legislators—Professional Politicians: The Consequences of Party-Centered Electoral Rules in a Federal System." *American Journal of Political Science* 46, no. 3 (2002): 656–69.

Kacewicz, Ewa, James W. Pennebaker, Matthew Davis, Moongee Jeon, and Arthur C. Graesser. "Pronoun Use Reflects Standings in Social Hierarchies." *Journal of Language and Social Psychology* 33, no. 2 (2014): 125–43.

Kathlene, Lyn. "Power and Influence in State Legislative Policymaking: The Interaction of Gender and Position in Committee Hearing Debates." *American Political Science Review* 88, no. 3 (1994): 560–76.

Katznelson, Ira, Kim Geiger, and Daniel Kryder. "Limiting Liberalism: The Southern Veto in Congress, 1933–1950." *Political Science Quarterly* 108, no. 2 (1993): 283–306.

Kawakami, Kerry, John F. Dovidio, and Simone van Kamp. "Kicking the Habit: Effects of Nonstereotypic Association Training and Correction Processes on Hiring Decisions." *Journal of Experimental Social Psychology* 41, no. 1 (2005): 68–75.

Keen, Suzanne. "Empathetic Hardy: Bounded, Ambassadorial, and Broadcast Strategies of Narrative Empathy." *Poetics Today* 32, no. 2 (2011): 349–89.

Kelly Garrett, R., et al. "Implications of Pro- and Counterattitudinal Information Exposure for Affective Polarization." *Human Communication Research* 40, no. 3 (2014): 309–32.

King, David C. *Turf Wars: How Congressional Committees Claim Jurisdiction*. Chicago: University of Chicago Press, 1997.

King, Desmond S., and Rogers M. Smith. "Racial Orders in American Political Development." *American Political Science Review* 99, no. 1 (2005): 75–92.

King, Gary, Robert O. Keohane, and Sidney Verba. *Designing Social Inquiry: Scientific Inference in Qualitative Research.* Princeton, NJ: Princeton University Press, 1994.

Kipling, Rudyard. *The English Flag.* 1891.

Kornberg, Maya, et al. *2022 Global Parliamentary Report.* Geneva: Inter-Parliamentary Union and United Nations Development Program, 2022.

Kraft, Patrick W., Milton Lodge, and Charles S. Taber. "Why People 'Don't Trust the Evidence': Motivated Reasoning and Scientific Beliefs." *ANNALS of the American Academy of Political and Social Science* 658, no. 1 (2015): 121–33.

Krehbiel, Keith. *Information and Legislative Organization.* Ann Arbor: University of Michigan Press, 1992.

Landy, Marc Karnis, Marc J. Roberts, and Stephen Richard Thomas. *The Environmental Protection Agency: Asking the Wrong Questions.* Oxford: Oxford University Press, 1990.

LaPira, Timothy M., Lee Drutman, and Kevin R. Kosar. *Congress Overwhelmed: The Decline in Congressional Capacity and Prospects for Reform.* Chicago: University of Chicago Press, 2020.

Lascher Jr, Edward L. "Assessing Legislative Deliberation: A Preface to Empirical Analysis." *Legislative Studies Quarterly* 21, no. 4 (1996): 501–19.

——. *The Politics of Automobile Insurance Reform: Ideas, Institutions, and Public Policy in North America.* Washington, DC: Georgetown University Press, 1999.

Lauderdale, Benjamin E., and Alexander Herzog. "Measuring Political Positions from Legislative Speech." *Political Analysis* 24, no. 3 (2016): 374–94.

Laver, Michael, and John Garry. "Estimating Policy Positions from Political Texts." *American Journal of Political Science* 44, no. 3 (2000): 619–34.

Lawrence, John A. *The Class of '74: Congress After Watergate and the Roots of Partisanship.* Baltimore, MD: Johns Hopkins University Press, 2018.

Lee, Frances. *Beyond Ideology: Politics, Principles, and Partisanship in the U.S. Senate.* Chicago: University of Chicago Press, 2009.

——. "How Party Polarization Affects Governance." *Annual Review of Political Science* 18 (2015): 261–82.

Leech, Beth L. "Lobbying and Influence." In *The Oxford Handbook of American Political Parties and Interest Groups*, ed. Sandy Maisel and Jeffrey Berry. Oxford: Oxford University Press, 2010.

Lees, John David, and Malcolm Shaw. *Committees in Legislatures: A Comparative Analysis.* Durham, NC: Duke University Press, 1979.

Levendusky, Matthew. *How Partisan Media Polarize America.* Chicago: University of Chicago Press, 2013.

Lewallen, Jonathan. *Committees and the Decline of Lawmaking in Congress.* Ann Arbor: University of Michigan Press, 2020.

Lewallen, Jonathan, et al. "Congressional Dysfunction: An Information Processing Perspective." *Regulation and Governance* 10, no. 2 (2016): 179–90.

Lewallen, Jonathan, Sean Theriault, and Bryan Jones. "The Senate's Disastrous Process for Crafting the AHCA Fits a Historic Pattern." *Vox*, June 21, 2017.

Leyden, Kevin M. "Interest Group Resources and Testimony at Congressional Hearings." *Legislative Studies Quarterly* 20, no. 3 (1995): 431–39.

Loewenberg, Gerhard, Peverill Squire, and D. Roderick Kiewiet, eds. *Legislatures: Comparative Perspectives on Representative Assemblies*. Ann Arbor: University of Michigan Press, 2002.

Longley, Lawrence, and Roger Davidson. *The New Roles of Parliamentary Committees*. London: Frank Cass, 1998.

Maass, Arthur. *Congress and the Common Good*. New York: Harper Collins, 1983.

Macedo, Stephen, *Deliberative Politics: Essays on Democracy and Disagreement*. Oxford: Oxford University Press, 1999.

Mackie, Diane, and Joel Cooper. "Attitude Polarization: Effects of Group Membership." *Journal of Personality and Social Psychology* 46, no. 3 (1984): 575–85.

Maliniak, Daniel, Ryan Powers, and Barbara F. Walter. "The Gender Citation Gap in International Relations." *International Organization* 67, no. 4 (2013): 889–922.

Maltzman, Forrest. *Competing Principles: Committees, Parties, and the Organization of Congress*. Ann Arbor: University of Michigan Press, 1998.

Mann, Thomas E., and Norman J. Ornstein. *The Broken Branch: How Congress Is Failing America and How to Get It Back on Track*. Oxford: Oxford University Press, 2006.

Mannes, Albert E., Jack B. Soll, and Richard P. Larrick. "The Wisdom of Select Crowds." *Journal of Personality and Social Psychology* 107, no. 2 (2014): 276.

Mansbridge, Jane. "Deliberative Polling as the Gold Standard." *Good Society* 19, no. 1 (2010): 55–62.

Marcellino, William M. "Talk Like a Marine: USMC Linguistic Acculturation and Civil–Military Argument." *Discourse Studies* 16, no. 3 (2014): 385–405.

Martin, Shane. "Committees." In *Oxford Handbook of Legislative Studies*, ed. Shane Martin, Thomas Saalfeld, and Kaare Strom. Oxford: Oxford University Press, 2014.

Maslow, Will. "The Witness Before the Congressional Committee." *Journal of Social Issues* 13, no. 2 (1957): 12–6.

Massey, Andrew. *Technocrats and Nuclear Politics: The Influence of Professional Experts in Policy-Making*. Avesbury: Aldershot, 1988.

Masters, Nicholas A. "Committee Assignments in the House of Representatives." *American Political Science Review* 55, no. 2 (1961): 345–57.

Mattson, Ingvar, and Kaare Strøm. "Parliamentary Committees." In *Parliaments and Majority Rule in Western Europe*, ed. H. Döring, 249–307. Frankfurt: Campus Mannheim, 1995.

Mayhew, David. *Congress: The Electoral Connection*. New Haven, CT: Yale University Press, 1974.

——. "Divided Party Control: Does It Make a Difference?" *PS: Political Science & Politics* 24, no. 4 (1991): 637–40.

McCarty, Nolan, Keith T. Poole, and Howard Rosenthal. *Polarized America: The Dance of Ideology and Unequal Riches*. Cambridge, MA: MIT University Press, 2008.

Mcclurg, Scott D., Lawrence R. Jacobs, Fay Lomax Cook, and Michael X. Delli Carpini. *Talking Together: Public Deliberation and Political Participation in America*. Chicago: University of Chicago Press, 2009.

McCubbins, Mathew, and Terry Sullivan. *Congress: Structure and Policy*. Cambridge: Cambridge University Press, 1987.

Mill, John Stuart. *Considerations on Representative Government*. Project Gutenberg Literary Archive Foundation, 1859.

Montieth, Margo, et al. "The Self-Regulation of Prejudice: Toward Understanding Its Lived Character." *Group Processes & Intergroup Relations* 13, no. 2 (2010): 183–200.

Moore, Robert L., Cherng-Jyh Yen, and F. Eamonn Powers. "Exploring the Relationship Between Clout and Cognitive Processing in MOOC Discussion Forums." *British Journal of Educational Technology* 52, no. 1 (2021): 482–97.

Mosley, Layna. *Interview Research in Political Science*. Ithaca, NY: Cornell University Press, 2013.

Mucciaroni, Gary, and Paul J. Quirk. *Deliberative Choices: Debating Public Policy in Congress*. Chicago: University of Chicago Press, 2006.

Murray, Rainbow, and Réjane Sénac. "Explaining Gender Gaps in Legislative Committees." *Journal of Women, Politics & Policy* 39, no. 3 (2018): 310–35.

Myers, David, and George Bishop. "Discussion Effect on Racial Attitudes." *Science* 169, no. 3947 (1970): 778–79.

National Archives. "Progressive Reform: Speaker Cannon." Washington, DC: National Archives. https://www.archives.gov/exhibits/treasures_of_congress/text/page16_text.html.

National Democratic Institute. "Committees in Legislatures: Legislative Research Series." Washington, DC: National Democratic Institute, 1996. https://www.ndi.org/sites/default/files/030_ww_committees.pdf.

Newburger, Emma. "There's a Gender Pay Gap for Congressional Staffers—and It's Worse Among Republicans." *CNBC*, January 16, 2019.

Nittrouer, Christine L., Michelle R. Hebl, Leslie Ashburn-Nardo, Rachel C. E. Trump-Steele, David M. Lane, and Virginia Valian. "Gender Disparities in Colloquium Speakers at Top Universities." *Proceedings of the National Academy of Sciences* 115, no. 1 (2018): 104–8.

Nutley, Sandra, and Isabel Walter. *Using Evidence: How Research Can Inform Public Services*. Bristol: Policy Press, 2007.

O'dea, Bridianne, Mark E. Larsen, Philip J. Batterham, Alison L. Calear, and Helen Christensen. "A Linguistic Analysis of Suicide-Related Twitter Posts." *Crisis: The Journal of Crisis Intervention and Suicide Prevention* 38, no. 5 (2017): 319.

Oliver, Kathryn, et al. "A Systematic Review of Barriers to and Facilitators of the Use of Evidence by Policymakers." *BMC Health Services Research* 14, no. 1 (2014): 1–12.

Olson, David. *The Legislative Approach*. New York: Harper & Row, 1980.

Ornstein, Norman. "Congress Would Get More Done with a Better Schedule." *New York Times*, January 29, 2014.

Owens, Ryan J., and Justin P. Wedeking. "Justices and Legal Clarity: Analyzing the Complexity of US Supreme Court Opinions." *Law & Society Review* 45, no. 4 (2011): 1027–61.

Parker, David C. W., and Matthew Dull. "Divided We Quarrel: The Politics of Congressional Investigations, 1947–2004." *Legislative Studies Quarterly* 34, no. 3 (2009): 319–45.

Pedersen, Helene Helboe, Darren Halpin, and Anne Rasmussen. "Who Gives Evidence to Parliamentary Committees? A Comparative Investigation of Parliamentary Committees and Their Constituencies." *Journal of Legislative Studies* 21, no. 3 (2015): 408–27.

Pennebaker, James W., Ryan L. Boyd, Kayla Jordan, and Kate Blackburn. *The Development and Psychometric Properties of LIWC 2015*. Austin: University of Texas, 2015.

Perna, Laura W., Kata Orosz, and Daniel C. Kent. "The Role and Contribution of Academic Researchers in Congressional Hearings: A Critical Discourse Analysis." *American Educational Research Journal* 56, no. 1 (2019): 111–45.

Pettigrew, Thomas F., and Linda R. Tropp. "A Meta-Analytic Test of Intergroup Contact Theory." *Journal of Personality and Social Psychology* 90, no. 5 (2006): 751–83.

Pierson, Paul. "The Costs of Marginalization: Qualitative Methods in the Study of American Politics." *Comparative Political Studies* 40, no. 2 (2007): 146–69.

Pildes, Richard H. "Why the Center Does Not Hold: The Causes of Hyperpolarized Democracy in America." *California Law Review* 99, no. 2 (2011): 273–333.

Polsby, Nelson W. *Congressional Behavior*. New York: Random House, 1971.

——. *How Congress Evolves: Social Bases of Institutional Change*. Oxford: Oxford University Press, 2004.

——. "The Institutionalization of the US House of Representatives." *American Political Science Review* 62, no. 1 (1968): 144–68.

Polsby, Nelson W., et al. "The Growth of the Seniority System in the U.S. House of Representatives." *American Political Science Review* 63, no. 3 (1969): 787–807.

Poole, Keith, and Howard Rosenthal. *Ideology and Congress*. Piscataway, NJ: Transaction, 2007.

Powell, Eleanor, and Justin Grimmer. "Money in Exile: Campaign Contributions and Committee Access." *Journal of Politics* 78, no. 4 (2016): 974–88.

Power, Timothy Joseph, and Nicol C. Rae, eds. *Exporting Congress? The Influence of the US Congress on World Legislatures*. Pittsburgh, PA: University of Pittsburgh Press, 2006.

Primosch, Anna. "Hoops Star Defends Food Stamps Program." *The Hill*, October 27, 2015.

Quinn, Kevin M., Burt L. Monroe, Michael Colaresi, Michael H. Crespin, and Dragomir R. Radev. "How to Analyze Political Attention with Minimal Assumptions and Costs." *American Journal of Political Science* 54, no. 1 (2010): 209–28.

Quirk, Paul J., and William Bendix. "Deliberation in Congress." In *The Oxford Handbook of the American Congress*, ed. George C. Edwards III, Frances E. Lee, and Eric Schickler. Oxford: Oxford University Press, 2011.

Ray, Victor. "A Theory of Racialized Organizations." *American Sociological Review* 84, no. 1 (2019): 26–53.

Resnik, Philip, Anderson Garron, and Rebecca Resnik. "Using Topic Modeling to Improve Prediction of Neuroticism and Depression in College Students." *Proceedings of the 2013 Conference on Empirical Methods in Natural Language Processing*. Seattle, WA: Association for Computational Linguistics, 2013, 1348–53.

Reynolds, Molly. "The Decline in Congressional Capacity." In *Congress Overwhelmed: The Decline in Congressional Capacity and Prospects for Reform*, ed. Timothy M. LaPira, Lee Drutman, and Kevin R. Kosar. Chicago: University of Chicago Press, 2020.

Robinson, Michael J., and Kevin R. Appel. "Network News Coverage of Congress." *Political Science Quarterly* 94, no. 3 (1979): 407–18.

Rohde, David W. "Committee Reform in the House of Representatives and the Subcommittee Bill of Rights." *ANNALS of the American Academy of Political and Social Science* 411, no. 1 (1974): 39–47.

Roller, Emma, Stephanie Stamm, and National Journal. "Here Are America's Most Wanted (House Committee Chairs)." *The Atlantic*, June 5, 2014.

Rush, Michael. "Committees in the Canadian House of Commons." In *Committees in Legislatures: A Comparative Analysis*, ed. John David Lees and Malcolm Shaw. Durham, NC: Duke University Press, 1979.

Sawi, Ali. "Assess—to Assist: A Preliminary Analysis of Committees Arab Parliaments." In *Parliamentary Committees in the Policy Process*, ed. Sven T. Siefken and Hilmar Rommetvedt, 38–60. London: Routledge, 2022.

Scher, Seymour. "Conditions for Legislative Control." *Journal of Politics* 25, no. 3 (1963): 526–51.

Schick, Allen. "Informed Legislation: Policy Research Versus Ordinary Knowledge." In *Knowledge, Power, and Congress*, ed. William Robinson and Clay Wellborn, 99–119. Washington, DC: CQ Press, 1991.

Schickler, Eric. "The Development of the Congressional Committee System." In *The Oxford Handbook of the American Congress*, ed. George C. Edwards III, Frances E. Lee, and Eric Schickler. Oxford: Oxford University Press, 2011.

Schickler, Eric, and Ruth Bloch Rubin. "Congress and American Political Development." In *The Oxford Handbook of American Political Development*, ed. Richard Valelly, Suzanne Mettler, and Robert Lieberman. Oxford: Oxford University Press, 2016.

Schreier, Margrit. *Qualitative Content Analysis in Practice*. London: Sage, 2012.

Schultz, Kenneth A. "Perils of Polarization for US Foreign Policy." *Washington Quarterly* 40, no. 4 (2017): 7–28.

Scott, Elsie L., Karra W. McCray, Donald Bell, and Spencer Overton. "Racial Diversity Among Top US House Staff." Washington, DC: Joint Center for Political and Economic Studies, 2020.

Settle, Jaime E., et al. "From Posting to Voting: The Effects of Political Competition on Online Political Engagement." *Political Science Research and Methods* 4, no. 2 (2016): 361–78.

Sexton, J. Bryan, and Robert L. Helmreich. "Analyzing Cockpit Communications: The Links Between Language, Performance, Error, and Workload." *Human Performance in Extreme Environments* 5, no. 1 (2000): 63–68.

Shaw, Malcolm. "Conclusion Chapter." In *Committees in Legislatures: A Comparative Analysis*, ed. John David Lees and Malcolm Shaw. Durham, NC: Duke University Press, 1979.

——. "Parliamentary Committees: A Global Perspective." In *The New Roles of Parliamentary Committees*, ed. Lawrence Longley and Roger Davidson, 225–51. London: Frank Cass, 1998.

Shepsle, Kenneth A. *The Giant Jigsaw Puzzle*. Chicago: University of Chicago Press, 1978.

Shepsle, Kenneth A., and Barry R. Weingast. "The Institutional Foundations of Committee Power." *American Political Science Review* 81, no. 1 (1987): 85–104.

——. *Positive Theories of Congressional Institutions*. Ann Arbor: University of Michigan Press, 1995.

Sherif, Mazafer. *Group Conflict and Cooperation: Their Social Psychology*. Abingdon: Routledge & Kegan Paul, 1967.

Sherwood, Peta-Gay, and Stephanie Denardo. "Congressman Yoho Speaks About Food Stamp Program." *WUFT*, September 24, 2013.

Siefken, Sven T., and Hilmar Rommetvedt. *Parliamentary Committees in the Policy Process*. London: Routledge, 2022.

Skowronek, Stephen, and Karen Orren. "Pathways to the Present: Political Development in America." In *The Oxford Handbook of American Political Development*, ed. Richard Valelly, Suzanne Mettler, and Robert Lieberman. Oxford: Oxford University Press, 2016.

Smith, Christine M., R. Scott Tindale, and Bernard L. Dugoni. "Minority and Majority Influence in Freely Interacting Groups: Qualitative Versus Quantitative Differences." *British Journal of Social Psychology* 35, no. 1 (1996): 137–49.

Smith, Lamar. "Overheated Rhetoric on Climate Change Hurts the Economy." *Washington Post*, May 19, 2013.

Smith, Steven S. *Call to Order: Floor Politics in the House and Senate.* Washington, DC: Brookings Institution Press, 1989.

Solomon, Stephan Marc. "Listen Carefully: Public Hearings in the German Bundestag." PhD diss., University of Mannheim, 2015.

"Statistics and Historical Comparison." *Govtrack.* https://www.govtrack.us/congress/bills/statistics.

Steiner, Jürg, et al. *Deliberative Politics in Action: Analyzing Parliamentary Discourse.* Cambridge: Cambridge University Press, 2004.

Stevens, Alex. "Telling Policy Stories: An Ethnographic Study of the Use of Evidence in Policymaking in the UK." *Journal of Social Policy* 40, no. 2 (2011): 237–55.

Stewart III, Charles, and Tim Groseclose. "The Value of Committee Seats in the United States Senate, 1947–91," *American Journal of Political Science* 43, no. 3 (1999): 963–73.

Stoker, Laura, and M. Kent Jennings. "Of Time and the Development of Partisan Polarization." *American Journal of Political Science* 52, no. 3 (2008): 619–35.

Sunstein, Cass. *Going to Extremes: How Like Minds Unite and Divide.* Oxford: Oxford University Press, 2009.

Taber, Charles S., and Milton Lodge. "The Illusion of Choice in Democratic Politics: The Unconscious Impact of Motivated Political Reasoning." *Political Psychology* 37, no. 1 (2016): 61–85.

Tausczik, Yla R., and James W. Pennebaker. "The Psychological Meaning of Words: LIWC and Computerized Text Analysis Methods." *Journal of Language and Social Psychology* 29, no. 1 (2010): 24–54.

Tetlock, Philip E. "Identifying Victims of Groupthink from Public Statements of Decision Makers." *Journal of Personality and Social Psychology* 37, no. 8 (1979): 1314–24.

——. "Social Psychology and World Politics." In *The Handbook of Social Psychology*, ed. D. Gilbert, S. Fiske, and G. Lindzey, 868–912. New York: McGraw Hill, 1998.

Touhy, Carolyn Hughes. "Epics, Anecdotes, and the Bounds of Solidarity. Policy Narratives of the Welfare State." Policy Narratives, Populism and the Institutions of Liberal Democracy: Challenge and Response Conference, University College London, February 11–12, 2019.

Tropp, Linda R., and Ludwin E. Molina. "Intergroup Processes: From Prejudice to Positive Relations Between Groups." In *The Oxford Handbook of Personality and Social Psychology*, ed. Kay Deaux and Mark Snyder. Oxford: Oxford University Press, 2012.

Tumasjan, Andranik, Timm Oliver Sprenger, Philipp G. Sandner, and Isabell M. Welpe. "Predicting Elections with Twitter: What 140 Characters Reveal About Political Sentiment." *International Conference on Web and Social Media* 10, no. 1 (2010): 178–85.

Turner, Rhiannon N., Miles Hewstone, and Alberto Voci. "Reducing Explicit and Implicit Outgroup Prejudice via Direct and Extended Contact: The Mediating Role of Self-Disclosure and Intergroup Anxiety." *Journal of Personality and Social Psychology* 93, no. 3 (2007): 369.

Van der Linden, Sander L., Anthony A. Leiserowitz, Geoffrey D. Feinberg, and Edward W. Maibach. "The Scientific Consensus on Climate Change as a Gateway Belief: Experimental Evidence." *PloS One* 10, no. 2 (2015).

Van Der Slik, Jack R., and Thomas C. Stenger. "Citizen Witnesses Before Congressional Committees." *Political Science Quarterly* 92, no. 3 (1977): 465–85.

Volden, Craig, and Alan E. Wiseman. "How Term Limits for Committee Chairs Make Congress Less Effective." *Washington Post*, January 4, 2017.

——. *Legislative Effectiveness in the United States Congress: The Lawmakers.* Cambridge: Cambridge University Press, 2014.

——. "Legislative Effectiveness in the United States Senate." *Journal of Politics* 80, no. 2 (2018): 731–35.

Wallach, Philip. "How Congress Fell Behind the Executive Branch." In *Congress Overwhelmed: The Decline in Congressional Capacity and Prospects for Reform*, ed. Timothy M. LaPira, Lee Drutman, and Kevin R. Kosar. Chicago: University of Chicago Press, 2020.

Warren, Mark. "Deliberative Democracy." In *Democratic Theory Today*, ed. April Carter and Geoffrey Stokes. Cambridge: Polity Press, 2002.

Waxman, Olivia. "Supreme Court Confirmation Hearings Weren't Always Such a Spectacle: There's a Reason That Changed." *Time Magazine*, September 6, 2018.

Weingast, Barry R. "A Rational Choice Perspective on Congressional Norms." *American Journal of Political Science* 23, no. 2 (1979): 245–62.

Weiss, Carol. "Congressional Committees as Users of Analysis." *Journal of Policy Analysis and Management* 8, no. 3 (1989): 411–31.

——. "Research and Policymaking: A Limited Partnership." In *The Use and Abuse of Social Science*, ed. Frank Heller, 214–35. London: Sage, 1986.

Weiss, Robert S. *Learning from Strangers: The Art and Method of Qualitative Interview Studies.* New York: Simon and Schuster, 1995.

Whiteman, David. *Communication in Congress: Members, Staff, and the Search for Information.* Lawrence: University Press of Kansas, 1995.

Wilson, Woodrow. *Congressional Government: A Study in American Politics.* Boston: Houghton Mifflin, 1885.

Wines, Michael. "Though Scorned by Colleagues, a Climate-Change Skeptic Is Unbowed." *New York Times*, July 15, 2014.

Young, Iris Marion. "Communication and the Other: Beyond Deliberative Democracy." In *Democracy and Difference*, ed. Seyla Benhabib, 120–36. Princeton, NJ: Princeton University Press, 1996.

Young, James Sterling. *The Washington Community, 1800–1828.* Vol. 69. New York: Columbia University Press, 1966.

Zhu, Meina, Susan C. Herring, and Curtis J. Bonk. "Exploring Presence in Online Learning Through Three Forms of Computer-Mediated Discourse Analysis." *Distance Education* 40, no. 2 (2019): 205–25.

INDEX

bipartisan nature of, 135; clout and certainty scores, 65; diversity, 39; 114th Congress witness profession data, 55, 56, 57, 57
House Ways and Means Committee, 19, 20, 86; balance scores by term, 97; chair changes in 2018, 96
HuffPost, 142
human rights, 124

implicit attitudes, 101–2
impossibility theorem, 107
informal hearings, 89, 119–20, 155–56; as bipartisan condition, 160–62; structure of, 161
Information Technology Laboratory, 108
Inhofe, Jim, 135
institutionalization: "Institutionalization of the US House of Representatives, The" (Polsby), 3, 8; *Men and Manners* (Hamilton), 3
Integrated Risk Information System (IRIS) program, 148
Intelligence Committee, as classified, 151
interest groups, 21
Internet Association, 80
internet trafficking, personal story of, 78, 80
interns, 38–39, 52; "Diversity on Capitol Hill Starts with Paying Interns" (Henson), 39
Inter-Parliamentary Union, 22
interviewees: committee staffers, 180, 183–85; list of, 181–88; number of, 180; other actors as, 188; personal staffers, 180, 185–86; proxy, 180; representatives, 181 83; senators, 17, 179–80, 183; witnesses, 187–88
interview sample, 17–18, 48, 83; details and overview of, 179–81; list of interviewees, 181–88; purposive sampling method, 179
"The Iran Nuclear Agreement: One Year Later" Hearing, 137–40
Iraq War, hearing on, 74

IRIS. *See* Integrated Risk Information System
ISIS. *See* Islamic State of Iraq and Syria

Johns Hopkins Bioethics Institute, 188
Johns Hopkins University, 148
Joint Center for Political and Economic Studies, 52
Joint Comprehensive Plan of Action (JCPOA). *See* Iran Nuclear Agreement Hearing
joint lists, of witnesses, 28, 93

Kahn, Jeffrey, 125, 126–27
Kavanaugh, Brett, nomination hearing of, 145–47
killer charts, 62
Kilmer, Derek, 113
Klobuchar, Amy, 28
Kryptos Logic, 108

labeled experts, 73–75, 108, 134; in climate change hearing, 140–41; in Iran Nuclear Agreement hearing, 138–39
Language Inquiry and Word Count (LIWC) software, 19; metrics, 63; 114th Congress witness analysis using, 59–66, 61, 63, 69; positive and negative words, 69; psychological analysis by, 63; text analysis in, 59, 65–66; word count scoring in, 61
Lawrence, John A., 9
leading questions, 132–33, 141
Leahy, Patrick, 131, 149
learning, legislative, 7, 8, 127–28; affirmations, 114–15; effect, 83; research function and, 16; Science and Ethics hearing, 127; staff education and, 121–25; staff members impacted by, 122–25; STEM hearing and, 129; term limits and, 120–21; when and how of member, 129–30
Lees, John, 2
legislation: fewer pieces of, 1–2, 11; hearing link with, 88–89; hearings decline linked to specific, 26; legislative effectiveness